Database Design and Development Simplified for Access 2007

HIM 3113

Cindy Joy Marselis

CENGAGE
Learning™

Australia • Brazil • Japan • Korea • Mexico • Singapore • Spain • United Kingdom • United States

Database Design and Development Simplified for Access 2007: HIM 3113

Cindy Joy Marselis

Executive Editors:
Maureen Staudt
Michael Stranz

Project Development Manager:
Linda deStefano

Senior Marketing Coordinators:
Sara Mercurio

Senior Production / Manufacturing Manager:
Donna M. Brown

PreMedia Services Supervisor:
Joel Brennecke

Rights & Permissions Specialist:
Kalina Hintz
Todd Osborne

Cover Image:

Getty Images*

* Unless otherwise noted, all cover images used by Custom Solutions, a part of Cengage Learning, have been supplied courtesy of Getty Images with the exception of the Earthview cover image, which has been supplied by the National Aeronautics and Space Administration (NASA).

For product information and technology assistance, contact us at
Cengage Learning Customer & Sales Support, 1-800-354-9706

For permission to use material from this text or product, submit all requests online at **cengage.com/permissions**
Further permissions questions can be emailed to
permissionrequest@cengage.com

ISBN-13: 978-1-111-03329-3

ISBN-10: 1-111-03329-3

Cengage Learning
5191 Natorp Boulevard
Mason, Ohio 45040
USA

Cengage Learning is a leading provider of customized learning solutions with office locations around the globe, including Singapore, the United Kingdom, Australia, Mexico, Brazil, and Japan. Locate your local office at:
international.cengage.com/region

Cengage Learning products are represented in Canada by Nelson Education, Ltd.

For your lifelong learning solutions, visit **custom.cengage.com**

Visit our corporate website at **cengage.com**

Printed in the United States of America

Database Design and Development Simplified for Access 2007

TABLE OF CONTENTS

Database Design and Development Simplified for Access 2007

TABLE OF CONTENTS

Database Design and Development Simplified for Access 2007

TABLE OF CONTENTS

Database Design and Development Simplified

ACCESS PRACTICE EXERCISES

Section 1: Database Design and Entity Relationship Diagrams (ERDs)

Chapter 1: Why is database design important?

I. Data, Information and Knowledge

Businesses collect and store data on a variety of things such as a price, a supplier, a product, or a sale. But the data doesn't really mean anything at this point. When the organization summarizes the information, applies context it, and presents the data in a fashion which is useful to the organization, the data has been transformed into information. Information is useful and typically provides answers to "who", "what", "where", and "when" questions.

While information is vital for organizations, firms that convert information into knowledge excel in their work. Knowledge answers "how" questions.

Finally, if you move up to the top of the knowledge pyramid, you achieve wisdom or true understanding.[1]

As business people, we try and move up the pyramid to move towards wisdom. Sounds like a Jedi in Star Wars, huh? So how do organizations do this? To start, organizations need good databases that facilitate the collection, storage, and dissemination of information within the organization.

II. Why do we need good design?

An organization's success is often tied to the efficient and effective flow of information. If the data of an organization is not stored in a properly designed database, the organization cannot make good business decisions based on data. If the data is stored in a flawed manner, the user can retrieve inconsistent results and the data is said to lack integrity. The user cannot be confident with the information retrieved. If the user doesn't trust the results received, he will not be able to make a decision with certainty.

Consider the following. What if you wanted to take the Temple shuttle bus from the Health Sciences Campus to Main Campus. You look at the schedule on Temple's portal and it says the bus will arrive at HSC at 8:15 AM. You arrive at the stop at 8:10 AM and wait for the bus. It finally arrives at 10:15 AM, and now you've missed your 9:40 AM class. It turns out that the schedule isn't updated regularly so you can't rely on it. Sometimes the bus arrives at 8:05, sometimes at 8:17, and sometimes it is cancelled, but these changes are not reflected on the website. What will you do next time? Will you look at the online schedule or will you just go to the stop super early in the hopes that you'll catch the bus whenever it arrives?

---

[1] http://www.systems-thinking.org/dikw/dikw.htm

Database Design and Entity Relationship Diagrams

The ERD is a model (a representation) of how the database is structured. The ERD is designed to allow the database designer to optimize the manner in which the data is stored to facilitate the use of the data within the organization.

A. Data Anomalies

We've all had situations where we've talked to a company and found out that the information stored isn't correct. Maybe you've called a store to confirm an item you want is in stock. You are told that there are 10 items in inventory. When you get there, it turns out they are out of stock.

For example, I received a book in the mail from a publisher. The book had been sent to my old house, and I had moved over a year ago. While this seems reasonable, the publisher knew that I had moved because they've sent other books to my new address. Why would some books be sent to the correct address and some routed to the old location? The most common reason for these kinds of situations is that organizations have many databases and many tables within each database, and these tables hold redundant data.

What if the publisher had a faculty table that listed each faculty member to whom they send books? The publisher also has an order table that shows which books that a faculty member ordered and this table includes the address to which the order was sent.

This is a perfect environment for breeding data anomalies. An anomaly is an abnormality in our data and we want to avoid abnormalities in database design. There are three types of data anomalies that plague us.

1. Insertion (add) anomaly

   In an insert anomaly a row cannot be inserted (added) to one table unless it is added somewhere else. This means there is a forced dependency between two tables that should not exist. In our publisher example it might be that a faculty member cannot be added to the database until he/she places an order. This is not an appropriate dependency. The publisher should be able to add a new faculty member, and then add orders as they are placed.

2. Deletion anomaly

   A deletion anomaly is just the reverse of an insertion anomaly. In other words a table is deleted and the data from another table cannot be retrieved. For instance, if we store information about the customer such as the address in the order table and then we delete an order, the information about the customer's account including the address will also be lost.[2] We don't want to lose the customer's address. We just want to remove an order.

3. Modification (update) anomaly

   In a modification anomaly, values of an attribute must be duplicated multiple times in a table. If the publisher stored my address each time an order was placed (rather than storing my address once), when I moved the publisher would need to update each row where my old address appears. An even worse scenario involves organizations which only update the address on some of the rows while others are left unchanged. This would lead to data retrievals that are inconsistent with some rows showing a new address and others showing an older location. As we've learned, inconsistent retrievals lead to loss of integrity in the database.

   If the database had been properly designed, my address would have been stored once for each location where I receive books (work or home). When my home address changed, the organization would only need to update my home location once, and all of

---

2

http://books.google.com/books?id=8TpWEIA9sEcC&pg=PT171&lpg=PT171&dq=insert+anomaly&source=web&o
ts=2scsXXmSuu&sig=ScpWtxjfbIbji-PWCo45x76H8XU&hl=en&sa=X&oi=book_result&resnum=8&ct=result

the rows related to this home address would be updated appropriately. The key is to capture the value of an attribute once, store it once, and use that one data value consistently.

Typically, companies would prefer to collect the value of an attribute for a row consistently wrong, as opposed to sometimes accurately and sometimes inaccurately. This may seem odd but really makes sense if you think about it. If the information is sometimes correct you falsely assume it is always right and rely on it until you are faced with a situation where the data is clearly inaccurate. At that point, you realize you may have made decisions on poor quality information. This situation is more difficult to correct as well since you need to consider each individual row and assess whether that row's data is correct or not.

Conversely, if the information is consistently inaccurate, it is more likely you'll note the error earlier and initiate the process to correct it faster. Also, with a consistent error, you may be able to globally update the information, and that is much simpler then considering each row on a case by case basis.

B. We always want to avoid data anomalies and maintain data in one location which is accurate and timely. When users of the data can rely and trust the results to be updated and accurate, they feel more confident making a business decision since the veracity of the data is not questioned.

Chapter 2: Background to ERD

I.   What's an ERD?

An ERD is an Entity Relationship Diagram. Just as the name implies, an ERD shows entities and their relationships to one another. An ERD shows the data elements stored in a database and in what manner the data is stored.

II.   Business Rules for Glenside Bank

One of the key aspects of an ERD is that it models the data needs of the organization as it relates to how the business operates. The policies regarding how the business works are called the "business rules" of the organization.

In this section, we will consider the case of Glenside Bank. Glenside Bank is a fictitious, local bank with just a few branches. Glenside would like to improve the way the bank stores information about customers and their accounts. The bank functions like this.

- The bank has customers and it collects basic demographic information for each customer such as name, address, social security number, gender, date of birth, phone number.

- The bank offers a number of accounts such as a checking account, savings account, money market account, CD, etc.

- The bank has a number of branches. The bank needs to track where each account was opened.

- A customer can have many accounts (you could have a checking and a savings account). For each account, the bank needs to track the type of the account (i.e. checking, savings, money market) and the date the account was opened.

- An account can have multiple customers associated with it (a husband and wife could have a joint checking account). The bank needs to track the customers associated with each account and the date that customer was added to the account. If the customer was removed from the account, the bank needs to track the date this occurred.

- Every time the customer interacts with one of the accounts it is considered a transaction. The bank needs to track a number of aspects of the transaction including the type (i.e. withdrawal, transfer, deposit), the amount, the date and time, the customer, and the location (ATM, check, branch, electronic fund transfer)

These business rules will be the basis for a new database which we'll call the Account database.

III.   Components of an ERD

An ERD has two main components: Entities and Relationships

A. Entity:

An entity is something about which the organization wants to collect data. We typically think of an entity as a noun (person, place, or thing).   For instance, in the Glenside bank scenario, you would need to keep information about a number of people, places, and things like the customer, branch, bank account, respectively.   Most people find it useful to think of an entity as table which holds rows. Each row is one row in the table or one occurrence of the entity.

1. An entity (table) is a two-dimensional structure with rows and columns

2. Column:

a.   The column in a table represents a piece of information called an attribute. Sometimes an attribute will be called a field, data element, or parameter. We'll learn more about attributes later including what the columns marked PK and Null mean.

For now, let's focus on the first column in the table below contains some of the attributes in the customer table.

Column Name ▼	ID ▼	Pk ▼	Null? ▼	Data Type ▼
CUSTOMER_ID	1	1	N	NUMBER (5)
CUSTOMER_LNAME	2		N	VARCHAR2 (30 Byte)
CUSTOMER_FNAME	3		N	VARCHAR2 (30 Byte)
ADD1	4		N	VARCHAR2 (30 Byte)
CITY	5		N	VARCHAR2 (25 Byte)
STATE	6		N	CHAR (2 Byte)
ZIP	7		N	CHAR (5 Byte)
GENDER	8		Y	CHAR (1 Byte)
DOB	9		Y	DATE
HOMEPHONE	10		Y	CHAR (10 Byte)

b. Column values (the information stored in an attribute) all must have the same data format (data type). We'll learn more about data types in the Access and SQL tutorials later in this book. As you can see above, all of the customer_id values must be of a number data type while all of the customer_lname values must be a varchar2.

c. An attribute has a range of values called the attribute domain. This indicates the range of acceptable values for that attribute. For instance, we could say that the domain for zip is 00001 – 99999 if there are no zip codes issued after 99999 and no negative zip codes are issued. For date of birth (DOB), you may decide to make the domain 1/1/1900 – today's date. This would indicate that there are no customers born on or before 12/31/1899 and the youngest bank customer was born today (such as when a savings account is opened as a present for a newborn).

3. Row:

a. An entity holds rows. Each row is one instance of an entity. As you can see below, a row holds the values for each attribute for that instance. Our first customer, Frank Sinatra, has an customer_id of 10000. He lives at 144 Woodstream Blvd in Hoboken, is male, and was born on 1/11/1943, etc.

b. Each piece of information in an attribute in the row holds the specific value for that field for that row.

4. Row/Column Intersection:

The intersection of a row and a column represents a single value for that attribute for that row.

OMER_ID	CUSTOMER_LNAME	CUSTOMER_FNAME	ADD1	CITY	STATE	ZIP	GENDER	DOB	HOMEPHONE
10000	Sinatra	Frank	144 Woodstream Blvd.	Hoboken	NJ	08703	M	1/11/1943	2141515551
10100	Martin	Dean	454 St. Orange Street	Philadelphia	PA	19115	M	5/16/2025	2156757777
10200	Patty	Davis	8921 Circle Drive	Huntingdon Valley	PA	19006	F	7/30/1964	6109879876
10300	Mobey	Amanda	1716 Summerton Avenue	Warrington	PA	19004	F	8/12/1954	2138765656

5. Other aspects of entities:

a. Entity names:

b. An entity must have a unique name in a database. Let's say that Glenside likes to track the different kinds of customers including personal customers and business customers. We could not have two tables in the Account database called customer. However, there could be a customer table in different database.

c. An entity name should be singular. Accordingly, we would have a table called customer, not customers.

d. An entity is depicted with a box in an ERD

e. Tables must have an attribute to uniquely identify each row in the table. This attribute is called the primary key. We'll discuss this soon.

f. The order of the rows and columns is irrelevant to the Database Management System (DBMS).

B. Relationship:

The relationship describes how entities are related to one another. A relationship is typically described as a verb. In the Glenside Bank example, the customer owns many bank accounts. The account is owned by many customers.

In an ERD, a relationship is depicted by a line that joins two (or more) entities.

There are three types of relationships: one to one, one to many, and many to many.

1. Example of a one to one relationship (abbreviated as 1:1) in Glenside Bank:

   ▪ An account is identified by one account number.
   ▪ An account number identified one account

2. Example of a one to many relationship (abbreviated as 1:M) in Glenside Bank:

   ▪ An account is classified into one account type such as checking, savings, money market
   ▪ An account type has many accounts (i.e. there are many checking accounts at Glenside Bank)

3. Example of a many to many relationship (abbreviated as M:N – yes the second letter is N) in Glenside Bank:

   ▪ An account can be owned by many customers
   ▪ A customer can own many accounts

C. Attributes:

Attributes are really part of an entity as we've already discovered. Let's think a bit more about attributes and an important concept – Atomicity.

Let's consider the customer at Glenside Bank. If we want to collect information about the customer, we'll need to know the customer's name. You might decide to create an attribute in the customer table called name and have the first and last name of the customer added to this one attribute. We'll use me as an example. Let's say I decide to update my account and change my last name to my husband's last name. I tell the bank I want to change my last name from Marselis to Lundeen on my account from now on. It's much more difficult to take my name which was stored in one attribute apart to update just the second name. They'd need to retrieve my name, Cindy Joy Marselis, and try and figure out which part of it is my first name, middle name, and last name. This isn't too hard if my name is typically spaced and capitalized. But what happens if I have a suffix to my name, like the third (III) or my name was hyphenated. It would get increasingly difficult to figure out which part is which. To alleviate this problem, we store attributes in their most atomic (smallest) parts. Accordingly, we'll keep my first name in one attribute, last name in another attribute, etc.

For instance, we don't store an address in just one attribute. We'll keep the first line of the address in one attribute, the second line (for a suite, an apartment number, etc.) in another attribute, the city in a separate attribute, and state in yet another attribute. Some folks like to keep the zip code as 2 attributes, one to store the 5 digit zip and another to store that 4 digit extension.

E. F. Codd, the father of relational databases, said the following, "values in the domains on which each relation is defined are required to be atomic with respect to the DBMS." Codd defines an atomic value as one that "cannot be decomposed into smaller pieces by the DBMS (excluding certain special functions)."[i]

IV. ERD Styles

There are a number of styles you can use to model a database, the most common of which are the Chen and the Crow's Foot approaches. In addition to the Chen and the Crow's Foot, we will also explore the infinity model (for lack of a better name) as this is the approach used by Access, our main modeling tool for this class. In general, it really doesn't matter which style you use, but your approach should be consistent within one ERD.

A. Chen Model

1. For a 1:1 relationship, a number 1 is placed on the relationship line close to the both entity boxes

2. For a 1:M relationship, a number 1 is placed on the relationship line close to the entity which is the one side of the relationship and a letter M is placed next to the entity which is the many side of the relationship

3. For a M:N relationship, a letter M is placed next to one entity (doesn't matter which one) and a letter N is placed next to the other entity

B. Crow's Foot Model

1. For a 1:1 relationship, a number 1 is placed on the relationship line close to the both entity boxes

2. For a 1:M relationship, a number 1 is placed on the relationship line close to the entity which is the one side of the relationship and a little symbol that looks like a crow's foot (◁) is placed next to the entity which is the many side of the relationship

3. For a M:N relationship, a crow's foot is placed next to both entities

C. Infinity Model

1. For a 1:1 relationship, a number 1 is placed on the relationship line close to the both entity boxes

2. For a 1:M relationship, a number 1 is placed on the relationship line close to the entity which is the one side of the relationship and an infinity symbol (∞) is placed next to the entity which is the many side of the relationship

3. For a M:N relationship, an infinity symbol is placed next to both entities

Database Design and Entity Relationship Diagrams

The table below illustrates how relationships are represented in the three ERD Styles.

Type	Example of Relationship	Chen	Crow's Foot	Infinity
1 to 1	• An account is identified by one account number. • An account number identified one account	Account —1——1— Account Number	Account —1——1— Account Number	Account —1——1— Account Number
1 to Many (1:M)	• An account is classified into one account type such as checking, savings, money market • An account type has many accounts	Account Type —1——M— Account	Account Type —1——<— Account	Account Type —1——∞— Account
Many to Many (M:N)	• An account can be owned by many customers • A customer can own many accounts	Account —M——N— Customer	Account —>——<— Customer	Account —∞——∞— Customer

V. Keys

A. Primary key:

A primary key is an attribute that uniquely identifies each row in a table. A primary key must satisfy three requirements:

- Unique. Each row's primary key must be different. For instance, if you wanted to create a primary key for the student table, you might select TUID since every student has a unique identifier for Temple. It wouldn't be wise to select the student's first name as there could be more than one person with that name. Similarly, last name wouldn't be a good idea.

- Not null. The value of the primary key cannot be blank. Why? Because its purpose is to identify each row. If you wanted to look a student up in Owlnet, how could you do that if the primary key (the attribute used to identify each student) was blank? So a primary key must have a value stored in it.

- Indexed. Indexing improves the speed required to find the desired row. As described in Wikipedia

---

[3] http://www.dbmsmag.com/9605d15.html

:

The classic analogy to help you understand database indexes is the index in the back of reference books. Sure, if you wanted to find everything in the book about a particular subject you could start at the beginning and scan every page, but it is much faster to look in a smaller, alphabetized subject index that directs you to a list of pages. Then you need to scan only those pages to find information about your chosen subject. Not everything in the book is indexed, however, so if your subject is not mentioned in the index, you must still scan for it. Likewise, a database index is a look-up mechanism that helps a DBMS find the information you request faster than it could with a full scan. As with book indexes, not everything in the database is indexed, so an occasional scan may still be necessary.

The primary reason to build an index is to improve performance. But it is not the only reason to build an index. The second reason has to do with enforcing uniqueness among rows stored in a database table. Tables in a SQL database are usually designed with a primary key; that is, a set of columns with a unique value that identifies a row in the table. When a new row is inserted into a table defined with a primary key, it is up to the DBMS to ensure that the primary key value for that row is unique. Performance would be unacceptable if the DBMS had to scan the entire table each time a new row was inserted. Therefore, the accepted solution is to build a unique index on the primary-key columns and let the DBMS use that as the physical enforcement mechanism for the primary key uniqueness requirement.

1. What makes a good primary key?

   Any attribute or combination of attributes that satisfy the three requirements above (unique, not null, and indexed) can be a primary key. However, some attributes are more appropriate to be select as the primary key than others. For instance, if all of my students have unique first names I could make student first name as the primary key for the student table. But that doesn't happen very often. Each semester I have a few students named John and a couple students named Michael. What about last name you might ask. Again, if I could be sure it would be unique so I never have more than one student with the last name of Patel or Smith or Jones, that would be fine. But again, that doesn't happen most semesters and we want our primary key to ALWAYS be unique. So what can I do? We can start adding attributes together. For instance, instead of making the student's last name the primary key, I could make a combination of first name, last name, and date of birth. It is unlikely I would have two students who have the same name and birthday.

   While it is acceptable to have a primary key which is a text or a date type or some combination thereof, it is easier to have a primary key that is an integer. As well learn later, we use primary keys and foreign keys to "join" tables (more about this in the SQL tutorial) and it is easier to join two attributes that have an integer data type.

   So what do you do if you don't have an attribute for a table that is unique and not null and an integer? No problem. Just create a new attribute and enforce those rules.

2. Composite key:

   As I've noted, a primary key does not have to be made of just one attribute. Whenever a primary key is composed of more than one attribute it is called a composite key. As long as it meets the requirement to be unique not null and indexed, you can add as many attributes together to make a composite key as you like. The only limitation is that it becomes increasingly difficult to join tables. We'll talk about joins later

In the bank example, a customer can have numerous accounts at a bank and an account can have numerous customers associated with it. For instance, spouses may have a checking and a saving account at a bank and both spouses' names may be on both accounts. Let's say the bank creates a table called the Account_Assignment table. This table shows the relationship between the accounts and the account holders. The primary key for this table is a composite key which is two attributes that together make the primary key: the account_id and the customer_id.

3. Rules about primary keys:

- A primary key is used to uniquely identify each row and the values of its attributes in a table.
- If a column is defined as primary key, it cannot contain duplicate values and cannot be null.
- A primary key can be a single attribute or a combination of more than one attribute (if a primary key is made of two or more attributes, it is called a composite key).
- You can add a primary key to a table when the table is first created as part of the create table statement

B. Foreign Key:

As we've learned, redundant data leads to insert, delete, and modification anomalies. Wherever possible, we want to avoid redundant data. By designing a database carefully, we can do a very nice job of keeping information once and only once to ensure that if it needs to be added, changed, or deleted, we can perform the function one time, and all of the rows in a table that use that data will refer to the correctly inserted, updated, or deleted information.

We've also learned that we keep information about a particular item in a table, and a database can be composed of a number of tables which are related to each other in some way, all pertaining to an aspect of a business. So how do we make these tables related to each other? That's the beauty of the foreign key.

A foreign key is an attribute in a table which is repeated in another related table. Wait, didn't we just say we didn't want redundant data? Yup! But, this is a form of CONTROLLED redundancy. In other words, we don't want to keep all kinds of duplicate data but we can keep just one piece of information (i.e. the primary key) of one table, and repeat it as a foreign key in another table and now we can link the tables together.

Here's an example. Imagine I'm designing a database that houses information about courses at a college. Here is just a piece of the database model. You can see there is a course table that has a number of attributes related to a course. There is a discipline table that holds information about the various majors (disciplines) offered, and there is a school table that describes the schools at the university.

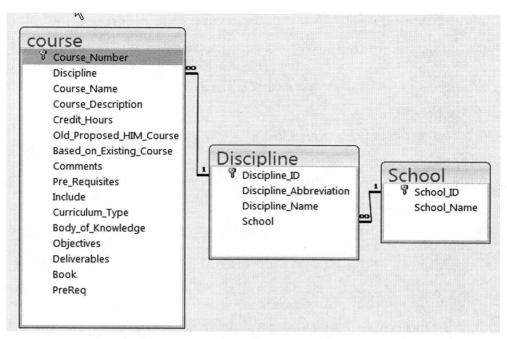

Let's take a look at the data in the discipline and the school tables.

Discipline:

Discipline_ID	Discipline_Abbr	Discipline_Name	School
1	OT	Occupational Therapy	1
2	Nursing	Nursing	1
3	MIS	Management Information Systems	2
4	HM	Health Management	2
5	HIM	Health Information Management	1
6	PT	Physical Therapy	1
7	MSOM	Management Science Operations Management	2
8	BA	Business Administation	2
9	CIS	Computer Information Systems	3
10	SOC	Strategic and Organizational communication	4
11	HRM	Human Resource Management	2
12	PH	Public Health	1
13	HIM/MIS	HIM and MIS	5
15	RM	Risk Management	2
16	HIM/HM	HIM and HM	5

School

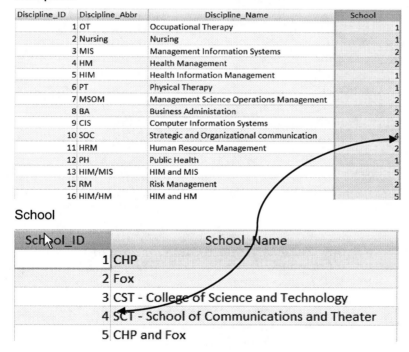

School_ID	School_Name
1	CHP
2	Fox
3	CST - College of Science and Technology
4	SCT - School of Communications and Theater
5	CHP and Fox

We can see that the number stored in the school attribute of the discipline table matches to the school_id value in the school table. Now let's consider row 10 in the discipline table. The school associated with SOC is 4 – or SCT-School of Communications and Theater. What would happen if there was a big reorganization at the university and all of the disciplines that were at Fox were transferred to SCT? We'd need to type SCT- School of Communications and Theater 6 times. That's a lot of typing! What if we mistyped it on a few occasions? Can you see how easy it would be to have errors in the data whenever there is an addition, modification or deletion of a value? But if you just use a foreign key (school) in the discipline table to the school_id (primary key) of the school table, all you need to do is add, update or delete the value of 1 row. Isn't that much easier? Sure! That's the beauty of foreign keys!

We'll discuss foreign keys in more detail in just a bit.

VI. Integrity Rules

There are two essential integrity rules that we follow when building ERDs

A. Entity Integrity:

Entity integrity is imposed on a database to ensure that each table's primary key is unique and not null. Consider the following customer table which has Customer ID as the primary key:

CustomerID	FirstName	LastName	Address	City	State	ZipCode	Telephone
4	David	Bowie	1515 Imam Way	Philadelphia	PA	19121-	(215) 415-3555
5	Cyrus	Miley	1234 Breaky Hear	Philadelphia	PA	19141-	(215) 468-6868
6	John	Alvizures	56566 Guat Road	Cherry Hill	NJ	08002-	(856) 194-1858
7	Barack	Obama	4444 Johnson Way	Philadelphia	PA	12939-1999	(215) 606-0606
8	Bob	Smith	8248 Walnut Avenue	Trenton	NJ	08205-	(856) 777-7777

Do you think I can enter the following 3 rows into the database?

8	Cindy	Marselis	1810 N. 13th St	Phila	PA	19122	215.204.3077
	Munir	Mandviwalla	1810 N. 13th St	Phila	PA	19122	215.204.8172
9	Bob	Smith	8248 Walnut Ave.	Trenton	NJ	080205	856.777.7777

1. If I try and enter the first row, I'd would violate entity integrity. Entity integrity ensures the primary key cannot be null and must be unique. Since a row already has a primary key of 8, the first row cannot be added. It doesn't matter that the data in the row is different since entity integrity is concerned with the primary key and this is a duplicate.

2. The second row has a null primary key, so this also should not be added

3. What about the third row? This has the same **data** as customerID 8. Would this be excluded as well? No. Entity integrity ensures that the primary key is not duplicated or null. Since there are no rows with a primary key of 9 and the field is populated (not null) it does not violate entity integrity. Also, isn't it possible that there are two Bob Smiths (perhaps Bob Senior and Bob Junior) who live in the same house? It could be that this is duplicated data and that is not desirable but it also is possible that there are indeed two people with the same name and address in the database. There are methods that organizations use to try to determine if rows such as these are duplicates but that discussion is outside of the scope of this class.

B. Referential Integrity

Referential integrity ensures that a foreign key matches to a primary key. Let's look at the following example. As we saw earlier, each discipline is in a school within Temple. Now let's say I add a new discipline for Dentistry into the discipline table, and I want this to be added to school 7. The database will not allow this row to be stored since the foreign key (7) does not have a matching primary key in its parent table School.

Note, a primary key may match a foreign key <u>or</u> a null value. For example, you see that SCT in the School Table (School_ID 4) does not have any corresponding rows in its child table Discipline. That is acceptable. Think of it like this. A school can be created and then its children (disciplines) will be added to it but a child cannot be added to a non-existent parent. So a discipline cannot be added if it doesn't have a school to go to. A row with a primary key of 7 must be created first in the school table first before it can be referenced by a child row in another table.

1. The referential integrity rules are:

   - A foreign key must match to a primary key
   - A primary key must match to a foreign key or a null value

Discipline Table

Discipline_ID	Discipline_Abbr	Discipline_Name	School
1	OT	Occupational Therapy	1
2	Nursing	Nursing	1
3	MIS	Management Information Systems	2
16	HIM/HM	HIM and HM	5
18	DENT	Dentistry	7 ˅

School Table

School_ID	School_Name
1	CHP
2	Fox
3	CST - College of Science and Technology
4	SCT - School of Communications and Theater
5	CHP and Fox

2. Highlights of key information relative to foreign keys and referential integrity

   - Foreign Keys represent relationship between tables. A foreign key is a column or group of columns whose value is derived from the primary key of another table. Foreign key constraints are used to enforce referential integrity, which means you can only place a value in table B if the value exists as a primary key in table A.
   - If a column is defined as a foreign key in a table, any inserts or updates will be rejected if a corresponding value does not exist in the primary key table. The referential integrity constraint specifies that the attribute in the referring table must refer to a primary key value that exists in the referenced table. The foreign key can also be null. (Remember a foreign MUST match to a primary key).
   - For example in the bank scenario, the account table has a field which refers to the Branch_ID in athe Branch table. Thus referential integrity would mean that the values of Branch_ID in the Account table must already exist in the Branch table or they should be null. This prevents the Account table from referring to Branches that do not exist!
   - The referencing column and referred column need not have the same name but MUST be of same data type and size.

VII. **Relationship Rules**

Now that we understand a bit about integrity rules, let's explore the rules related to relationships. Relationships must be defined into one of three types (1:1, 1:M, M:N). Once it is defined, the relationship must be resolved (converted into a format that can be stored in a database). Here's how we handle the relationship type and resolution. We will see examples of this in Chapter 3 but for now, just try and digest the concepts.

A. Determine relationship using this terminology: (i.e. relationship between student and dorm rooms)

- 1 of A is related to X (1 or many) of B
  i.e. 1 student is assigned to 1 dorm room
- 1 of B is related to X (1 or many) of A
  i.e. 1 dorm room is assigned to many students

The decision will be as follows:

1. 1:1

   a. 1 of A is related to 1 of B

   b. 1 of B is related to 1 of A

2. 1:M

   a. 1 of A is related to many of B

   b. 1 of B is related to 1 of A

3. M:N

   a. 1 of A is related to many of B

   b. 1 of B is related to many of A

B. Resolve the relationship

1. If the relationship is a 1:1, it is assumed that the entity is just another attribute for that table. Add it as another attribute to an existing entity.

   For instance, if you have TUID and student, a student can have only one TUID and a TUID is assigned to one student. Include the TUID as an attribute to the student table.

2. If the relationship is a 1:M, **the primary key of the one** side is duplicated as the **foreign key on the many side**. The rule is that the foreign key ALWAYS goes on the many side.

   a. The names of the primary key and the foreign key do not need to match. Only the data type needs to be the same.

   b. Of course, the values of the data stored in the field must match as well or there cannot be a join.

3. If the relationship is a M:N, resolve the M:N relationship into two 1:M relationships. To resolve the M:N relationship into two 1:M relationships:

   a. Create a new table which is an associative entity (AKA composite entity or bridge entity). The purpose of the associative entity is to function as a bridge between the two entities. This table must include the primary keys of the two entities as foreign keys. This makes sense since the associative entity is now the many side of both 1:M relationships. Since the foreign key ALWAYS goes on the many side of a relationship and the associative entity is ALWAYS the many side of the relationship, both of the foreign keys would be placed in the associative entity.

b. If the combination of the 2 foreign keys is unique, it can be used as the primary key of the associative entity. Since the primary key will be composed of 2 primary keys, it is called a composite key.

c. If the combination of the 2 foreign keys is not unique, leave the 2 foreign keys in the associative entity and create a new primary key for the associative entity.

Chapter 3: Example of Creating an ERD

We'll start off with a small example. Let's design a database for Glenside Bank. We'll consider each of the business rules step by step. We'll also explore some database design concepts as we go.

I. **1:1 Relationships**

The bank has customers and it collects basic demographic information such as name, address, social security number, gender, date of birth, phone number, for each customer.   Customer seems a good candidate for an entity as it is a noun and we are collecting information about that customer. So let's create a bank customer table.   There can be no spaces in between the words in attributes or tables names, so the name of this table will be bank_customer.

Let's consider what information (attributes) we'll keep about our customers.

A. Our first step is to identify a good primary key for our table. You might be tempted to use a person's social security number, but a social security number isn't always unique since at one point duplicate numbers were issued. Also, in the past, not everyone was issued an SS#, so the value can be null. This violates 2 of the 3 rules about a primary key. We woulc also consider some combination of the customer's first name, last name, and date of birth as the primary key but this might get a bit cumbersome. To make it easier for ourselves later, let's just create a new attribute called Customer_ID

B. Now we'll consider social security number, date of birth, phone number and name. The social security number is unique to one customer (hopefully) and a customer should have only one social security number (again hopefully). This is clearly a 1:1 relationship.   If we review our relationship rules, if a relationship is 1:1, it is assumed that the entity is just an attribute for that table. Add it as an attribute to the bank_customer entity.

C. Derived (calculated) field:

1. What about date of birth? A customer can only have one birth date, right? But it is possible for more than one customer to have the same birthday.   Is this a 1:M relationship? You could say that, but this type of data is virtually always handled as a 1:1 relationship so we'll just add date of birth to the bank_customer table.

2. Why am I collecting the date of birth rather than the customer's age? Unfortunately, we are all getting older every nano-second, and your current age will not be the same at this moment as it will be a second, month, or year from now. However, you date of birth stays the same. We can always calculate (derive) your age by taking the current date and subtracting your birth date so it is better to keep your birthdate. Storing the birthdate has another advantage over storing age. What if we want to send a birthday message to anyone whose birthday is in July. If I store age I won't be able to do this but if I store birthday, that's an easy calculation.

3. You'll find there are numerous times where you'll be tempted to store a derived field (subtotals, totals, calculations, etc.) but it is always preferable to store the raw attribute and do the math as a calculation. In the SQL section of this book you'll learn how to handle calculations.

D. What about address? Address is like the date of birth in that there could be multiple customers with the exact same address (such as spouses or parents and children) but it is common to keep this information within the customer table. Remember with address we want to keep the attribute atomic, so we'll keep address 1, city, state, and zip as separate attributes.

E. We'll handle phone number the same way as address and keep the phone in the bank_customer table. Although it is true the customer can have lots of phone numbers, from the bank's perspective, it really only needs one.   We'll just have one telephone number per customer.

F. We also want to keep personal information such as the person's gender. Try to avoid calling this attribute sex as that has a number of different connotations. Rather, we'll name this attribute gender.

G. Of note, you can add attributes to a table in any order you wish but makes more sense to group the attributes into similar areas and in a logical order. As such, we put the components of the address lumped together and place the attributes in the same order as a typical mailing address.

H. There could be lots of other pieces of information we'd like to keep about the customer but let's go with this. Our customer table now appears as follows with customer_id as the primary key (delineated by the key symbol to the left of the attribute name):

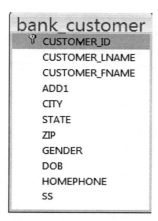

II. 1:M Relationships

The next two business rules coincide with one another so I'm going to consider them together. The bank offers a number of accounts such as a checking account, savings account, money market account, CD, etc. The bank has a number of branches. The bank needs to track where each account was opened.

Looks like we need an account table. What type of information will we need in our account table? Certainly we'll need a primary key to uniquely identify each account in the account table. Account_Number seems like a good one since it is unique and shouldn't be null. We also need to store the state where the account was opened. In addition, we need to track the type of the account (checking, savings, money market, CD, etc.), the branch where the account was opened, and the billing cycle date (that's the day of the month when you get your statement like the 15th of the month so the value is 15). Let's start with this list of attributes:

- Account_number
- State_opened
- Account_type
- Branch_opened
- Billing_cycle_day

We could add an attribute for account type with a data type of varchar2 (text). In this situation, the user would need to type in the word "checking", "savings", "money market", etc. each time a new row was added to the account table. But that's quite a bit of typing! Also, what happens when someone types Checking and someone else types checking, and a third person types check? If I want to see all of the checking account customers, I'll only see a subset of them. Why? To a computer upper case is different than lower case. To make it easier for the user to enter information and to ensure information is entered in a consistent manner to facilitate data retrieval it would be better to give the user a drop down box which has a list of the acceptable values for that field. The user then just has to click on one and the value will be filled into the field. It's like when you order something on the web. You don't type your state in to the state field when you enter your address. You typically see a drop down list and you click on your state.

A. When to use a look up table?

It is wise to consider a lookup table when the possible values of the attribute are not limitless. Therefore, we don't usually give a lookup table for birthdates, street addresses, first names or last names. However, you will typically see them for products and anything where the item is categorized or grouped into a particular type like country, region or ethnicity, student class type, etc.

B. What does a lookup table include?

A lookup table can include any attribute, but most commonly it will include 2 fields, the primary key and a description. For instance, when you pick your state when ordering something online, the state lookup table typically has a primary key which is the 2 letter state abbreviation and the state's full name.

Here is the structure of the state table as well as a subset of some of the values stored in the table.

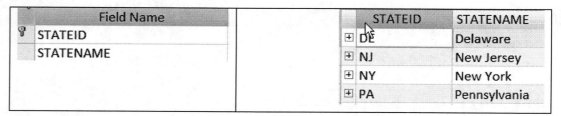

C. Building a relationship with a look up table.

A lookup table is really just an example of a 1:M relationship.

- A customer lives in one state.
- A state includes many customers.

- State is the 1 side of the relationship)
- Bank_customer is the many side of the relationship

As the relationship rules tell us, in a 1:M relationship, **the primary key of the one** side is duplicated as the **foreign key on the many side**. Remember the rule is that the foreign key ALWAYS goes on the Many side. The names of the primary key and the foreign key do not need to match – only the data type needs to be the same.

To make the relationship, we'll take the primary key of the 1 side (state) and make it a foreign key in the many side of the relationship (bank_customer). This means we'll take stateid from the state table and add this attribute to the bank_customer table. We don't have to call it stateid and in fact, I've just called it state. Now our relationship appears as follows:

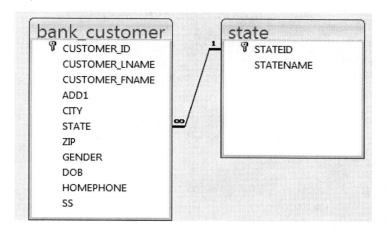

When user is entering information into the bank_customer table, he will select a value from the state table. The primary key (stateid) of the state table will be duplicated in the bank_customer table as a foreign key (state).

D. Additional examples of lookup tables related to the account table.

   1. Account type: We've seen we need to track the account type. Here's an example of what the account type would look like in the structure as well as the values:

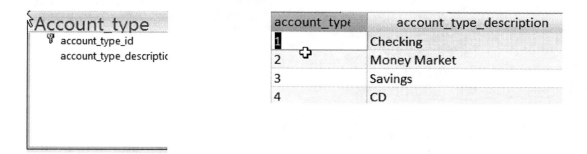

Just like before, this is a 1:M relationship. An account is of one type. An account type includes many accounts. We'll take the primary key (account_type_id) of the one side (account type table) and make it a foreign key (account_type) on the many side of the relationship (account table).

Here's what the structure looks like:

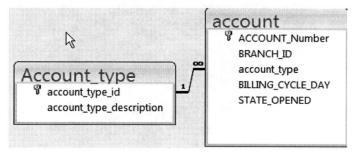

Here's what the corresponding data looks like:

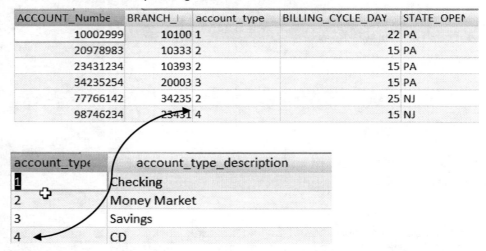

ACCOUNT_Numbe	BRANCH_I	account_type	BILLING_CYCLE_DAY	STATE_OPEI
10002999	10100	1	22	PA
20978983	10333	2	15	PA
23431234	10393	2	15	PA
34235254	20003	3	15	PA
77766142	34235	2	25	NJ
98746234	23431	4	15	NJ

account_type	account_type_description
1	Checking
2	Money Market
3	Savings
4	CD

You can see here that account_number 98746234 has an account_type of 4 so it must be a CD.

2. Branch: You'll note we need to store the branch where the account was opened. The Account was opened at one branch. A branch had many accounts opened at its location.

   For branch, we need to keep additional pieces of information other than just the primary key (I'll call this branch_id) and description (branch_name). We also need to keep the branch's address as well as the date the branch was opened. Its design will look like this:

branch
- BRANCH_ID
- BRANCH_NAME
- BRANCH_ADD1
- BRANCH_CITY
- BRANCH_STATE
- BRANCH_ZIP
- DATE_OPENED

The data stored in the table will look like this:

BRANCH_ID	BRANCH_NA	BRANCH_ADI	BRANCH_CIT	BRANCH_ST/	BRANCH_;	DATE_OPENE
10100	Abington	10101Highland ,	Abington	PA	19007	1/1/2005
10333	Huntingdon Vall	1111Huntingdor	Huntingdon Vall	PA	19006	5/16/2006
10393	Feasterville	1003 Street Roa	Feasterville	PA	19053	11/12/2006
20003	Ambler	9888 Meetinghc	Ambler	PA	19064	11/15/2006
23431	Ft. Washington	23423 Commer(	Ft. Washington	PA	19871	2/4/2006
34235	Cherry Hill	12495 Brace Ro	Cherry Hill	NJ	08002	5/6/2006

Now branch_state can use same state lookup table that is linked to the bank_customer table. Similarly, state_opened attribute in the account table can use the stateid in the state table as a lookup table. If we look at our relationships at this point, if we look at our database design at this point, it will look like the following:

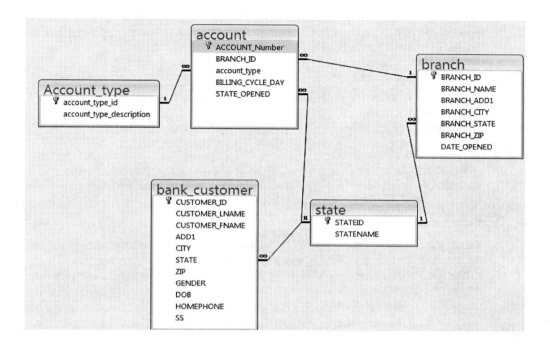

III. **M:N Relationship**

We know from our business rules that a customer can have many accounts (i.e. a checking and a savings account) and an account can be associated with multiple customers (a husband and wife could have a joint checking account). The bank needs to track the customers associated with each account and the date that customer was added to the account. If the customer was removed from the account, the bank needs to track the date this occurred.

A. Resolving M:N Relationships

Clearly, we have a many to many relationship here between bank_customer and accounts. Upon review of our relationship rules:

- If you have a M:N relationship, you need to resolve it into two 1:M relationships. To do this, create an associative entity (AKA composite entity or bridge entity) which has the primary keys of the two entities as foreign keys.

Here are our two entities:

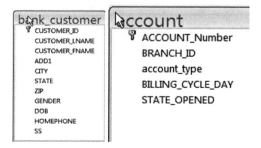

1. We need to make a new table which has the primary keys of the bank_customer table (customer_id) and the account table (account_number) as foreign keys to the new table. In addition to the foreign keys from the account and the bank_customer table, we need to add an attribute to collect the date this account was opened. Let's call this new table account_assignment. It will look like this:

Field Name	Data Type
BANK_ACCOUNT_ID	Number
BANK_CUSTOMER_ID	Number
DATE_OPENED	Date/Time

2. Since the foreign key ALWAYS goes on the many side of a relationship and the associative entity is ALWAYS the many side of the relationship, the foreign key for both of the original entities must go on the associative entity.

B. Composite key:

1. Bank_account_id is the foreign key to the customer_id primary key in the bank_customer table. Customer_id is the foreign key to the account_number primary key in the account table. Bank_account_id and Bank_customer_id are a composite primary key in the account_assignment table. Remember a composite key is a primary key made up of more than one attributes.

2. If the combination of these attributes is unique, the combination of the foreign keys is the primary key of the associative entity. In this case, can a customer open the same account on a day? No – then it is unique. Therefore, the primary key can be the composite key of bank_account_id and bank_customer_id.

   Here is the resolved M:N relationship:

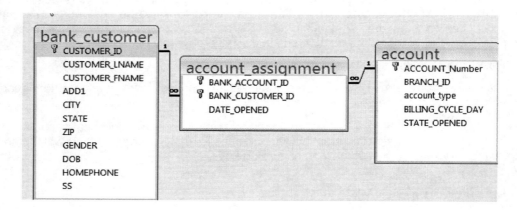

3. Let's take a look at the data for these tables:

Bank_Customer

CUSTOMER_	CUSTOMER_	CUSTOMER_	ADD1	CITY	STATE	ZIP	GENDER	DOB	HOMEPHONE	SS
10000	Sinatra	Frank	144 Woodstrea	Hoboken	NJ	08703	M	1/11/1943	2141515551	222-22-0202
10100	Martin	Dean	454 St. Orange	Philadelphia	PA	19115	M	5/16/2025	2156757777	187-37-3737
10200	Patty	Davis	8921 Circle Driv	Huntingdon Vall	PA	19006	F	7/30/1964	6109879876	193-94-1221
10300	Mobey	Amanda	1716 Summerto	Warrington	PA	19004	F	8/12/1954	2138765656	199-19-1919

Account_Assignment

BANK_ACCOUNT_ID	BANK_CUSTOMER_ID	DATE_OPENED
10002999	10100	1/3/2007
20978983	10100	12/19/2006
20978983	10300	12/19/2006
23431234	10200	1/15/2007
34235254	10300	10/13/2006
77766142	10200	6/22/2006
98746234	10000	12/15/2006

Account

ACCOUNT_Numbe	BRANCH_	account_type	BILLING_CYCLE_DAY	STATE_OPEN
10002999	10100	1	22	PA
20978983	10333	2	15	PA
23431234	10393	2	15	PA
34235254	20003	3	15	PA
77766142	34235	2	25	NJ
98746234	23431	4	15	NJ

This is showing that the first row in the account_assignment table is for customer 10100. If we look at the bank_customer table we can see that this number corresponds with Dean Martin. He has an account which was opened at branch 10100 on 1/3/2007 in PA.

If we look at the next row, which is also for Dean Martin, we can see he also opened an account with the number of 20978983 in PA on 12/19/2006. This account is jointly owned by customer 10300 – Amanda Mobley.

IV. Final ERD

When we put all of the entities and their appropriate relationships together into one diagram, we develop the following ERD model of our database. Note that all of the relationships are now 1:M since all of the M:N relationships have been resolved into 1:M relationships.

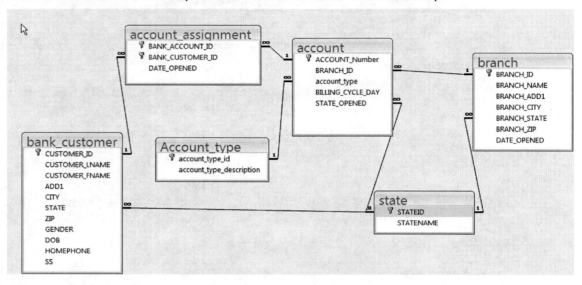

V. Placements of attributes in tables

One area where new database designers can get confused is the placement of attributes in tables. In this scenario you'll notice I added an attribute, date_opened, into the account_assignment table. You may wonder why I put the attribute in that table.

A. When you are considering attributes you need to come back to the definition of a primary key. A primary key's purpose is to uniquely identify every row in a table and to allow the user to retrieve the values of all the attributes in that row. If I put the date_opened field in the bank_customer table, it would mean that the value of the date_opened field (i.e. what date the account was opened) is determined solely by the customer. Since a customer can have more than one account and each could be opened on different dates the value of date_opened is determined by more than the customer.

   1. What if we put the date_opened attribute in the account table? This makes sense except that multiple customers can be on one account. For instance, a husband and wife can open an account, and both go and sign the paperwork on different days. In this situation, the date that the customer opened the account would be different for both customers. Therefore, date opened is not solely determined by the account.

   2. Clearly, date_opened is determined by both the customer AND the account, and therefore it must be placed in the associative entity, the account_assignment table.

B. Most of the time people run into problems with the placement of attributes when working with a M:N relationship. If you find yourself confused, just consider each table independently and decide if the value of the attribute is determined by only one side of the relationship. If it is determined by both sides of the relationship, place the attribute in the bridge entity.

Chapter 4: Invoice Example

Now that we've seen a full ERD example, we'll go one step farther. Organizations typically exist to make and or provide a product or a service for a customer or client. As such, companies typically need to make an invoice or a receipt which is given to the customer for payment. Since the requirement to create an invoice is basically universal in all organizations, let's explore how to handle this through a database.

In a new scenario, what if you order books online from a publisher for next semester. When you receive the book in the mail, it will have an invoice that looks something like this:

Customer:	**Invoice # 3211**			Shipped From:	
	Order Date: 6/3/2008				
Bruce Springsteen	Order Clerk: 144444			Publisher's R Us	
1818 Rock and Roll Way				8181 Education Way	
Rumsford, NJ 08045	Ship Date: 6/5/2008			Smartsville, PA 19888	

		Line Items			
ISBN	Item Description	Product Type	Unit Price	Quantity	Subtotal
141414	Databases R Amazing	IS	100.00	3	300.00
333333	The History of Rock and Roll	Music	200.00	1	200.00
455050	How to Make a Lot of Money	Finance	500.00	1	500.00
	TOTAL				1,000.00
	Tax				60.00
	Grand Total				1,060.00

I.   **Entities and Attributes:**

Let's decompose each piece of the order. Invoices typically include 4 main pieces which correspond to the sections of the invoice above:

- Customer
- Shipper
- Invoice Information
- Items purchased

A. Customer Information

1. When you place an order, the company needs to know basic information about you. This might include your full name, home address, credit card information (number, type of card, expiration date, etc.) and your shipping information.   Of course, the company needs to uniquely identify each customer, so it will typically issue a customer identifier.

2. Not all invoices will have customer information. For instance, imagine you go to 7-Eleven and buy some munchies for lunch. On the receipt you receive it will not include customer information since you don't typically give any data about yourself when you shop at a store. But what about if you shop at a place that uses a frequent shopper card like a

super market? In that case, your customer information will probably show up on the receipt. The presence of customer information will be driven by the needs of the organization.

B. Seller Information:

An invoice typically includes basic information about the store from which you purchased the item. If it is a purchase at 7-Eleven, it might just say 7-Eleven and show the store number and address. Again, the amount of the information displayed will be driven by the needs of the organization.

C. Product Information

An invoice or receipt will normally show the products that were purchased. Typically it will include the product identifier (such as a SKU or an ISBN), a description about the product, and perhaps some information as to the type of the product.

1. In the invoice above you see information such as subtotal, total, and tax. All of these are derived or calculated fields as described earlier. These attributes would not be stored in the database, but rather would appear on a report based on a calculation you perform.

2. For product type, we probably want a lookup table since we don't want the user to enter free text. Rather, we'd like to have the user pick the value from a list to ensure there is consistency in the information collected and to minimize data entry. As you'll recall, when we add a lookup table it is simply a 1:M relationship. A product is of one type, and a type has many products associated with it.

D. Invoice Information

Virtually all receipts and invoices have some basic identifying information about the purchase which includes an invoice or receipt number, perhaps a barcode, an invoice date and time, and possibly the name of the person who placed the order. If the item was shipped it might include the shipping date. At a store it might include the cashier's identifying number.   All of this type of information will be housed in a table that you might call invoice, receipt, or order.

II.   **Relationships:**

Now that we've identified the basic entities, we'll move on to determining their relationships.

A. Customer to Invoice

An invoice is issued for one customer. A customer can purchase items or services from an organization on multiple occasions and each purchase is tracked through an invoice. Therefore, a customer can have many invoices but an invoice is for only 1 customer. The relationship between customer and invoice is 1 to many, with invoice as the many side of the relationship.

B. Seller to Invoice

An invoice is created by one seller. A seller creates many invoices (or they wouldn't stay in business too long). The relationship between a seller and an invoice is also 1 to many, respectively.

C. Product to Invoice

When we buy something at a store or online we can purchase more than one item during the visit or transaction. It would be cumbersome and very time consuming if the store had to create a different invoice for each item purchased so the store adds all the products purchased during that one transaction on one invoice. For instance, in the example above, Bruce Springsteen bought three books and all appear on one invoice.

Now Bruce Springsteen is not the only person who might purchase a copy of Databases R Amazing or The History of Rock and Roll. Therefore, a product can be on multiple invoices. Accordingly, the relationship between product and invoice is M:N.

1. Be careful when thinking through these relationships. You might have thought that only one person could buy a book. It is true that an individual copy of a book could only be purchased by one person but what we are tracking in this database is a product, not an instance of a product. In other words, the bookstore has a bunch of copies of Databases R Amazing, It doesn't track each individual copy of the book. Rather, it only knows there were X number of copies of the book. With RFID (radio frequency ID) you can in fact track each individual instance of an item. However, most stores still work on bar coding which just tracks a product and the number in stock.

2. Now that we know that the relationship between product and invoice is M:N, we need to review our relationship rules. As you'll recall, if you have many to many relationships, you must resolve it into 2 one to many relationships. We resolve it by creating a new entity called a bridge or associative entity (it bridges or associates the two entities).

   a. The bridge entity must include the primary keys of the two tables as foreign keys.

   b. If the combination of these attributes is unique, the combination of the foreign keys can be used as the primary key of the bridge entity. If you use the 2 foreign keys as a primary key, the primary key is a composite key as it is composed of more than one attribute.

   c. If the combination of the foreign keys is not unique, then you need to create a new attribute to be the primary key.

3. In industry, the bridge entity between the invoice and the product table is typically called the invoice detail table. That is because it shows the line items (details) on the invoice.

III. **ERD**

Below is an example of what the basic entity relationship diagram for an invoice database would look like. As you'll note, it typically includes tables pertaining to the

- Product
- Customer
- Seller
- Transaction (the invoice, receipt, or order table)
- Order details (the bridge/associative entity between invoice and product showing the invoice detail).

You'll have a number of other tables as required by the specific needs of an organization but this is the basic design of invoicing systems.

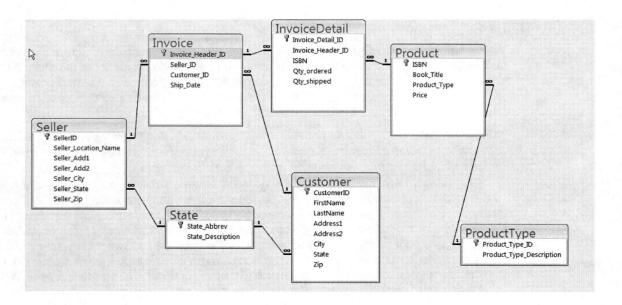

IV. Variations on a theme

Based on the business, some of these basic tables would be called different things. For example, if you were creating a system for the Bursar's office at Temple, the customer would be called Student. The Product would be Course. You would probably delete the Seller table since all of the services (courses) are provided from one "store" (Temple). The Invoice Detail table will not include quantity ordered or shipped since we don't ship courses or take multiple sections of the same class.

If the business was a doctor's office, the Product might be service (i.e. chest x-ray, physical exam, vaccination), the Customer would be called Patient, and the Seller might be Clinic since one doctor could practice in multiple locations. The Invoice table might be called Patient Bill and the Invoice_Detail table will not include quantity shipped or ordered.

Clearly, additional tables and attributes could be added to collect more information based on the organization's needs. But in general, this invoicing structure is fairly stable across all types of firms.

Chapter 5: Data Dictionary

I. What is a data dictionary?

We've spent some time discussing ERDs and while the design is critical to the functionality of the database, the data dictionary is essential as well. The data dictionary is just what the name implies – a dictionary about the data housed in the database. The data dictionary holds metadata, or data about the data. Hmpf, was that confusing?

Let me give you an example. I'm a new database developer at Glenside Bank. The manager comes to me and asks me to write a report of all of the accounts opened in Abington in the prior month. That seems easy enough. But, when I write the report I return no rows. Upon closer inspection of the data, I realize that Glenside stores dates in military format (i.e. MMM-DD-YYYY such as JUN-17-2008) and I had written the query assuming the date was stored as MM/DD/YYYY (such as 06/17/2008). How would I know the format of the attributes – just look it up in the data dictionary!

A. Although there is no standard for what should be contained in the metadata, you might find the following information for each table in the database. Some of these items will be explained more fully in the Access and SQL Tutorials.

- Table description (explaining the basic kind of information stored in the table)

- If the table comes from an outside source, it may include the format in which the table was received, the date of receipt, the date it was loaded into the database, and when an update may be expected.

- Attribute name, field size, data type, whether it is a primary key, and if it is required (cannot be left null), formats for the value, levels of precision, and input masks

- Information relating to relationships such as whether an attribute is a foreign key. If so, what table it references.

This is an example of a piece of a data dictionary:

Table	Product			Created	2/23/2007		Modified	4/13/2007	Fields	4	Records	0

Table Description

Field Name	Caption	Indexed	Field Type	Size	Default Value	Reqd	ZLgth	Validation Rule	Description
Product_ID	Product ID	Duplicates OK	Long	4	None	No	No		PRIMARY KEY for the Product Table
Product_Name	Product Name		Text	50	None	No	Yes		Various products and services the company is providing
Product_Type	Product Type	Duplicates OK	Long	4	0	No	No		FOREIGN KEY reference to Product_Typ from the Product_Type Table
Product_Unit_Price	Product Unit Price		Currency	8	None	Yes	No	<0	This is price of each product or service the company is providing

B. Many database management systems are considered to be self-describing. In other words, they document the information which is stored in the data dictionary automatically when tables and attributes are added to the database. It is simply a matter of querying the data to retrieve the information.

C. A data dictionary can also be used to create an ERD of a database if one has not been provided. Since the metadata typically shows which attribute is a primary key, which attributes are foreign keys and the table referenced, you could take a dictionary and recreate the ERD.

Section 2: Access Tutorial

Chapter 6: Introduction

I. **Access 2007 Interface**

A. The Ribbon

Microsoft Access 2007 offers a new user interface that includes a standard area called the Ribbon, which contains groups of commands that are organized by feature and functionality. The Ribbon replaces the layers of menus and toolbars found in earlier versions of Access.

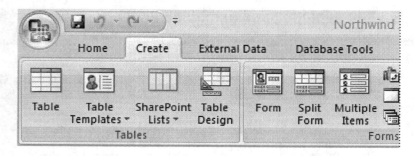

Use the Ribbon to locate groups of related commands faster. For example, if you need to create a form or report, use one of the commands on the Create tab. Commands are placed closer to the surface, which means that you do not need to dig for them in menus or memorize their locations.

B. Navigation Pane

The Navigation Pane lists and provides easy access to all of the objects in the currently open database. Use the Navigation Pane to organize your objects by object type, date created, date modified, related table (based on object dependencies), or in custom groups that you create. You can easily collapse the Navigation Pane so that it takes up little space, but still remains available. The Navigation Pane replaces the Database window that was used in versions of Access earlier than Access 2007.

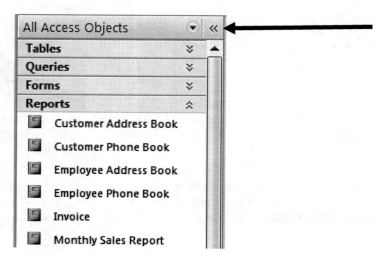

Chapter 7: Tables

I. Introduction to Tables

Tables are grids that store information in a database similar to the way an Excel worksheet stores information in a workbook. Access provides three ways to create a table for which there are icons in the Database Window. Double-click on the icons to create a table. For our purposes, we will create a table in design view.

A. Create a Table in Design View Design View allows you to define the fields in the table before adding any data to the datasheet. The window is divided into two parts: a top pane for entering the field name, data type, and an optional description of the field, and a bottom pane for specifying field properties.

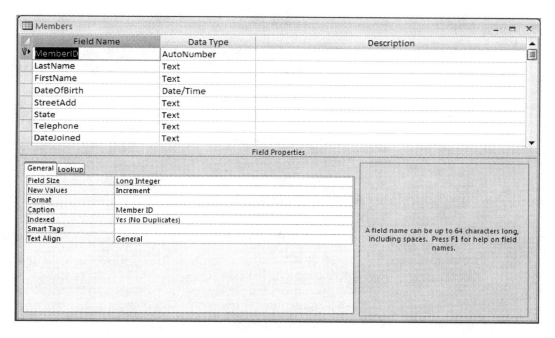

B. Field Properties

Field Name	This is the name of the field and should represent the contents of the field such as "FirstName", "Address", "Final Grade", etc. The name cannot exceed 64 characters in length and may include spaces. Access has a few "words" that are considered reserved field names including the word "Name". If you try and add an attribute with a reserved field name, Access will not allow you to save the attribute. If you run into this situation, simply enter a different name for that attribute.

Data Type		
Data Type	The type of value that will be entered into the fields. Below are some of the data types available in Access	

Data Type	Description
Text	The default type, text type allows any combination of letters and numbers up to a maximum of 255 characters per field row
Memo	A text type that stores up to 64,000 characters.
Number	Any number can be stored.
Date/Time	A date, time, or combination of both
Currency	Monetary values that can be set up to automatically include a dollar sign ($) and correct decimal and comma positions.
AutoNumber	When a new row is created, Access will automatically assign a unique integer to the row in this field. From the General options, select Increment if the numbers should be assigned in order or random if any random number should be chosen. Since every row in a datasheet must include at least one field that distinguishes it from all others, this is a useful data type to use if the existing data will not produce such values.
Yes/No	Use this option for True/False, Yes/No, On/Off, or other values that must be only one of two possible values
OLE Object	An OLE (Object Linking and Embedding) object is a sound, picture, or other object such as a Word document or Excel spreadsheet that is created in another program. Use this data type to embed an OLE object or link to the object in the database.
Hyperlink	A hyperlink will link to an Internet or Intranet site, or another location in the database. The data consists of up to four parts each separated by the pound sign (#): DisplayText#Address#SubAddress#ScreenTip. The Address is the only required part of the string. Examples: • Internet hyperlink example: FGCU Home Page #http://www.fgcu.com# • Database link example: C:\My Documents\database.mdb#mytable
LookupWizard	The LookupWizard isn't really a data type but Access provides you an easy way to allow you to create foreign keys to lookup tables. Make sure you review the section on lookup tables in the ERD section of this book to gain a better understanding of what lookup tables offer. The lookup wizard can read values from 2 main sources. You can tell the wizard to look up the values from an existing table or query OR you can type the acceptable values into a list that is stored with the field. In general, it is preferable to look the values up from a table since the user can just update that table whenever a new value needs to be added or a value needs to be changed. While the same is true if the value is typed in a list, this approach is more cumbersome and difficult to maintain. You will need to have the lookup table created first. As an example, let's say I have an address table and I want the user to be able to pick a state from a lookup table (as you typically would if you were completing a form online). For our example, the table is called State and its structure looks as follows:

Field Name	Data Type
State_abbeviation	Text
State_name	Text

Here's a few rows stored in the table:

State_abbevi	State_name
DE	Delaware
NJ	New Jersey
NY	New York
PA	Pennsylvania

To use the lookup wizard

1. Select LookupWizard from the data type drop down box

2. Select "I want the lookup column to look up the values in a table or query" in the first screen of the wizard.

3. In the next screen, select the table which is the lookup table. In our case, you would select Table: State from the list of tables in the database.

4. In the next screen, select the values to appear in the lookup column. In this scenario, we would probably want to select both the abbreviation as well as the description. This will help in case the user isn't entirely sure what is the 2 letter abbreviation for desired state (particularly useful with all those I states like Idaho, Indiana, Illinois, etc.)

5. In the following screen, you will be asked how you want the lookup values to be sorted. Typically you'll want it in alphabetic or numeric order. You get to select whether the order should be ascending or descending. In this case, we'll ask for it be sorted by the 2 letter abbreviation in ascending order.

6. In the next screen you can modify the appearance of the lookup columns. Note that there is a checkbox which indicates that the primary key will be hidden. This option is useful since many times the primary key doesn't provide meaningful information to the user. For instance, if the lookup table was something like a product table, it would be difficult to remember all the different product identifiers so it would be better to show the product description. In our case, the 2 letter abbreviation is useful so we'll uncheck the box.

7. In the last screen, you get to give the column a name. We'll use state. Then click Finish.

8. Now whenever the user wants to enter a row and the user gets to the field with the data type of lookup, a drop down list will appear with the values in the lookup table in the selected order. The user will just need to click on the proper value and the value will be populated (stored) in that field.

Description	(optional) – Allows user to enter a brief description of the contents of the field
Field Properties-	Select any pertinent properties for the field from the bottom pane of the Design View window. See Field Properties Table below.

Field Properties:	
Field Size	Used to set the number of characters needed in a text or number field. The default field size for the text type is 50 or 255 characters based on how your application was configured. If the rows in the field will only have two or three characters, you can change the size of the field to save disk space or prevent data entry errors by limiting the number of characters allowed. Likewise, if the field will require more than 50 characters, enter a number up to 255. The field size is set in exact characters for Text type. The following are the options available for number type fields.

Size	Description
Byte	Positive integers between 1 and 255
Integer	Positive and negative integers between -32,768 and 32,768
Long Integer (default)	Larger positive and negative integers between -2 billion and 2 billion.
Single	Single-precision floating-point number
Double	Double-precision floating-point number
Decimal	Allows for Precision and Scale property control

Format	Ensures the data entered into a field is consistent for each row entered. For text and memo fields, this property has two parts that are separated by a semicolon. The first part of the property is used to apply to the field and the second applies to empty fields.

Some formats are pre-established and the user does not need further specification. For instance, in the currency format, there is a standard currency option. However, the user has the capability to change that standard to further customize the output. Examples are provided below to demonstrate how customization can be achieved. |

Text and memo format.

Text Format			
Format	**Datasheet Entry**	**Display**	**Explanation**
@@@-@@@@	1234567	123-4567	@ indicates a required character or space
@@@-@@@&	123456	123-456	& indicates an optional character or space
<	HELLO	hello	< converts characters to lowercase
>	Hello	HELLO	> converts characters to uppercase
@\!	Hello	Hello!	\ adds characters to the end

Number format. Select one of the preset options from the drop down menu or construct a custom format using symbols explained:

Field Properties:			

Number Format

Format	Datasheet Entry	Display	Explanation
###,##0.00	123456.78	123,456.78	0 is a placeholder that displays a digit or 0 if there is none.
$###,##0.00	0	$0.00	# is a placeholder that displays a digit or nothing if there is none.
###.00%	.123	12.3%	% multiplies the number by 100 and added a percent sign

Currency format: This formatting consists of four parts separated by semicolons: format for positive numbers; format for negative numbers; format for zero values; format for Null values.

Currency Format

Format	Explanation
$##0.00;($##0.00)[Red];$0.00;"none"	Positive values will be normal currency format, negative numbers will be red in parentheses, zero is entered for zero values, and "none" will be written for Null values.

Date format. In the table below, the value "1/1/01" is entered into the datasheet, and the following values are displayed as a result of the different assigned formats.

Date Format

Format	Display	Explanation
dddd","mmmm d","yyyy	Monday, January 1, 2001	dddd, mmmm, and yyyy print the full day name, month name, and year
ddd","mmm ". " d", "'yy	Mon, Jan. 1, '01	ddd, mmm, and yy print the first three day letters, first three month letters, and last two year digits
"Today is " dddd	Today is Monday	
h:n:s: AM/PM	12:00:00 AM	"n" is used for minutes to avoid confusion with months

Yes/No	Fields are displayed as check boxes by default on the datasheet. To change the formatting of these fields, first click the Lookup tab and change the Display Control to a text box. Go back to the General tab choices to make formatting changes. The formatting is designated in three sections separated by semicolons. The first section does not contain anything but the semicolon must be included. The second section specifies formatting for Yes values and the third for No values.

Format	Explanation
;"Yes"[green];"No"[red]	Prints "Yes" in green or "No" in red

Default	There may be cases where the value of a field will usually be the same for all. In this case, a changeable default value can be set to prevent typing the same thing numerous times. Set the Default Value property.

	Field Properties:
Primary Key	Every row in a table must have a primary key that differentiates it from every other row in the table. In some cases, it is only necessary to designate an existing field as the primary key if you are certain that every row in the table will have a different value for that particular field. A social security number is an example of a row whose values will only appear once in a database table. By default, Access automatically names the first field **ID** and indicates it as the primary key field. However, you can designate a primary key field by right-clicking on the attribute and selecting **Primary Key** from the shortcut menu or selecting primary key from the Ribbon or Menu Bar 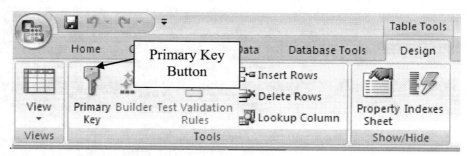 The primary key field will be noted with a key image to the left. To remove a primary key, repeat one of these steps. **Table1** |	Field Name	Data Type
---	---	---
🔑	Actor_ID	AutoNumber
	Actor_FName	Text
	Actor_LName	Text	 If none of the existing fields in the table will produce unique values for every row, a separate field must be added. Access will prompt you to create this type of field at the beginning of the table the first time you save the table and a primary key field has not been assigned. The field is named "ID" and the data type is "autonumber". Since this extra field serves no purpose to you as the user, the autonumber type automatically updates whenever a row is added so there is no extra work on your part. You may also choose to hide this column in the datasheet as explained on a later page in this tutorial.
Indexed	Creating indexes allows Access to query and sort rows faster. To set an indexed field, select a field that is commonly searched and change the Indexed property to Yes (Duplicates OK) if multiple entries of the same data value are allowed or Yes (No Duplicates) to prevent duplicates.
Validation Rules	Validation Rules specify requirements for the data entered in the datasheet. A customized message can be displayed to the user when data that violates the rule setting is entered. Click the expression builder ("...") button at the end of the Validation Rule box to write the validation rule. An example of field validation rules include <> 0 to not allow zero values in the row.
Input Masks	An input mask controls the value of a row and sets it in a specific format. They are similar to the Format property, but instead display the format on the datasheet before the data is entered. For example, a telephone number field can formatted with an input mask to accept ten digits that are automatically formatted as "(999) 888-7777". The blank field would look like (___) ___-____. An input mask can be applied to a field by as shown below: 1. In design view, place the cursor in the field that the input mask will be applied to. 2. Click in the white space following **Input Mask** under the **General** tab. 3. Click the "..." button to use the wizard or enter the mask, (@@@) @@@-

	Field Properties:	
	@@@@, into the field provided. The following symbols can be used to create an input mask from scratch:	

Symbol	Explanation
A	Letter or digit
0	A digit 0 through 9 without a + or - sign and with blanks displayed as zeros
9	Same as 0 with blanks displayed as spaces
#	Same as 9 with +/- signs
?	Letter
L	Letter A through Z
C or &	Character or space
<	Convert letters to lower case
>	Convert letters to upper case

Practice 1 – Create Tables in Access:

1. Download the Video Database from Blackboard.
2. Create the following tables in Design View.

													VideoDistributor

Attribute	PK	Data type	Size	Required	Validation Rule	Validation Text	Format	Default Value	Caption	FK	Referenced Table
Distributor_ID	Y	AutoNumber							Distributor ID	N	
Distributor_Name	N	Text	35	Y					Distributor	N	

											VideoCategory

Attribute	PK	Data type	Size	Required	Validation Rule	Validation Text	Format	Default Value	Caption	FK	Referenced Table
Category_ID	Y	AutoNumber							Category ID	N	
Category_Name	N	Text	35	Y					Category	N	

VideoTitle

Attribute	PK	Data type	Size	Required	Validation Rule	Validation Text	Format	Default Value	Caption	FK	Referenced Table
Title_ID	Y	AutoNumber							Title ID		
Video_Title	N	Text	50	Y					Video Title		
Release_Date	N	Date/Time		Y	>=#01/01/1900#		Short Date		Release Date		
Video_Duration	N	Number(Long Integer)		N					Duration		
Distributor_Name	N	(LookUp)		Y					Distributor	Y	Video Distributor
Category_Name	N	(LookUp)		Y					Category	Y	Video Category

3. Populate (enter the following rows into) the tables:

VideoCategory

Category_ID	Category
1	Action
2	Horror
3	Thriller
4	Sci-Fi
5	Drama

VideoDistributor

Distributor_ID	Distributor Name
1	Crazy Video
2	SBC Video
3	DVDNow
4	East Park Media
5	Scary Entertainment

VideoTitles

Title ID	Video Title	Release Date	Duration	Distributor	Category
3	Freedom Day	01/12/2006	140	Crazy Video	Action
4	Sea Trek	12/3/2000	190	Crazy Video	Sci-Fi
5	Gone with the Air	11/20/1964	300	DVDNow	Drama
6	Ex-Terminator	06/13/1999	200	SBC Video	Action
7	Buccaneers of the Caribbean	10/16/2006	119	East Park Media	Action

II.   **Table Relationships**

   A.   Introduction to Table Relationships

A primary key in one table should match the foreign key in the corresponding table and the two attributes must be of the same data type.

   B.   Create Relationships

     1.   To view the relationships tool, select Database Tools→ Relationships on the Ribbon or Menu Bar.

     2.   The Show Table Dialog should appear listing all of the tables in the database as below.

        a.   If the dialog doesn't appear, click on the show table icon.

        b.   If you have created relationships with foreign keys, you will note that those relationships will automatically appear in the ERD. You'll find that the tables I created will be related already

     3.   Highlight the tables you created in Practice 1 and click on Add.

     4.   If the relationships do not create automatically, the user can create relationships on demand. Click on name of attribute which is primary key in a table.

     5.   Click and drag to corresponding foreign key in the child table.

     6.   The Edit relationships dialog will appear showing the tables and associated attributes selected.

     7.   The relationship type will appear automatically based on information entered when tables created

     8.   To minimize data anomalies, enforce referential integrity for all relationships

        a.   Right click on the relationship line

        b.   The edit relationship dialog box will appear as shown below.

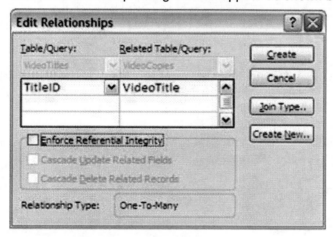

        c.   Click on enforce referential integrity.

        d.   Cascade on Update and Cascade on Delete will appear. Select both.

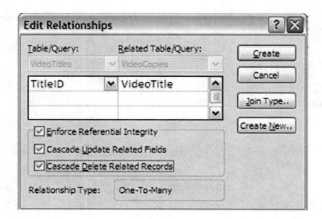

9. A line now connects the two fields in the Relationship window.

10. Expand the tables by clicking and dragging each table to ensure that each table is completely visible, there are no scroll bars, and relationships cross at a minimum.

11. Below are examples of the table with additional attributes not visible and then all the attributes visible (and no scroll bars).

Example with Scroll Bars:

Example with No Scroll Bars:

12. The datasheet of a relational table will provide expand and collapse indicators to view sub datasheets containing matching information from the other table. In the example below, the VideoTitle table and VideoCopy tableswere related and the two can be shown simultaneously using the expand feature.

13. To expand or collapse all sub datasheets at once, from the Ribbon select Home -> Records ->More->Subdatasheet->Expand All or Collapse All.

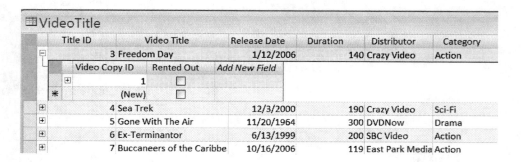

Practice 2 - Create an ERD:

1. If you haven't already done so, add the tables that you created in Practice 1 to the ERD in the Video Database.
2. Make sure that the tables that were provided in the download are shown and that all the tables are related as shown below:
3. Make sure to enforce referential integrity.

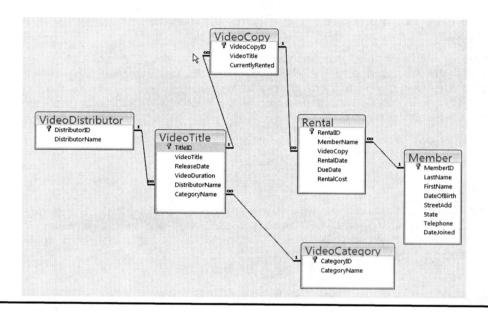

Chapter 8 Queries

I.   Introduction

Queries select rows from one or more tables in a database so they can be viewed, analyzed, and sorted on a common datasheet. The resulting collection of rows is saved as a database object and can therefore be easily used in the future. This database is called a dynaset, short for dynamic subset. The query will be updated whenever the original tables are updated. There are various types of queries. The most typical is the select query that extracts data from tables based on specified values, find duplicate queries that display rows with duplicate values for one or more of the specified fields, and find unmatched queries display rows from one table that do not have corresponding values in a second table.

Queries are used to view, change, and analyze data in different ways. You can also use them as a source of rows for forms, reports, and data access pages (data access page: A Web page, published from Access that has a connection to a database. In a data access page, you can view, add to, edit, and manipulate the data stored in the database. A page can also include data from other sources, such as Excel).

There are several types of queries in Microsoft Access:

II.   Select Queries

A select query is the most common type of query. It retrieves data from one or more tables and displays the results in a datasheet where you can update the row(s), with some restrictions. You can also use a select query to group rows and calculate sums, counts, averages, and other types of totals.

A. Wildcards:

The following table provides examples for some of the wildcard symbols and arithmetic operators that may be used. The Expression Builder ⚒ can also be used to assist in writing the expressions.

Query Wildcards and Expression Operators	
Wildcard / Operator	**Explanation**
? Street	The question mark is a wildcard that takes the place of a single letter.
43rd*	The asterisk is the wildcard that represents a number of characters.
<100	Value less than 100
>=1	Value greater than or equal to 1
<>"FL"	Not equal to (all states besides Florida)
Between 1 and 10	Numbers between 1 and 10
Is Null	Finds attributes with no value
Is Not Null	Finds all attributes that have a value
Like "a*"	All words beginning with "a"
>0 And <=10	All numbers greater than 0 and less than 10
"Bob" Or "Jane"	Values are Bob or Jane

B. Example - Select query to display all videos in the database with category of drama, sorted by distributor.

    1. From the Ribbon or Menu Bar, click on the Create tab then select Query Design in the Other section.

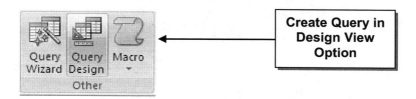

    2. In the Show Table window, add the tables you created in Part 1.

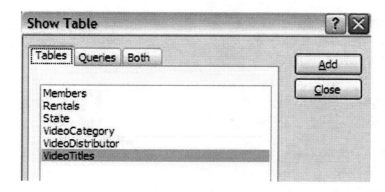

    3. Note the asterisk (*) in the tables you created. This is a SQL special character that tells the system that you wish to include ALL the attributes in the table to appear in the output. You can also select individual attributes to print out. The order of the attributes you select corresponds to the order that those attributes will appear in the output.

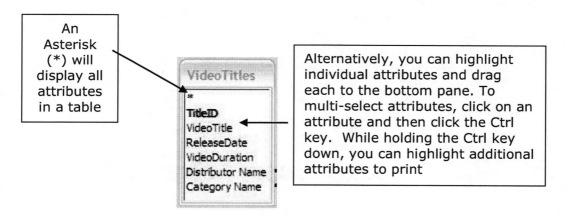

       a. For example, if you wanted to write a SQL statement which would display all the attributes in the Category table, you would write the following:

       b. SELECT * FROM VideoCategory

       c. Access actually allows you to write SQL directly without using QBE (Query by Example).

       d. To write SQL, click on the drop down next to Design ->Results->View.

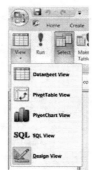

e. Select SQL View

f. The SQL statement that corresponds to the query you are writing in QBE will appear

```
SELECT
FROM VideoCategory;
```

4. Add the following attributes to the lower pane from each table:

Table	Attributes
VideoTitle	TitleID, VideoTitle, ReleaseDate , VideoDuration.
VideoDistributor	DistributorName
VideoCategory	CategoryName

5. In the DistributorName column, select Ascending for the Sort property.

6. In the CategoryName column, enter "Sci-Fi" for the Criteria. Note, you don't need to enter the word in quotes as Access will add them automatically.

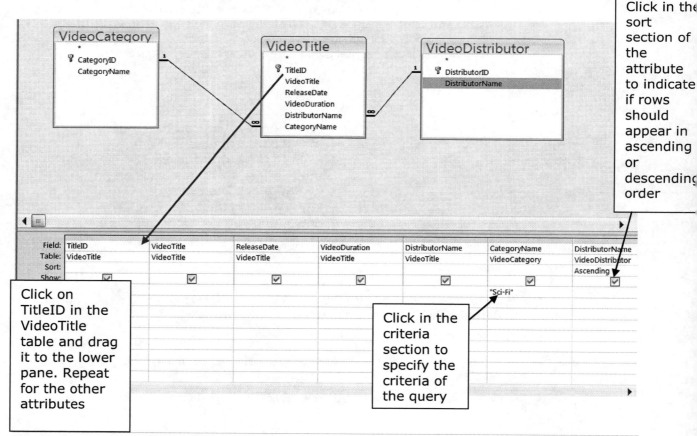

7. Under the Results section on the Ribbon or Menu Bar, click the button to run the query.

8. The results should appear as follows:

Title ID	Video Title	Release Date	Duration	Distributor	Category	VideoDistribu
4	Sea Trek	12/3/2000	190	Crazy Video	Sci-Fi	Crazy Video
(New)						

III. Parameter Queries

A parameter query is a special type of query in which the user has the ability to limit the output to specified rows which correspond to values of rows stored in the data of the table. For instance, let's say you have a student table which has information such as first name, last name, address, status (i.e. freshman, sophomore, junior, senior). You want the user to be able, on demand, limit the output based on the status without having to write a custom query each time. Essentially, you want the user to be able to pick a value from the status attribute (a parameter) and limit the output to just those rows that have that value in the attribute.A query parameter (often called just a parameter) is a placeholder for an actual value.

Although Access' parameter query function, it is cursory at best. Essentially when the parameter query runs, a dialog box will appear prompting the user to enter a value while will limit the rows retrieved. You can design the query to prompt you for more than one piece of information; for example, you can design it to prompt you for two dates. Access can then retrieve all rows that fall between those two dates.

Parameter queries are handy when used as the basis for forms, reports, and data access pages. For example, you can create a monthly earnings report based on a parameter query. When you print the report, Access displays a dialog box asking for the month that you want the report to cover. You enter a month and Access prints the appropriate report.

A. Example of Parameter Query:

In this example, we are going to write a query that allows the user to show the video title, release date and category name. What makes this different than a typical select query is that the user can limit the output to a specific category which can be entered as a parameter at run time. This means that the user can create a custom query without having to rewrite the select query each time the query is to run.

1. Click on Create ->Other-> Query Design.

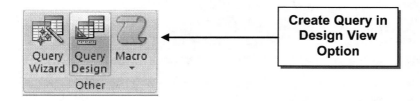

Create Query in Design View Option

2. In the Show Table window, add the VideoCategory and VideoTitle tables.

3. Drag the following attributes to the bottom pane of the query: VideoTitle, ReleaseDate, and CategoryName

4. In the criteria section of the Category Name column, enter the following: [Enter Category Name].

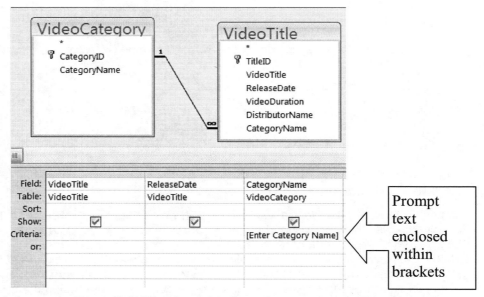

5. Click the run button and a dialog box with the text you entered in brackets will appear

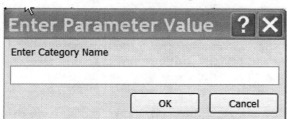

a. When you run the query, Access sees the bracketed parameter and prompts you to enter a value in the Enter Parameter Value dialog box. The value you enter is passed to the query as the parameter. It's as if you typed the value directly into the query design grid— but you didn't have to modify the query.

b. The text you supply within the brackets of the parameter becomes the prompt that you see in the Enter Parameter Value dialog box, so you should choose your phrase carefully and make sure it clearly indicates the information that needs to be entered. The phrase also serves as the name that Access uses to identify the parameter.

6. Enter in a value for which you would like to search. For this example, enter Action and click OK

Video Title	Release Date	Category
Freedom Day	1/12/2006	Action
Ex-Terminantor	6/13/1999	Action
Buccaneers of the Caribbe	10/16/2006	Action

a. After you enter the value, Access processes the query, selects the matching data, and presents the results in a datasheet.

b. Remember the value you enter must match exactly to the value stored in the table (including that the case must be identical) or no rows will return.

c. If you press ENTER without supplying a value, Access displays an empty datasheet as you are essentially telling the database to return rows with a null category.

IV.   **Crosstab Queries**

You use crosstab queries to calculate and restructure data for easier analysis of your data. Crosstab queries calculate a sum, average, count, or other type of total for data that is grouped by two types of information— one down the left side of the datasheet and another across the top. When creating a crosstab query, you must specify one or more Row Heading(s) options, one Column Heading option, and one Value option.

- **Row Heading:** This crosstab option is represented vertically in your dataset. Good candidates for this grouping are product types or other categories of data you want to aggregate. You can have multiple row heading columns, so multiple column aggregations are allowed.

- **Column Heading:** This crosstab option is represented horizontally in your dataset. Good candidates for this grouping are sales quarters or other categories of data for which you want only one grouping aggregation, because only one column heading is allowed in a crosstab query.

- **Value:** This crosstab option is the data that's typically summarized in your crosstab query. It's the product of cross-referencing your Row Heading(s) and your Column Heading aggregation.

A. Examples:

This example will create a crosstab query that will display the total number of movies that a distributor filmed in a specific category.
1.   Select Create ->Other-> Query Design.

2.   In the Show Table window, add the VideoCategory, VideoTitle and the VideoDistributor tables.

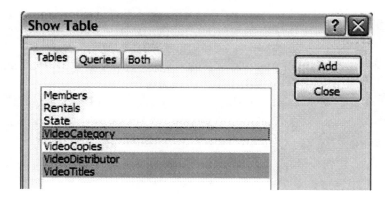

3.   In order to change the query into a crosstab query, under the Query Type section on the Ribbon or Menu Bar, select Crosstab.

4. Double-click the VideoTitle attribute in the VideoTitle table to add the attribute to the lower pane. Select Count for the Total property and Value for the Crosstab property.

5. Double-click the DistributorName attribute in the VideoDistributor table to add the attribute to the lower pane. Select Group By for the Total property and Column Heading for the Crosstab property.

6. Double-click the CategoryName attribute in the VideoCategory table. Select Group By for the Total property and Row Heading for the Crosstab property.

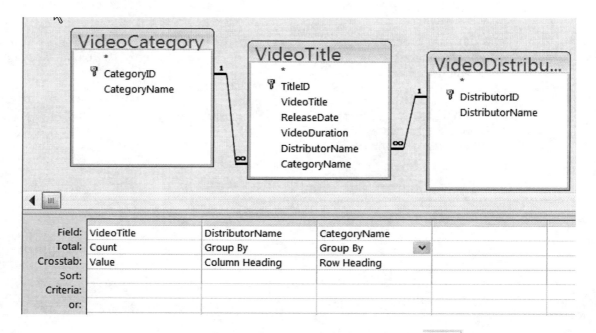

7. Under the **Results** section on **Ribbon or Menu Bar**, click the [Run] button to run the query. The results should appear as follows based upon the data you entered earlier:

Category	Crazy Video	DVDNow	East Park Me	SBC Video
Action	1		1	1
Drama		1		
Sci-Fi	1			

V.   Action Queries

An action query is a query that makes changes to or moves many rows in just one operation. There are four types of action queries

- Append
- Make table
- Update
- Delete.

A. Append Query

An append query adds a group of rows from one or more tables to the end of one or more tables. For example, suppose that you acquire some new customers and a database containing a table of information on those customers. To avoid typing all this information into your own database, you'd like to append it to your Customers table.

B. Make Table Query

A make-table query creates a new table from all or part of the data in one or more tables. Make-table queries are helpful for creating a table to export to other Microsoft Access databases (Microsoft Access database: A collection of data and objects (such as tables, queries, or forms) that is related to a particular topic or purpose. The Microsoft Jet database engine manages the data.) or a history table that contains old rows.

Let's consider the following scenario to explore the update and delete queries. Let's say we are working on a database for a hair stylist system (note – you do not have this database. I'm just providing an example). The customer table currently holds 29 rows and the structure looks like the following.

Field Name	Data Type	Description
Gender	Text	Customers' gender - Male or Female
Customer_LName	Text	Customers' last name.
Customer_FName	Text	Customers' first name.
Customer_Add1	Text	First line of customers address.
Customer_Add2	Text	Second line of customers address.
Customer_City	Text	City where customer currently resides.
Customer_State	Number	State where the customer lives from a drop down list.
Customer_Zip_Code	Text	Zip code of the town where the customer lives.
Customer_Phone_Number	Text	Customers' phone number.
Customer_E_Mail	Text	Customers email address.
Preferred_Stylist	Number	If applicable allows user to enter a customers' preferred stylist.
Status	Text	Displays whether the customer's appointment frequency is regular, occasional, or rare

C. Update Queries:

An update query makes global changes to a group of rows in one or more tables. The update statement changes the values of single rows, groups of rows, or all the rows in a table

If you have a update statement with no criteria clause you will update all the rows in the table. Accordingly, unless you truly want to update all the rows, consider a condition or filter.

1. Update Query with Criteria:

As you can see, the customer table has a gender attribute. The value of the field should be male or female. However, the current value of the field is a number (1 for male, 2 for female, and 3 for other). Let's write an update query to change the values of the field for women from a 2 to female.

a.   Select Create -> Query Design to display the show table dialog box

b.   Select the table(s) from which the rows are to be update. In this example, I'll select customer.

c.   Click on the update query icon Update on the toolbar. You'll note that the parameters in the lower pane of the query window change to limit the functionality to selection of the update criteria.

d.   Click on the attributes upon which the rows to be updated will be selected. For this update query, I'll click on gender as I only want to update rows from the customer table if the gender is a 2.

e.   In the Update To field – enter the value to which you want the current values changed. In the Criteria field – enter the current value of the field.

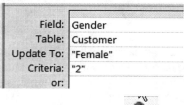

f.   Click the Run button Run

g.   The message below returns indicating the number of rows which are to be updated

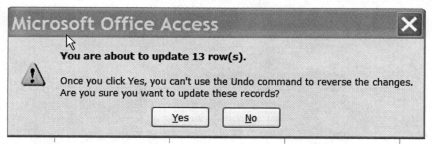

h.   Repeat steps to update rows with a value of 1 in the gender field to "Male" and a value of 3 to "Other".

2.   Update Query without Criteria:

We have a status field in our customer table which was designed to describe how frequently the customer comes to the salon. The field is currently not used. We'd like to populate (add data) to this field. Presently, our customer table is populated only with regular customers so we will update all of the rows to have a value of Regular in the status field.

All of the steps are the same to write the query except the criteria field will be left blank.

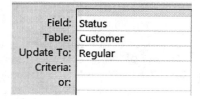

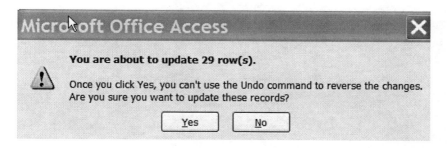

D. Delete Queries:

A delete query permanently deletes selected rows from one or more tables. For example, you could use a delete query to remove products that are discontinued or for which there are no orders. With delete queries, you delete entire rows, not just selected fields within rows.

If you have a delete statement with no criteria clause you will delete all the rows in the table. Accordingly, unless you truly want to delete all the rows in the table, it is essential to consider the condition or filter.

Remember – a delete statement only affects the rows in a table - even if you delete all the rows, the table structure still exists. In other words, the table is still there but there will be no rows in the table.

The process to write a delete query is essentially the same as with an Update Query.

1. Delete Query with Criteria

   Let's say the shop decides to market solely to men so they decide to remove all customers who are woman from the database.

   a. Select Create -> Query Design to display the show table dialog box

   b. Select the table(s) from which the rows are to be deleted. In this example, I'll select customer.

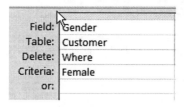

   c. Click on the delete icon ' Delete on the toolbar. You'll note that the parameters in the lower pane of the query window change to limit the functionality to selection of the delete criteria.

   d. Click on the attributes upon which the rows to be updated will be selected. For this update query, I'll click on gender as I only want to update rows from the customer table if the customer is female.

   e. In the Criteria field, enter the appropriate criteria. I'll enter "Female"

Field:	Gender
Table:	Customer
Delete:	Where
Criteria:	Female
or:	

   f. Click the Run button

2. Delete Query without Criteria

Let's say you decide to delete all the rows from the gender table:

VI. Aggregate Functions with Group By clause

A Group By clause specifies that you wish to perform some type of aggregations (sum, average, count, or other type of total for data that is grouped) but the grouping may not appear as a crosstab.

A. Example of Count and Group by Clause:

This example will show the total number of movies in a given category.

1. Select Create ->Other->Query Design.

2. In the Show Table window, add the VideoCategory and VideoTitle tables. Close the show table window.

3. Under the Show/Hide section of the Design Ribbon tab, click the Σ Totals button to add the Total property to the lower pane.

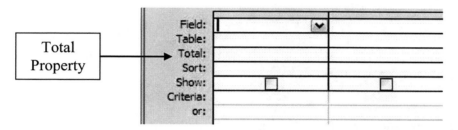

4. Add the following attributes to the lower pane:

Table	Attributes
VideoCategory	CategoryName
VideoTitle	TitleID

5. In the CategoryName column of the lower pane, select Group By for the Total property.

6. In the TitleID column of the lower pane, select Count for the Total Property.

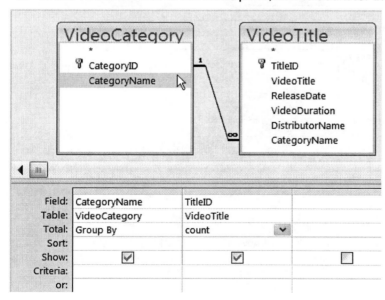

---

7. Click -> Results -> then the button to run the query. Your result should be similar the image below:

Category	CountOfTitle
Action	3
Drama	1
Sci-Fi	1

B. Example of a Query using the SUM function with the Group By clause: This example will show the video duration total in a given category.

1. Click Create ->Other ->Query Design.

2. In the Show Table window, add the VideoCategory and the VideoTitle tables. Close the Show Table Window.

3. In Design Tab ->Show/Hide ->click the **Σ** **Totals** button to add the Total property to the lower pane.

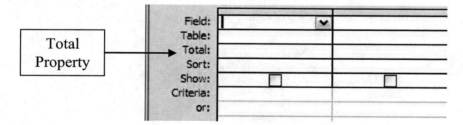

4. Add the following attributes to the lower pane:

Table	Attributes
VideoCategory	CategoryName
VideoTitle	VideoDuration.

5. In the CategoryName column of the lower pane, select Group By for the Total property.

6. In the VideoDuration column of the lower pane, select Sum for the Total Property.

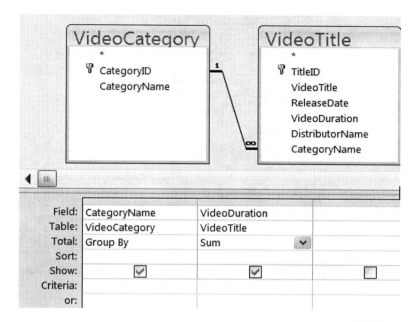

7. Under the Results section on Ribbon or Menu Bar, click the button to run the query. Your result should be similar the image below:

Query2	
Category	SumOfVideoDuration
Action	459
Drama	300
Sci-Fi	190

C. Example of a Query using the MAX function with the Group By clause: This example will show the max release date in a given category.

1. Click Create ->Other -> Query Design.

2. In the Show Table window, add the VideoCategory, and the VideoTitle tables. Close the Show Table Window.

3. Select ->Design-> Show/Hide->click the Totals button to add the Total property to the lower pane.

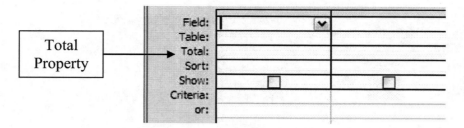

4. Add the following attributes to the lower pane:

Table	Attributes
VideoCategory	CategoryName
VideoTitle	ReleaseDate

5. In the CategoryName column of the lower pane, select Group By for the Total property.

6. In the ReleaseDate column of the lower pane, select Max for the Total Property.

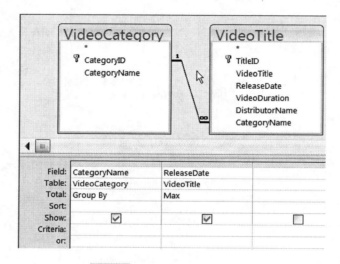

7. Click ->**Results** -> the [Run] button to run the query. Your result should be similar the image below:

Category	MaxOfReleas
Action	10/16/2006
Drama	11/20/1964
Sci-Fi	12/3/2000

Practice 3 - Create Queries:

Query the tables you created above based on the following criteria below. Examples of the output are provided

1. Create select query that will display all videos that have a category of Action, sort by VideoTitle. SAVE AS qrySelect

Video Title	Release Date	Duration	Distributor	Category
Buccaneers of the Caribbe	10/16/2006	119	East Park Media	Action
Ex-Terminantor	6/13/1999	200	SBC Video	Action
Freedom Day	1/12/2006	140	Crazy Video	Action

2. Create a crosstab query that will display the total number of movies that a distributor filmed in a specific category. SAVE AS qryCrosstab

Distributor	Action	Drama	Sci-Fi
Crazy Video	1		1
SBC Video	1		
DVDNow		1	
East Park Media	1		

3. Create a select query using the COUNT function with the Group by clause to display the total number of distributors in a given category. SAVE AS qryCount

Distributor	CountOfCate
Crazy Video	2
SBC Video	1
DVDNow	1
East Park Media	1

4. Create a query using the MIN function with the Group By clause to display the minimum release date of a video for each category. SAVE AS qryMIN

Category	MinOfReleas
Action	6/13/1999
Drama	11/20/1964
Sci-Fi	12/3/2000

5. Create a select query that will display the total number of videos in database. SAVE AS qryTotal

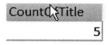

CountOfTitle
5

6. Create a parameter query for that shows the Video Title, Distributor Name and Duration and allows the user to pass the distributor's name as a parameter. SAVE AS Qry**Parameter.**

Chapter 9: Forms

I. Introduction to Forms

A user can enter data into a table directly through the datasheet view. However, this approach is not very user friendly. Accordingly, forms are used as an alternative way to enter data into a database table. Note: Every form must have a title pertaining to the topic that is meaningful. For instance, if the data entry form is to add, edit, or search for users, you may want to name the form "Manage Users". Also, the form should include the company's name and logo.

II. Create Form by Using Wizard

A. In the Ribbon, click Create tab -> Forms section ->More Forms button. In the drop-down box, select Form Wizard. The Form Wizard window opens.

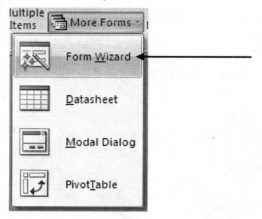

B. From the **Tables/Queries** drop-down menu, select the table or query whose datasheet the form will modify.

C. Select the fields that will be included on the form by highlighting each one of the **Available Fields** window and clicking the single right arrow button **>** to move the field to the **Selected Fields** window.

    1. To move all of the fields to Select Fields, click the double right arrow button **>>**.

    2. If you make a mistake and would like to remove a field or all of the fields from the Selected Fields window, click the left arrow **<** or left double arrow **<<** buttons.

D. After the proper fields have been selected, click the **Next >** button to move on to the next screen

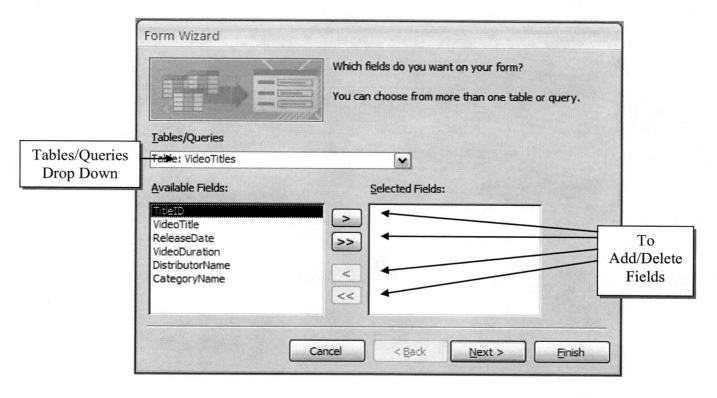

E. On the second screen, select the layout of the form.

- **Columnar** - A single record is displayed at one time with labels and form fields listed side-by-side in columns

- **Justified** - A single row is displayed with labels and form fields are listed across the screen

- **Tabular** - Multiple rows are listed on the page at a time with fields in columns and records in rows

- **Datasheet** - Multiple rows are displayed in Datasheet View

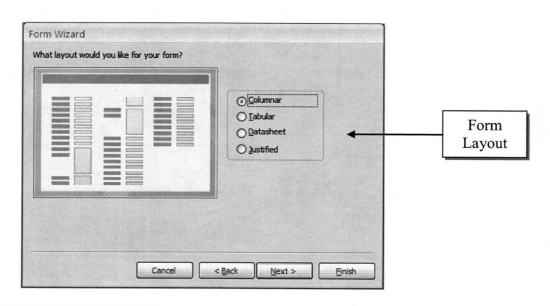

F. Click the **Next >** button to move on to the next screen.

G. Select a visual style for the form from the next set of options and click **Next >**.

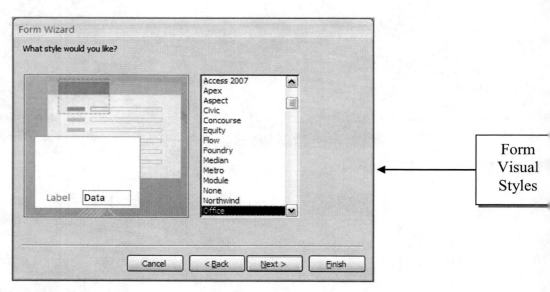

H. On the final screen, name the form in the space provided. Select "Open the form to view or enter information" to open the form in Form View or "Modify the form's design" to open it in Design View. Click **Finish** to create the form.

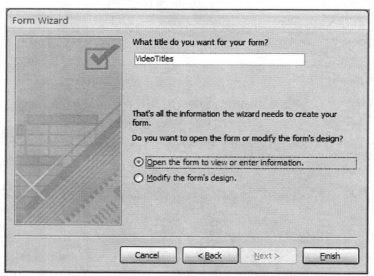

Practice 4 - Create a Data Entry Form Using Form Wizard:

1. Create a form that will display all the fields in the Member table by using the wizard. Save the form and call it Members.
2. When your form is complete, it should look similar to picture below:

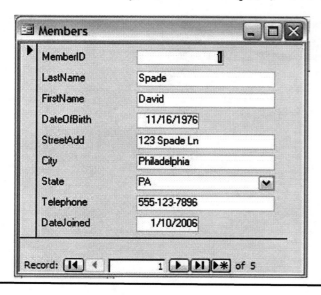

III.   **Create Form in Design View**

To create a form without the wizard, follow these steps. This options provides more control and flexibility.

A. Click the **Create** tab on the **Ribbon**, and then under the **Forms** section, click the **Form Design** button.

B. Notice that a new tab called Design is created on the Ribbon. This tab contains tools that can be used to design your form.

C. The **Field List** pane shows all of the other tables in your database, grouped into categories. To view the **Field List** window, on the **Design** tab on the **Ribbon**, in the **Tools** section, click **Add Existing Fields**.

1. In the **Field List** pane, when you click the plus sign (+) next to a table name, you see a list of all the fields available in that table.

2. To add a field to your table, drag the field that you want from the **Field List** pane to the form.

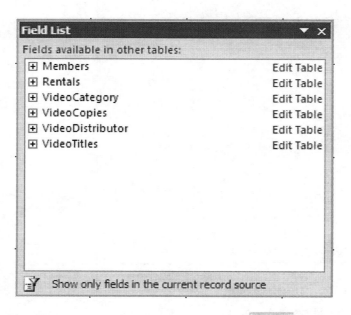

D. Once you have added the fields to the pane, click the  **Views** button on the **Ribbon** to view the form.

Practice 5 - Create a Data Entry Form in Design View:

1. Create a form that will display all the fields in the VideoTitles table by using the design view. Save the form and call it Video Titles.

2. When your form is complete, it should look like this:

IV. Adding Records Using a Form

A. To add information into the form, type the data into the appropriate fields of the form.

B. Press the **Tab** key to move from field to field

C. Create a new row by clicking **Tab** after the last field of the last row. A new row can also be created at any time by clicking the **New Record** button at the bottom of the form window.

D. Records are automatically saved as they are entered so no additional manual saving needs to be executed.

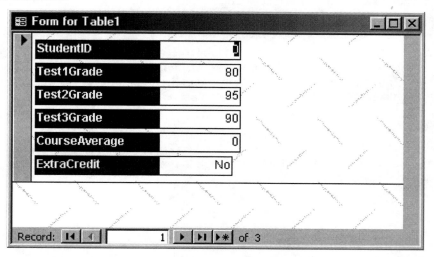

Practice 6 - Add Records to a Form:

1. Add the following row to the VideoTitles table using the form that you created in the last section. The system will automatically assign the Title ID as the primary key is an autonumber data type.

Video Title	Release Date	Duration	Distributor	Category
Spiderwoman	09/12/2002	100	East Park Media	Action

V. Editing Forms

The follow points may be helpful when modifying forms in Design View.

A. Grid lines:

By default, a series of lines and dots underlay the form in Design View so form elements can be easily aligned. To toggle this feature on and off click the Arrange tab on the Ribbon, in the Show/Hide section, click the button.

B. Snap to Grid:

Click the Arrange tab on the Ribbon, in the Control Layout section, click the Snap to Grid button to align form objects with the grid to allow easy alignment of form objects or uncheck this feature to allow objects to float freely between the grid lines and dots.

C. Resizing Objects:

Form objects can be resized by clicking and dragging the handles on the edges and corners of the element with the mouse.

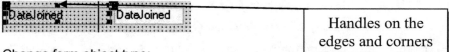

Handles on the edges and corners

D. Change form object type:

To easily change the type of form object without having to create a new one, right click on the object with the mouse and select Change To and select an available object type from the list.

E. Label/object alignment:

Each form object and its corresponding label are bounded and will move together when either one is moved with the mouse. However, to change the position of the object and label in relation to each other (to move the label closer to a text box, for example), click and drag the large handle at the top, left corner of the object or label.

F. Tab order:

Alter the tab order of the objects on the form by selecting View->Tab Order. Click the gray box before the row you would like to change in the tab order, drag it to a new location, and release the mouse button.

G. Form Appearance:

You can change the background color of the form by clicking the button on the Ribbon's Design -> Font section. Change the color of individual form objects by highlighting one and selecting a color from the button in the Font section of the Design tab on the Ribbon. The font and size, font effect, font alignment, border around each object, the border width, and a special effect can also be modified using the Design tab .

H. Page Header and Footer:

Headers and footers added to a form only appear when the form is printed. Click Arrange->Show/Hide->, the button to turn it off and on.

I.   Page numbers:

Page numbers be added to sections by selecting the Design -> Controls-> ▣ button. A date and time can be added by selecting the Design ->Control-> 🕒 button.

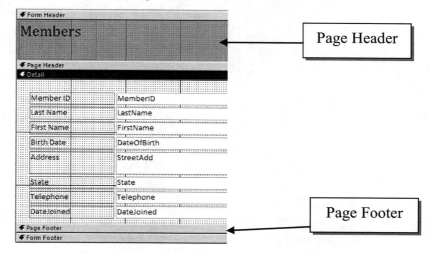

VI.   Form Controls

Access provides a number of controls to use on forms.   Some of the common form controls including lists, combo boxes, checkboxes, option groups, and command buttons are described below.

A. List and Combo Boxes

If there are small, finite number of values for a certain field on a form, using combo or list boxes may be a quicker and easier way of entering data. These two control types differ in the number of values they display. List values are all displayed while the combo box values are not displayed until the arrow button is clicked to open it as shown in these examples.

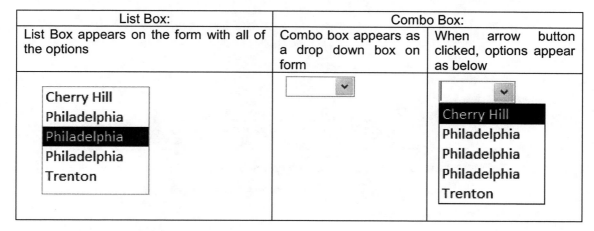

By using a combo or list box, the name of the academic building does not need to be typed for every row. Instead, it simply needs to be selected from the list. Follow these steps to add a list or combo box to a form:

1. Open a form in **Design View**.

2. Make sure the "Control Wizards" button is pressed in by clicking on the ⟋ button in the **Controls** section of the **Design** tab on the **Ribbon**.

3. Click the list or combo box tool button and draw the outline on the form. The combo box wizard dialog box will appear.

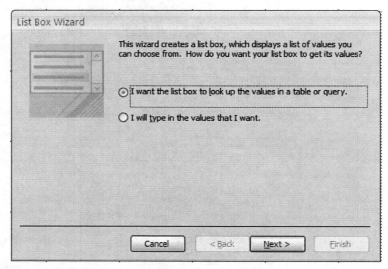

4. Depending on your choice in the first dialog box, the next options will vary. In this case, we will select the choice to look up values from a table or query. The following box will be displayed.

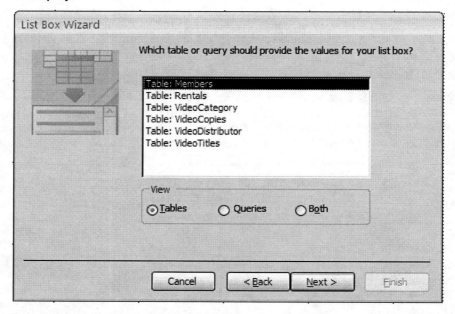

5. Select the table or query from which the values of the combo box will come.

6. Click **Next >** and choose fields from the table or query that was selected.

7. Click **Next >** to proceed.

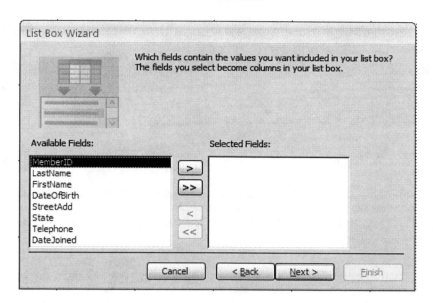

8. On the next dialog box, you have the option to sort the options in the combo box or list box in ascending or descending order. Click **Next.**

9. On the next dialog box, set the width of the combo box by clicking and dragging the right edge of the column.

10. If you selected the primary key field, it is recommended that you check the **Hide Key Column**. Click **Next >** to proceed to the final screen.

Hide
Primary
Key Option

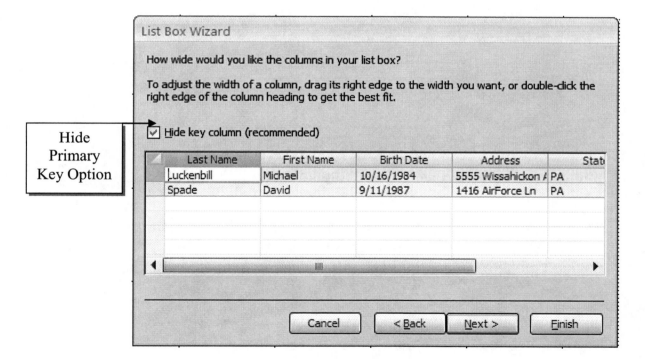

Practice 7 - Create a Combo Box:

1. If you haven't done so already, convert the foreign key State field in the Members form into a combo box. The combo box should display the states names in the States table.

B. Check Boxes and Option Boxes

Use check boxes and option buttons to display yes/no, true/false, or on/off values. Only one value from a group of option buttons can be selected while any or all values from a check box group can be chosen. Typically, these controls should be used when five or fewer options are available. Combo boxes or lists should be used for long lists of options. To add a checkbox or option group:

1. Click Design-> Controls ->Option Group 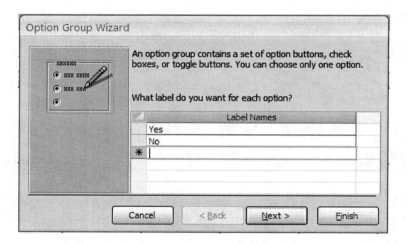 tool and draw the area where the group will be placed on the form with the mouse. The option group wizard dialog box will appear.

2. On the first window, enter labels for the options and click the tab key to enter additional labels. Click Next **>** when finished typing labels.

3. On the next window, select a default value if there is any and click **Next >**.

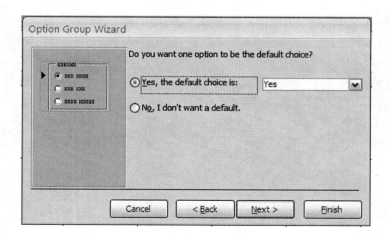

4. Select values for the options and click **Next >**.

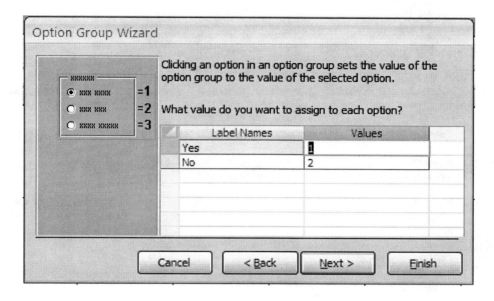

5. Save the values in a field

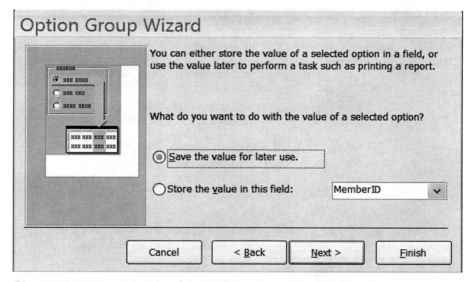

6. Choose the type and style of the option group and click **Next >**.

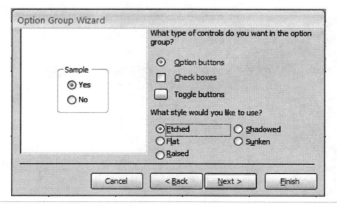

7. Type a caption (label) for the option group and click **Finish**. The option group will appear on the form and the data will be stored in the appropriate attribute in a table.

C. Command Buttons

In this example, a command button beside each row is used to open another form. This is a very common approach to add buttons to forms that allow the user to add a row, save a row, delete a row, cancel an operation, and lookup a row. We'll try it on the Member Form

1. Open the form in Design View and click on Design -> Controls -> Control Wizard .

2. Click Design-> Controls-> Command button icon and draw the button on the form. The Command Button Wizard will then appear.

3. On the first dialog window, action categories are displayed in the left list while the right list displays the actions in each category. Select an action for the command button and click **Next >**.

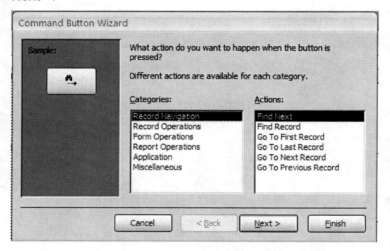

a. For our example, we want to add a button to add a member.

b. Click on Record operations and then Add New Record

4. On the next dialog window, you have the choice to either have a picture of the action on the button or just text. For our example, we'll add the text Add Member.

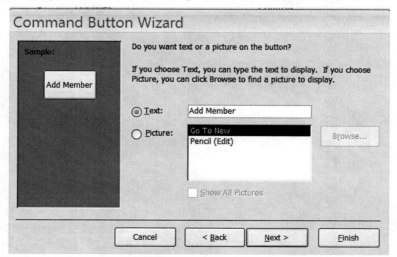

5. On the final window, give the button a name, such as cmdAddMember and click Finish.

6. Change to form view and click on the button. You will be presented with a blank form to enter a new member.

Practice 8 - Create Buttons on a Form:

1. Create buttons on the Members form to find a row, undo a row, and close the form.

VII.   Sub Forms for 1:M Relationships

A.   What is a Sub Form?

A sub form is a form that is placed in a parent form, called the main form. Sub forms are particularly useful to display data from tables and queries that have one-to-many relationships. For example, in the sample below, data on the main form is drawn from an item information table while the subform contains all of the orders for that item. The item row is the "one" part of this one-to-many relationship while the orders are the "many" side of the relationship since many orders can be placed for the one item.

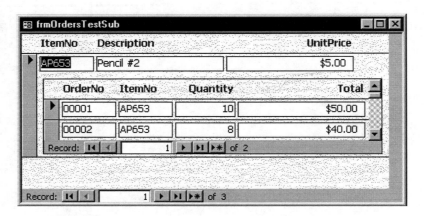

There are three methods to create sub forms. Each assumes that the data tables and/or queries have already been created.

B.   Create a Form and Sub Form at Once

Use this method if neither form has already been created. A main form and sub form can be created automatically using the form wizard if table relationships are set properly or if a query involving multiple tables is selected. For example, a relationship can be set between a table containing customer information and one listing customer orders so the orders for each customer are displayed together using a main form and sub form. Follow these steps to create a sub form within a form:

1.   Click the **Create** tab on the **Ribbon**, then in the **Forms** section, click the **More Forms** button. Finally, in the drop-down box, select **Form Wizard**. The Form Wizard window opens.

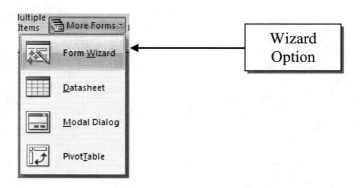

2. From the **Tables/Queries** drop-down menu, select the first table or query from which the main form will display its data.

3. Select the fields that should appear on the form by highlighting the field names in the **Available Fields** list on the left and clicking the single arrow **>** button or click the double arrows **>>** to choose all of the fields.

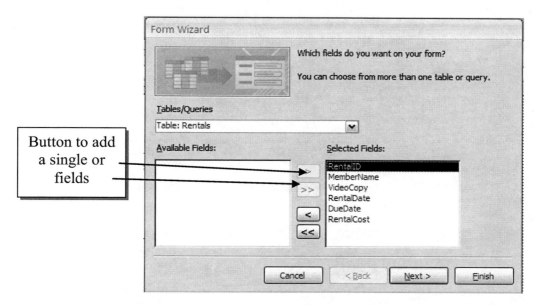

4. From the same window, select another table or query from the **Tables/Queries** drop-down menu and choose the fields that should appear on the form. Click **Next** to continue after all fields have been selected.

5. Choose an arrangement for the forms by selecting **form with subform(s)** if the forms should appear on the same page or **Linked forms** if there are many controls on the main form and a sub form will not fit. Click **Next** to proceed to the next page of options.

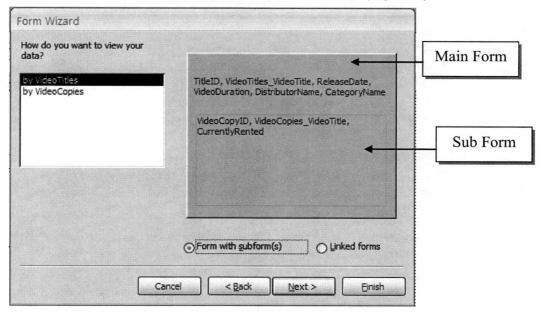

6. Select a tabular or datasheet layout (when you click on one of the radio buttons, an example of the form layout will appear to the left) and click **Next**.

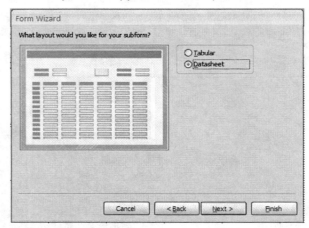

7. Select a style for the form (when you click a style, an example of the style will appear to the left) and click **Next**.

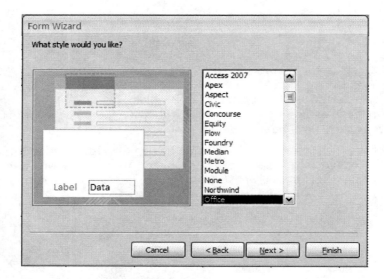

8. Enter the names for the main form and subform. Click **Finish** to create the forms. New rows can be added to either tables or queries at once by using the new combination form.

C. Create a Form and Sub Form at Once in Design View

If the main form or both forms already exist, the Subform Wizard can be used to combine the forms. Follow these steps to use the Subform Wizard:

1. Open the main form in **Design View** and make sure the "Control Wizards" button is pressed in by clicking on the ⚘ button in the **Controls** section of the **Design** tab on the **Ribbon**.

2. Click the **Subform/Subreport** icon ▦ in the **Controls** section of the **Design** tab on the **Ribbon** and draw the outline of the subform on the main form. The Subform Wizard dialog box will appear when the mouse button is released.

3. If the subform has not been created yet, select "Use existing Tables and Queries". Otherwise, select the existing form that will become the subform. Click **Next** to continue.

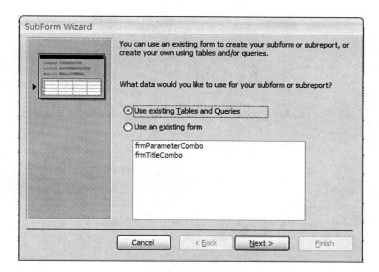

4. The next dialog window will display the relationship between the main and the subform assumed by Access. Select one of these relationships or define your own and click **Next**.

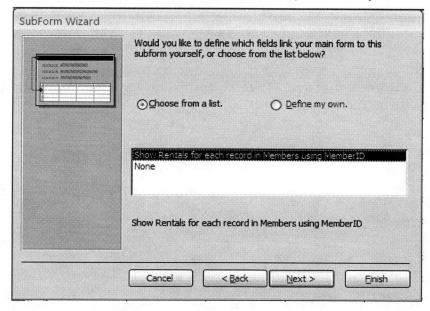

5. On the final dialog box, enter the name of the subform and click **Finish**.

D. Drag-and-Drop Method

Use this method to create subforms from two forms that already exist. Make sure that the table relationships have already been set before proceeding with these steps.

1. Open the main form in **Design View**

2. Drag the form icon beside the name of the subform onto the detail section of the main form design.

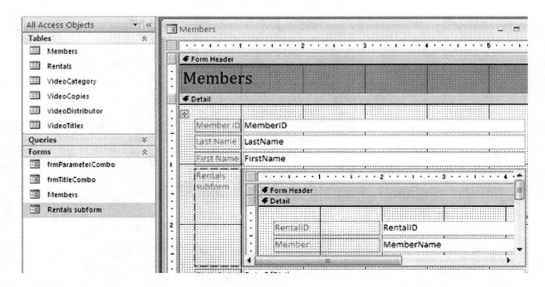

Practice 9 – Create a Form with a Subform:

1. Create a form with a subform at once using the VideoDistributor and VideoTitles tables.
2. When prompted how to view your data, select by VideoDistributor.
3. Save the form and call it VideoDistributor for the main form and VideoTitles Subform for the subform.
4. When your form is complete, it should look similar to picture below:

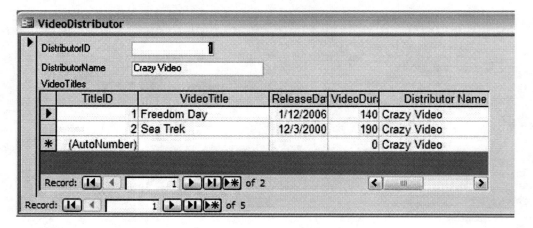

VIII. Sub Forms for M:M Relationships

The process for creating sub-forms with M:M relationships to other tables is basically the same as 1:M. The only difference is that you must decide what you want to be the main form.

For instance, in the video database, the main form could be movies and the subforms could be members and rentals. This would then show for each movie all of the members who rented the movie and the rental date. Alternatively, you might prefer to see for each member all of the movies rented. In this case, the member would be the main form and the movies and rentals would the subforms. Either approach is fine – it is completely determined by the needs of the organization. In some cases, you might want to create two forms: one with the Member as the main form and one with the Movie as the main form.

There is one rule to remember with M:M relationships. The main form must always be one of the entity tables, NOT the associative entity. If you think about it, this makes sense. For instance, you wouldn't want the rental to be the main form.

Refer to Subforms for 1:M relationships to create the relationships for both foreign keys.

A. Steps to create M:M Forms

1. Click the **Create** tab on the **Ribbon**, then in the **Forms** section, click the **More Forms** button. Finally, in the drop-down box, select **Form Wizard**. The Form Wizard window opens.

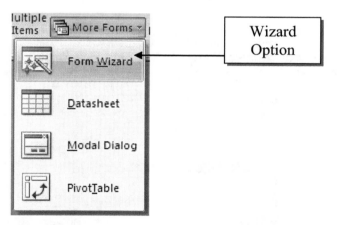

2. Click on the drop down menu next to display the tables and queries.

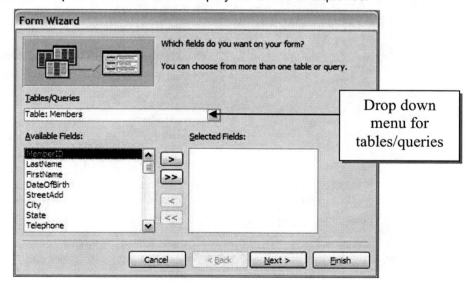

3. Select the Members table from the drop down list.

    a. The attributes for that table will appear below.

    b. Click >> to move all the fields into the Selected Fields section.

    c. Repeat for the Rentals and the VideoCopies table.

    d. All of the attributes for all three tables will appear in the Selected Fields panel. Click Next.

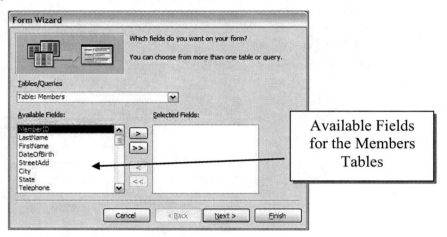

4. The wizard will ask how the data is to be viewed – this relates to which of the two entities will be the main form. Select the VideoCopies table and click Next.

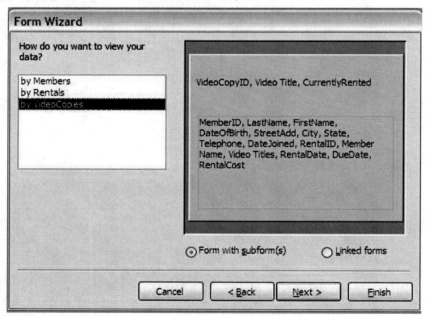

5. The next screens are the same as in the 1:M form. On the next window, you will be prompted to select a layout. For this example, choose the Datasheet layout.

6. Next select the style for the form.

7. On the next window, you will be prompted to enter titles of the both the main form and the subform. You will also be asked to open the form or to modify the form in design view.

For this example, the title of the main form will be VideoCopies and the subform Rentals Subform. Click Finish to open the form.

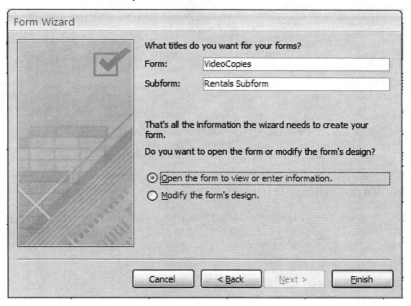

8. Below is a screenshot of the results:

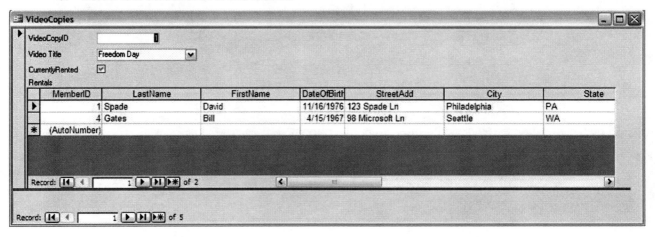

Practice 10 - Create a M:N Form

1. Create a form for M:N relationship using the VideoDistributor, VideoTitles and VideoCategory tables.
2. When prompted how to view your data, select by VideoCategory.
3. Save the form and call it VideoCategory for the main form and VideoTitles Subform 2 for the subform.
4. When your form is complete, the form should display VideoTitles and the VideoDistributor's fields in the subform and look similar to picture below:

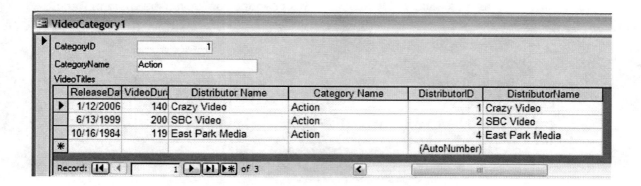

IX. Multiple-Page Forms Using Tabs

A tab control is the easiest and most effective way to create a form with multiple pages or multiple embedded subforms. With a tab control, you can build separate pages into one control. To switch pages, you click one of the tabs on the control. Create a tab control by following these steps:

A. Click the **Tab Control** icon in the **Controls** section of the **Design** tab on the **Ribbon** and draw the control on the form.

B. Add new controls to each tab page the same way that controls are added to regular form pages and click the tabs to change pages.

C. Existing form controls cannot be added to the tab page by dragging and dropping. Instead, right-click on the control and select **Cut** from the shortcut menu. Then right-click on the tab control and select **Paste**. The controls can then be repositioned on the tab control.

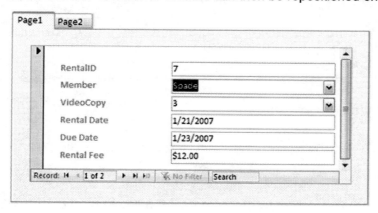

    1.   Add new tabs or delete tabs:

        a.   Right-click in the tab area.

       b.   Choose Insert Page or Delete Page from the shortcut menu.

2. Reorder tabs:

       a.   Right-click on the tab control.

       b.   Select Page Order.

3. Rename tabs:

       a.   Double-click on a tab

       b.   Select Name property under Other tab.

Practice 11 – Create a Form with Tab Control:

1. Create a new form called Tabs. The new form should include a tab control with two tabs (one for Members and the other for Video Titles)
2. Using the Member form and the VideoTitles form that you created earlier, attach these forms to their respective tabs.
3. When your form is complete, the form should look similar to picture below:

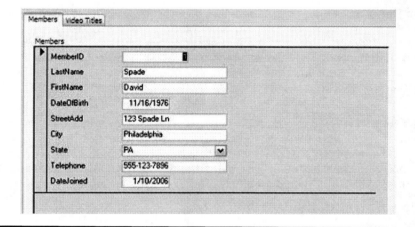

Chapter 10: Reports

I. Introduction to Reports

Reports will organize and group the information in a table or query and provide a way to print the data in a database. Note: Every report should have a title pertaining to the topic that is meaningful. For instance, if the report is to display all employees in the Human Resources Department, you may want to name the report "Human Resource Department Employees". Also, the report should include the company's name and logo.

II. Types of Reports

A. **Parameterized Reports**- A parameterized report is a report that uses input values to complete report processing. . Parameters are typically used to complete a query that selects data for the report. For instance, on online banking system may have a report that accept different parameters from the user including the bank account type (savings vs. checking) and the date range of transactions. It then returns a report of all the transactions from that account for the specified time period. The user does not typically get to decide what attributes will print on the report as this is predetermined. But the user does get to limit the output to the values entered into the parameters (the date range and the type of account).

B. **Ad hoc Reports** - An ad hoc (as needed) report is a customized query. The user has full contol over the attributes that appear on the report, the sort order of the report, and any criteria for the report. For instance, in our online banking example, the user might want to create a custom report that allows him to print only the transaction date, merchant, and dollar amount of the transaction for all transactions made between a certain time period and only of a particular transaction type. This is a fully customized report which may only be needed once.

C. **Canned Reports** – a canned report is a report that runs when a user pushes a button. It does not allow the user the ability to customize the report in any manner. A typical report might be a list of all transactions for an account. The button has code attached to it which determines what information will appear in the report including the attributes to print, the sort order, and any predetermined criteria.

III. Create Report Using the Wizard

Create a report using Access' wizard by following these steps:

A. Click the **Create** tab on the **Ribbon**, then in the **Reports** section, click the **Report Wizard** button. The Report Wizard window opens.

B. Select the information source for the report by selecting a table or query from the **Tables/Queries** drop-down menu.

C. Select the fields that should be displayed in the report by transferring them from the **Available Fields** menu to the **Selected Fields** window using the single right arrow button **>**

to move fields one at a time or the double arrow button **>>** to move all of the fields at once. Click the **Next >** button to move to the next screen.

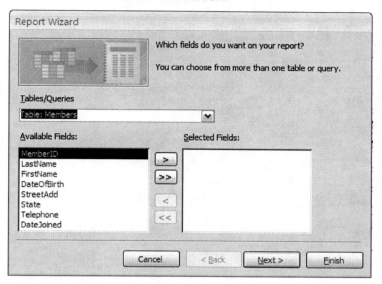

D. Select fields from the list that the rows should be grouped by and click the right arrow button **>** to add those fields to the diagram. For instance, let's say you want to see rows group by the member's last name. Use the **Priority** buttons to change the order of the grouped fields if more than one field is selected. Click **Next >** to continue.

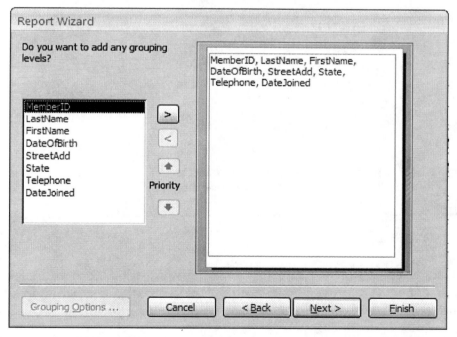

E. If the rows should be sorted, identify a sort order here. Select the first field by which the rows should be sorted and click the A-Z sort button to choose from ascending or descending order. Click **Next >** to continue.

F. Select a layout and page orientation for the report and click **Next >**.

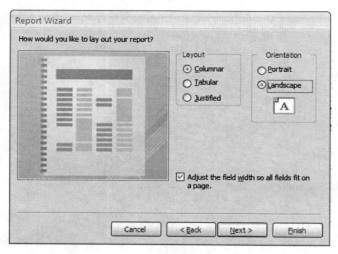

G. Select a color and graphics style for the report and click **Next >**

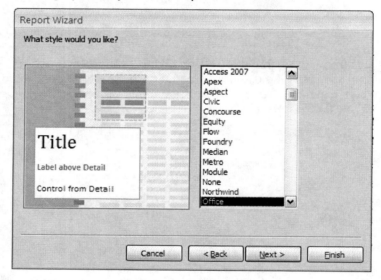

H. On the final screen, name the report and select to open it in either Print Preview or Design View mode. Click the **Finish** button to create the report.

Practice 12 - Create a Report:

1. Create a report called Members that will display a listing of all members as well as each member's address, phone, birth date, and date the member joined.
2. The report should display the last name in ascending order and landscape as the page layout.

IV. **Create Report in Design View**

A. To create a report from scratch (without a wizard), select **Create-> Reports ->Report Design** button.

B. You will be presented with a blank grid. Design the report in much the same way you would create a form. For example:

C. To view the Field List window, click Design ->Tools -> Add Existing Fields. In the Field List pane, when you click the plus sign (+) next to a table name, you see a list of all the fields available in that table. To add a field to your table, simply drag the field that you want from the Field List pane to the form.

D. Use the handles on the elements to resize them, move them to different locations, and modify the look of the report by using options on the formatting toolbar.

E. Click the View button at the top, left corner of the screen to preview the report.

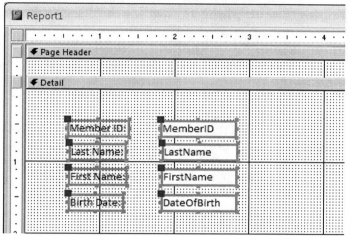

V. Printing Reports

A. Select Page ->Page Layout ->Page Setup button to modify the page margins, size, orientation, and column setup.

B. After all changes have been made, print the report by selecting the 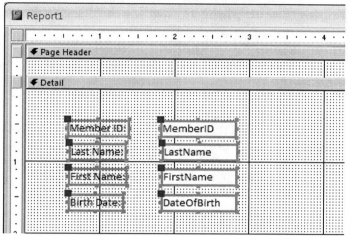 button on the Ribbon and select the Print ->Print button.

Chapter 11: Switchboard

I. **Introduction to Switchboards**

    A. A switchboard is essentially a Microsoft Access form that allows you to facilitate navigation or perform tasks within your database application. This form is basically a customized menu that contains user-defined commands; using either buttons, labels, images or hyperlinks, that invoke actions that will automatically carry out tasks for you such as opening other forms, running queries or printing reports.

    B. The form will typically contain various command (buttons), which users can then click on to carry out the pre-defined actions that have been associated with these commands.

    C. Using a switchboard form in your Microsoft Access database application allows you to tie together all of the other objects that you have created for your database users from a single form, and removes the need for the users to have to openly navigate from within the database window. You can also use this as the interface for your application, removing the chances of your users tampering with any of the objects that lie behind the scene of your application.

    D. Using buttons on your switchboard form can also replace the many possible steps that it would take the user to navigate around the objects in the database. To simply open a form in the database, the user may need to switch to the database window, choose the Forms tab and open the form from there. Using a command on the switchboard interface, the user now only has to click one button to carry out the same action.

    E. Most applications are organized into switchboards with submenus that have a button for data entry, administrative functions (manage users, manage lookup tables, etc.), and reports.

    F. Example: Below is a snapshot of a main switchboard that has four buttons: Administrative Settings, Customer Forms, Reports and Exit.

If the user selects the second option, Customer Forms, he will move to a submenu of forms pertaining to a customer as shown in the next picture. While the submenu screenshot is functional and very pretty, the user does not actually know that he is on the Customer Form menu. All submenus should have the company name and logo as well as the name of the submenu (i.e. Customer Form Menu)

II. Create a Switchboard

A. To create a switchboard, click the Database Tools->Database Tools->Switchboard Manager. For this example we are going to add one button onto our switchboard which will allow us to update (edit) a member's information.

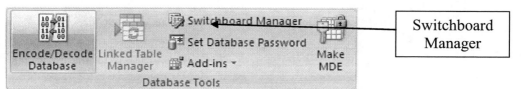

B. On the next screen, click Yes to create a new switchboard.

C. When the Switchboard Manager window appears, click on the Edit button.

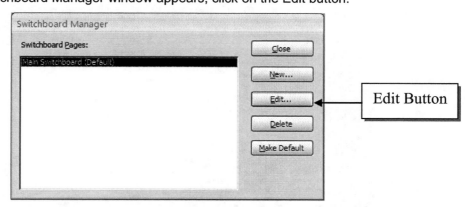

D. Next, you will need to add buttons to the switchboard. Click on the New button.

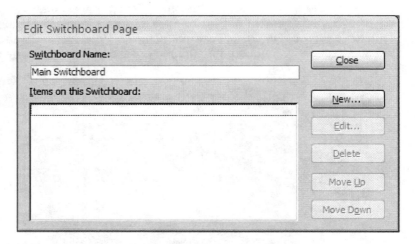

E. The Edit Switchboard Item dialog appears and you will need to complete three sections.

   1. Text:

      The Text field allows you to enter the text that will show as the label next to the button you are creating on the switchboard. In this example, we are Enter the text that will appear next to the button. We'll call this form Edit Member.Information.

   2. Command:

      The command option let's you select from a number of typical actions to be performed from a switchboard. Since we want to edit the member's information, we'll use the Open Form in Edit Mode option. The most common options are:

      a. Open Form in Add Mode: Opens a form so that the user can add a new row to the table. This option does not allow the user to modify the information that exists in a row.

      b. Open Form in Edit Mode: Opens a form so the user can edit information in a row in the table.

      c. Open Report: Allows the user to bring up a report. If the report is based on a query, the query will run when the button is selected and the report will appear with the updated data.

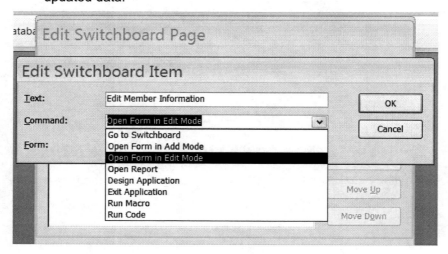

3. Form:

> The form option let's you select which form or report the command should be affected. The drop down will display all the forms and reports you have created in the database. In this case, we'll select the Member form.

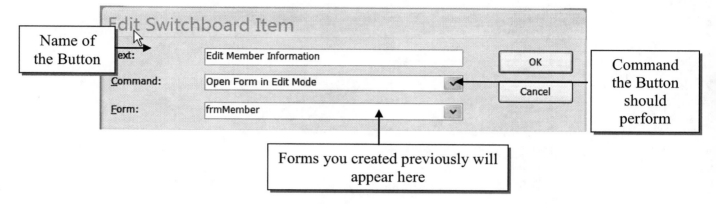

4. Select OK and then Close until the switchboard dialog box closes. Now you can click on the switchboard in your navigation pane and it should look similar to the image below. You can switch to design view to customize this form with images, logos, colors, etc.

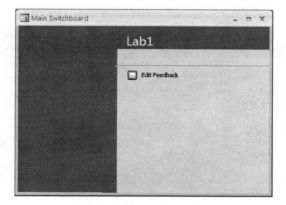

III. Create a Switchboard Within a Switchboard

This example assumes that there you have not created a switchboard for your database.

A. To create a switchboard, click the **Database Tools** tab on the Ribbon, then in the **Database Tools** section, click Switchboard Manager.

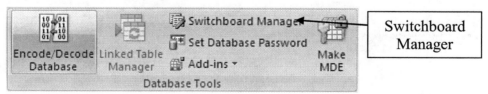

B. On the next screen, click Yes to create a new switchboard.

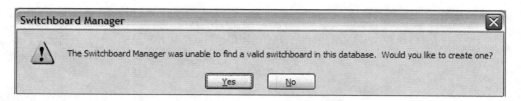

C. The Main Switchboard has already been created for you. To create another switchboard, click the New button.

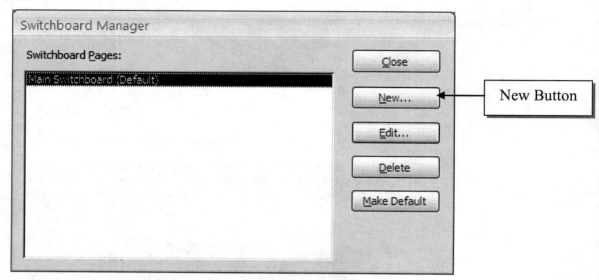

New Button

D. On the next screen, name the new switchboard Data Entry Forms and click OK.

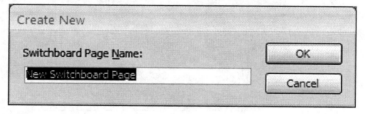

E. On the Switchboard Manager window, select the Main Switchboard and click the Edit button.

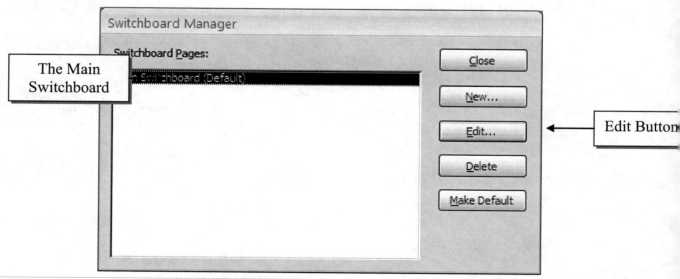

The Main Switchboard

Edit Button

F.   On the Edit Switchboard Page window, click the New button.

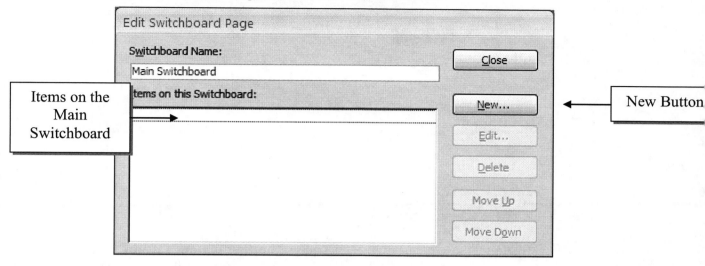

G.   On the Edit Switchboard Item window

   1.   Enter Edit **Forms for the Text**

   2.   **Select Go to Switchboard for the Command**

   3.   **Select Data Forms** for the Switchboard, Click OK and then Close twice.

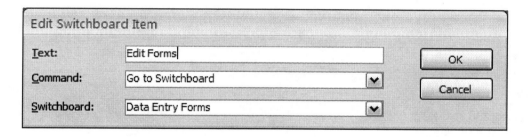

IV.   **Display Switchboard When Database Opens**

A.   To automatically display the Switchboard when the database is opened, follow these steps:

B.   From the **Ribbon**, click the ⬚ button and then select **Access Options**. The   **Access Options** window displays.

C.   Select the Current Database option.

D.   Under Application Settings, next to the Display Form label, select the Switchboard option from the drop   down menu and click OK.

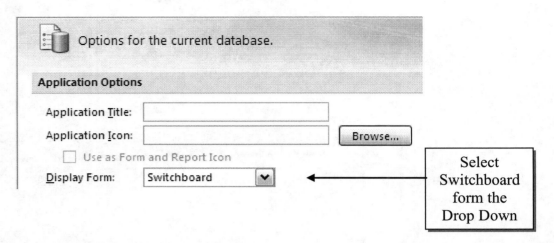

Options for the current database.

Application Options

Application Title: _____

Application Icon: _____ [Browse...]

☐ Use as Form and Report Icon

Display Form: [Switchboard ▼] ⟵ Select Switchboard form the Drop Down

Practice 13 – Create a Switchboard:

1. Create a switchboard that has 3 buttons. The first button, called Queries, takes the user to another switchboard that includes has buttons for all of the queries created so far. The next button, called Forms, takes the user to the M:N form created. The last button, called Exit, closes the application
2. Make the switchboard open automatically when the user opens the database.

Chapter 12: Keyboard Shortcuts Cuts

Keyboard shortcuts can save time and the effort of constantly switching from the keyboard to the mouse to execute simple commands. Print this list of Access keyboard shortcuts and keep it by your computer for a quick reference. Note: A plus sign indicates that the keys need to be pressed at the same time.

Action	Keystroke
Document actions	
Open existing database	CTRL+O
Open a new database	CTRL+N
Save	CTRL+S
Print	CTRL+P
Undo data changes made in current field	ESC
Display database window	F11
Find and Replace	CTRL+F
Copy	CTRL+C
Cut	CTRL+X
Paste	CTRL+V
Undo	CTRL+Z
Editing	
Toggle between editing and navigation mode	F2 function key
Open window for editing large content fields	SHIFT+F2
Switch from current field to current row	ESC
Move to next field in row	TAB
Other	
Insert line break in a memo field	CTRL+ENTER
Insert current date	CTRL+;
Insert current time	CTRL+:
Copy data from previous row	CTRL+'
Add a row	CTRL++
Delete a row	CTRL+-

Action	Keystroke
Formatting NOT ACCESS	
Select all	CTRL+A
Copy	CTRL+C
Cut	CTRL+X
Paste	CTRL+V
Undo	CTRL+Z
Redo	CTRL+Y
Bold	CTRL+B
Italics	CTRL+I
Left justified	CTRL+L
Center justified	CTRL+E
Right justified	CTRL+R
Decrease indent	CTRL+SHIFT+M
Increase indent	CTRL+M
Editing NOT ACCESS	
Find	CTRL+F
Replace	CTRL+H
Insert hyperlink	CTRL+K
Spell checker	F7
Macros	ALT+F8
Moving through a datasheet	
Next field	TAB
Previous field	SHIFT+TAB
First field of row	HOME
Last field of row	END
Next row	DOWN ARROW
Previous row	UP ARROW
First field of first row	CTRL+HOME
Last field of last row	CTRL+END

Chapter 13: Pivot Tables

I.   **Introduction to Pivot Tables**

You can download a very nice introduction to pivot tables at the following site: http://www.nacba.net/PDF_FILES/PivotTableIntroduction.pdf Here's a really short description as provided by Wikipedia:

A. What's a Pivot Table:

A pivot table is a data summarization tool found in data visualization programs such as spreadsheets (e.g. Microsoft Excel). Among other functions, they can automatically sort, count, and total the data stored in one table or spreadsheet and create a second table displaying the summarized data. Pivot tables are also useful for quickly creating cross tabs. The user sets up and changes the summary's structure by dragging and dropping fields graphically. This "rotation" or pivoting of the summary table gives the concept its name.

For typical data entry and storage, data is usually flat. Flat means that it consists of only columns and rows, such as in the following example:

	A	B	C	D	E	F	G
1	Region	Gender	Style	Ship Date	Units	Price	Cost
2	East	Boy	Tee	1/31/2005	12	11.04	10.42
3	East	Boy	Golf	1/31/2005	12	13	12.6
4	East	Boy	Fancy	1/31/2005	12	11.96	11.74
5	East	Girl	Tee	1/31/2005	10	11.27	10.56
6	East	Girl	Golf	1/31/2005	10	12.12	11.95
7	East	Girl	Fancy	1/31/2005	10	13.74	13.33
8	West	Boy	Tee	1/31/2005	11	11.44	10.94
9	West	Boy	Golf	1/31/2005	11	12.63	11.73
10	West	Boy	Fancy	1/31/2005	11	12.06	11.51
11	West	Girl	Tee	1/31/2005	15	13.42	13.29
12	West	Girl	Golf	1/31/2005	15	11.48	10.67

While there is quite a bit of information stored in such data, it is very difficult to gather the information you want out of it. A pivot table can help you quickly summarize the flat data, giving it depth, and get the information you want. The usage of a pivot table is extremely broad and depends on the situation. The first question to ask is, "what am I looking for?". In the example here, let's ask "How many Units did we sell in each Region for every Ship Date?":

Sum of Units	Ship Date					
Region	1/31/2005	2/28/2005	3/31/2005	4/30/2005	5/31/2005	6/30/2005
East	66	80	102	116	127	125
North	96	117	138	151	154	156
South	123	141	157	178	191	202
West	78	97	117	136	150	157
(blank)						
Grand Total	363	435	514	581	622	640

A pivot table usually consists of row, column, and data (or fact) fields. In this case, the row is Region, the column is Ship Date, and the data we would like to see is Units. These fields were dragged onto the pivot table from a list of available fields. Pivot tables also allow several kinds of aggregations including: sum, average, standard deviation, count, etc. In this case, we wanted to see the total number of units shipped, so we used a sum aggregation.

B. How a pivot table works:

Using the example above, it will find all distinct rows for Region. In this case, they are: North, South, East, West. Furthermore, it will find all distinct rows for Ship Date. Based on the aggregation type, sum, it will summarize the fact, and display them in a multidimensional chart. In the example above, the first data point is 66. This number was obtained by finding all rows where both Region was East and Ship Date was 1/31/2005, and adding the Units of that collection of rows together to get a final result.[4]

II.   Introduction to ODBC

ODBC is an:

Abbreviation of *Open DataBase Connectivity*, a standard database access method developed by Microsoft Corporation. The goal of ODBC is to make it possible to access any data from any application, regardless of which database management system (DBMS) is handling the data. ODBC manages this by inserting a middle layer, called a database *driver*, between an application and the DBMS. The purpose of this layer is to translate the application's data queries into commands that the DBMS understands. For this to work, both the application and the DBMS must be *ODBC-compliant* -- that is, the application must be capable of issuing ODBC commands and the DBMS must be capable of responding to them.[5]

What does this mean for you? All large database management systems including Oracle and SQL Server support ODBC. This means you can connect any application with an ODBC driver to the compliant DBMS. So, if you would like to attach to an Oracle DB using Access, you can query multiple databases of different types simultaneously provided they have common data.

This also means that you only need Access to connect to various ODBC client database management systems. So if you are at home but you don't have SQL Server or Oracle loaded onto your machine, you can still access them via Access!

III.   Background to Connecting Access to Other Data Formats:

Access was designed to function as a conduit which allows interaction between other data formats. As such, you can import and/or link data from a variety of other data sources noted below. You can find more information and instructions pertaining to working with the below data formats through the help function within Access.

- Access Files
- Text Files
- Spreadsheets
- Web Page
- Windows SharePoint Services
- SQL or another ODBC data source (described above)
- Mail programs including Microsoft Exchange and Outlook
- Another database
- Data Access Page
- XML

---

[4] http://en.wikipedia.org/wiki/Pivot_table
[5] http://www.webopedia.com/TERM/O/ODBC.htm

IV. Connect Excel to Access

You can share data between Access and Excel in many ways. You can copy data from an open worksheet and paste it into an Access datasheet, import a worksheet into an Access database, or simply load an Access datasheet into Excel using the Analyze it with Excel command.

If your goal is to store some or all data in one or more Excel worksheets in Access, you will typically import the contents of the worksheet into Access database. When you import data, Access creates a copy of the data in a new or existing table, without altering the source Excel file. Of note, any changes made to an imported table will NOT be reflected in the source data. The changes will affect only the imported table.

If you do not wish to maintain a copy of the data in your Access database, you can link to the Excel worksheet. Linking allows you connect to data in Excel without importing it, so that you can view the data in Access. When you link to a worksheet, Access creates a new table that is linked to the source cells. . You can update the data in the worksheet when you are working in Excel and your changes will be shown when you view the linked table in Access. Of note:

- You cannot create a link to an Access database from within Excel.

- You cannot link Excel data to an existing table in the database. When you create a link, Access creates a new table, often referred to as a linked table. The table shows the data in the source worksheet or named range, but it doesn't actually store the data in the database.

- A database can have multiple linked tables.

- Any change that you make to the data in Excel will be automatically reflected in the linked (source) table.

- When you open an Excel worksheet in Access (In the File Open dialog box, change the Files of Type list box to Microsoft Office Excel Files, and select the file you want), Access creates a blank database, and automatically starts the Link Spreadsheet Wizard.

V. Connecting Text Files to Access

In this section, we will explore importing text files of different types: delimited and fixed width. When you import data from another source, the recipient (in this case Access) needs to know what information to put into which column. In a delimited file, a character (called a delimiter) is used to indicate when the values of one field end and the next column begins. In a fixed width file, all the values in the column are a set width so if the value is always 5 characters long, the characters at the sixth position would be stored in the next column. As you might guess, delimited files are typically used with files with attributes of a variable length (such as last name) while fixed width files would be used for files containing data that is always the same length (such as a phone number or a zip code). If the file has both variable length and fixed width fields, a delimited file is routinely used.

Access allows you to import files of both delimited and fixed width type through a wizard. We will see examples of both in this exercise. When you import a file, you can do the following functions. In this exercise, we will import tables.

- append data to a table that already exists in Access

- import a new table which has column headings

- import a new table without column headings.

VI. Creating Queries across Multiple Data sources

Once you have a database that connects various file formats, you can use this database to write queries. It will appear as those the database houses all the information and that all of the files were actually Access tables but you know that some of these are linked files, some imported, and all of various formats. You are beginning to see the beauty of ODBC!!!

VII. Crosstab Queries:

A. Cross tabs in Access:

You use crosstab queries to calculate and restructure data for easier analysis of your data. Crosstab queries calculate a sum, average, count, or other type of total for data that is grouped by two types of information— one down the left side of the datasheet and another across the top. When creating a crosstab query, you must specify one or more Row Heading(s) options, one Column Heading option, and one Value option.

- Row Heading: This crosstab option is represented vertically in your dataset. Good candidates for this grouping are product types or other categories of data you want to aggregate. You can have multiple row heading columns, so multiple column aggregations are allowed.

- Column Heading: This crosstab option is represented horizontally in your dataset. Good candidates for this grouping are sales quarters or other categories of data for which you want only one grouping aggregation, because only one column heading is allowed in a crosstab query.

- Value: This crosstab option is the data that's typically summarized in your crosstab query. It is the product of cross-referencing your Row Heading(s) and your Column Heading aggregation.

Example: Let's consider a banking scenario. The bank holds information about each branch, each customer, the various accounts a customer may have as well as each transaction on each account. Let's say we want to see a report that shows the number of each account type by branch of the bank. If you look at a detailed listing of loans from each bank, it would be difficult to discern which branch is processing the most loans and of what type. But if you create a cross tab that will display by branch, the number of loans of each type and the total number of loans for each bank. The final output will appear as below. As you will note, with the cross tab you can quickly see that Ambler is processing the most loans.

LOAN_TYPE_DESCRIPTION	Abington	Ambler	Cherry Hill	Feasterville	Huntingdon
15 Year Fixed Mortgage	2	1		1	
30 Year Fixed Mortgage	1	4	1		5
30 Year Variable Rate Mortgage			1	1	5
Auto Loan		2			4
Home Equity	2	3	2	3	
Line of Credit				1	4

B. Crosstab queries in Excel 2007

You can create crosstabs in Access. You can also create them in Excel but Excel's crosstab functionality is even more extensive. You can apply styles, perform drill down function, click, drag and move all the attributes, include page settings, and much more.

Section 4: SQL

Chapter 14: Welcome to SQL

I. Introduction to SQL

As described in Wikipedia:

> "Structured Query Language…is a database computer language designed for the retrieval and management of data in relational database management systems (RDBMS), database schema creation and modification, and database object access control management.
>
> SQL is a standard interactive and programming language for querying and modifying data and managing databases….. The core of SQL is formed by a command language that allows the retrieval, insertion, updating, and deletion of data, and performing management and administrative functions…: [6]

Before starting, to ensure that you have all the necessary data entered correctly, a database has been developed for you. Download the database which has been posted to your student portal.

A snapshot of the ERD is provided below to assist you in navigating through the database.

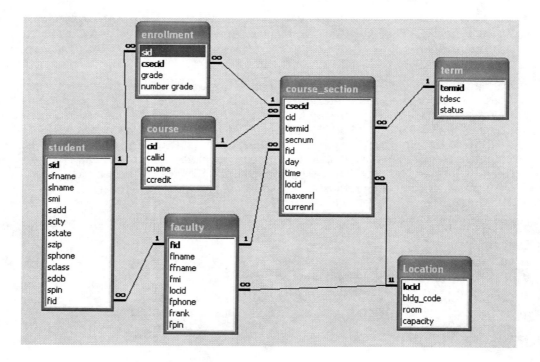

---

[6] http://en.wikipedia.org/wiki/SQL

II. DDL vs. DML

SQL has 2 components – the DDL(Data Definition Language) and the DML(Data Manipulation Language).

A. The DDL (Data Definition Language) deals with the management of objects themselves. DDL includes functions to allow the user to create a table, change the structure of a table, and delete a table. We will review the following statements so that you will become comfortable with them if you work on a database management systems (DBMS) which does not have a graphical user interface (GUI). However, in Access, you do not write these statements as they are automatically generated when you use the GUI. In other words, these statements are being generated automatically by Access as you work through the graphical front end.

Although all DBMS use these statements, there are slight variations in terms of the syntax when you move from one DBMS to another, such as between Oracle and SQL Server. In this book, the syntax is written for Oracle.

- CREATE TABLE - create a new database table
- DROP TABLE – delete a database table
- ALTER TABLE - alter (changes) a database table

B. The DML (Data Manipulation Language) deals with the data in the tables. DML allows the user to add rows to tables, query the data in a table, and change the information in a row. We will review the following statements. Again, some of these you will not need to write in Access as they are invoked automatically.

- INSERT INTO - insert new data into a database table
- SELECT – extract (retrieve) data from a database table
- UPDATE - update data in a database table
- DELETE - delete data from a database table
- COMMIT – permanently saves the changes to a database
- ROLLBACK – undo the uncommitted changes to a database

C. Qualifying column notation

1. When you refer to a column in a SQL statement, you specify the table first followed by a period and then the column name. This is known as qualifying the column name and uses tablename.attribute name notation.

    For instance, if there is an attribute in the student table called first_name, the attribute is called as student.first_name .

2. You can also call an attribute by just its column name (excluding the table name first) IF that attribute name is unique in the tables included in the query.

    a. For instance, if you are writing a query and the only table in the query is the student table. If you want the student's first name to appear on the output, you can just call first_name.

    b. If, however, if you included two tables in a query (student and faculty) and both had an attribute called first name, you would need to specify the table name first before the attribute as SQL wouldn't know which attribute you were referencing. Accordingly, if you wanted to call the first name in the student table, you'd have to write student.first_name.

3. It is always acceptable (and probably preferable) to use the full qualifying column notation. It just means more typing.

Chapter 15: DDL – Data Definition Language

NOTE: None of the DDL commands can be invoked directly through the SQL view in Access.

I.   Create Table

All the data in a database is stored in the form of 2 dimensional matrix called a table. A table consists of rows (also referred to as records) and columns (also known as fields/attributes/parameters). A table can be viewed as a container of data.

Each table has a structure. At a minimum, the table structure is defined by a table name and specific information about the attributes (columns) of the table including name, size and data type.

A. Format for Create Table:

1. The general format of the CREATE TABLE command appears below. Phrases in square brackets are optional, i.e. in this case the CONSTRAINT definitions are optional. You will learn about data declaration and constraint declaration as we go along. CONSTRAINTS can be also be defined separately after you have created a table.

   Syntax to create a table:

   CREATE TABLE <tablename>

   (<fieldname> <data declaration> …

   [CONSTRAINT <integrity constraint declaration>…

   );

2. Let's say we want to create a bank_customer table. In this table we want to add the following attributes shown on the left. Again, please note, the examples below are based on creating an Oracle database. The syntax and datatypes may change slightly if you use a different RDBMS. For instance, in Oracle there are two types of text datatypes, char and varchar. Char is used when the value of the field is always a set length (i.e. zipcode of 5 characters is a Char 5). A Varchar2 is a variable length data type (i.e. last name is not always a set number of characters). The syntax to create the table is shown on the right.

Attribute	Data Type	Size	CREATE TABLE bank_customer
Customer_ID	Number	5	(
Customer_ LastName	VarChar2	30	Customer_ID NUMBER(5) , Customer_LastName VARCHAR2(30) ,
Customer_ FirstName	VarChar2	30	Customer_FirstName VARCHAR2(30), Add1 VARCHAR2(30) ,
Add1	VarChar2	30	City VARCHAR2(25) ,
City	VarChar2	25	State CHAR(2) ,
State	Char	2	Zip CHAR(5)
Zip	Char	5	);

3. To create the table, we would write the statements noted above. The CREATE TABLE statement must start with the keywords "CREATE TABLE" followed by the table name. Of note, SQL will not allow spaces between words in a table name or attribute name. If you want to have a table or attribute name that is more than one word long, separate the words with underscores as shown above.

4. When you add an attribute you need to define its data type and size.

5. Each attribute added must be followed by a comma to indicate to SQL that there are additional attributes to be added.

6. The last attribute is NOT followed by a comma (since there are no more attributes to be added).

II. Drop Table

A. To remove a table from an Oracle database we drop it. This command deletes the table from the database.

You will often see a drop table statement appear before a create table command. As you know, each table in a database must have a unique name. If you are replacing a table with another with the same name, you must drop the existing table before you can recreate it.

B. Drop Table Syntax:

DROP TABLE <tablename>;	DROP TABLE manager;

C. Drop Table Cascade Constraints

If there are any foreign keys in other tables referring to the primary key of the table being dropped, the statement will generate an error message and the table will not be dropped. So what is a foreign key constraint? We'll learn more about foreign key constraints after we learn more about the drop statement. What is happening here is that the database is telling us that the table is related to another table and that by dropping one row which is related to another, you may create a delete anomaly.

If you cascade constraints, the database drops all referential integrity constraints that refer to primary and foreign keys in the dropped table and then drops the table from the database.

DROP TABLE <tablename> CASCADE CONSTRAINTS;	DROP TABLE manager CASCADE CONSTRAINTS;

III. Alter Table

The ALTER table statement is used to modify the structure of a table once it has been created. For instance, you'd use an alter table statement to add a new column to a table or to change a column's definition.

NOTE: the alter command is different from an update command. **Update** changes (updates) the **Data**. **Alter** changes the **table structure**. We will learn more about update later.

A. Restrictions on Alter table:

One key restriction of the ALTER TABLE statement involves adding a column with a not null constraint. As we'll learn later, a not null constraint indicates that an attribute must be populated (have data entered into it) and cannot be left blank. Most DBMS will not allow a not null column to be added to an existing table since we would automatically have null values for all rows that already exist in the table. Thus it would make it impossible for the constraint to be enforced by the DBMS. We'll explore null constraints further in a little bit.

B. Syntax:

   ALTER TABLE <tablename>
      ADD/MODIFY….

1. If you are adding something to a table (i.e. a new constraint or attribute), you will use the ADD keyword

Let's say we want to track a customer's date of birth and this is a newly added attribute to the table	ALTER TABLE customer ADD (customer_dob DATE);

2. If you are modifying something which is already in the table structure (changing a data type or size), you will use the MODIFY keyword.

Increase the size of the string column customer_add1 in the customer table from 35 to 50	ALTER TABLE customer MODIFY (customer_add1 VARCHAR2(50));

IV. Describe

The describe command allows you to show the attribute names and data types of a table as noted in the snapshot below.

Of note, the describe command does not show constraints with the exception of the Null constraint. However, if you look at the table design in Access, you can see all of the properties and constraints.

A. Syntax:

1. Describe <tablename>);

2. You can also use the shortcut Desc as in Desc <tablename>

| show the table structure of the bank_customer table<br><br>DESCRIBE bank_customer;<br><br>OR<br><br>DESC bank_customer; | ```
SQL> describe bank_customer;
 Name                             Null?    Type
 -------------------------------- -------- ----------------
 CUSTOMER_ID                      NOT NULL NUMBER(5)
 CUSTOMER_LNAME                   NOT NULL VARCHAR2(30)
 CUSTOMER_FNAME                   NOT NULL VARCHAR2(30)
 ADD1                             NOT NULL VARCHAR2(30)
 CITY                             NOT NULL VARCHAR2(25)
 STATE                            NOT NULL CHAR(2)
 ZIP                              NOT NULL CHAR(5)
 CUSTOMER_MI                               CHAR(1)
``` |
|---|---|
```

Chapter 16: Constraints (DDL continued)

I. Introduction to Integrity Constraints

In addition to the data content, a relational database consists of integrity constraints, a set of conditions that must be met or satisfied by the data content at all times. There are a few basic types of constraints. The concept of an integrity constraint is discussed in Section 1 of this book.

A. Integrity Constraint Syntax

   The general syntax for specifying constraints is as follows. Many developers give constraints constraint names. While this is often the preferred naming convention, it is not required.

```
[constraint <constraint_name>]
    unique  (<column> {, <column>}) |
    not null (<column> .{, <column>}) |
    primary key (<column> {, <column>}) |
    foreign key (<column> {, <column>})
            references <table_name> [(<column> {, <column>})]
                [on delete cascade]
```

II. Primary Key Constraints

A. As noted in early sections of this book, the primary key rules include:

   1. A primary key is used to uniquely identify each row and the values of its attributes in a table.

   2. If a column is defined as primary key, it cannot contain duplicate values and cannot be null.

   3. A primary key can be a single attribute or a combination of more than one attribute (if a primary key is made of two or more attributes, it is called a composite key).

   4. You can add a primary key to a table when the table is first created as part of the create table statement

   5. You can also add a primary key to a table after the table has been created using an Alter Table statement.

B. Syntax:

   1. Create primary key when creating table:

      <fieldname> data type CONSTRAINT (<fieldname> PRIMARY KEY)

Create a new table called city with the following attribute:	Attribute	Data Type	Size	Primary Key	CREATE TABLE city (
	city_id	Number	4	Y	city_ID NUMBER(4)
	city_description	VarChar2	30	N	CONSTRAINT city_ID PRIMARY KEY, city_description VARCHAR2(30));

   2. Add primary key to existing table:

      ALTER TABLE <tablename> ADD (PRIMARY KEY (<fieldname>));

Add monkey_id as the primary key to the monkey table.	ALTER table monkey ADD (PRIMARY KEY (monkey_id));

3. Create composite key when creating table:

PRIMARY KEY (<fieldname>, <fieldname>)

As we saw earlier, in the bank example, a customer can have numerous accounts at a bank and an account can have numerous customers associated with it. For instance, spouses may have a checking and a saving account at a bank and both spouses' names may be on both accounts. Let's say the bank creates a table called the Account_Assignment table. This table shows the relationship between the accounts and the account holders. The primary key for this table is a composite key which is two attributes that together make the primary key: the account_id and the customer_id.

Create a new table called account_assignment with the following attributes	Attribute	Data Type	Size	Primary Key	CREATE TABLE Account_Assignment
	customer_id	Number	5	Y	(customer_id NUMBER(5), account_id NUMBER(5), active CHAR(1), PRIMARY KEY (customer_id, account_id));
	account_id	Number	5	Y	
	Active	Char	1	N	

4. Create composite key for existing table

ALTER TABLE <tablename> add (primary key (<fieldname>, (<fieldname>)));

Make customer_id and account_id the primary key for the account_assignment table (this table already exists).	ALTER TABLE account_assignment ADD (PRIMARY KEY (customer_id, account_id));

III. Foreign Key Constraint:

A. Foreign Key rules:

1. Foreign Keys represent relationship between tables. A foreign key is a column or group of columns whose value is derived from the primary key of another table. Foreign key constraints are used to enforce referential integrity, which means you can only place a value in table B if the value exists as a primary key in table A.

2. If a column is defined as a foreign key in a table, any inserts or updates will be rejected if a corresponding value does not exist in the primary key table. The referential integrity constraint specifies that the attribute in the referring table must refer to a primary key value that exists in the referenced table. The foreign key can also be null. (Remember a foreign MUST match to a primary key).

For example in the bank scenario, the account table has a field which refers to the Branch_ID in the Branch table. Thus referential integrity would mean that the values of Branch_ID in the Account table must already exist in the Branch table or they should be null. This prevents the Account table from referring to Branches that do not exist!

3. The referencing column and referred column need not have the same name but MUST be of same data type and size.

4. A foreign key can be specified when the table is first created as part of the create statement or after the table has been created as part of an alter table statement.

5. It is often preferable to create tables without foreign keys and use an alter table command to add the foreign key later. In this manner, if you do refer to them from other tables, data entered satisfies the constraints. Also you cannot enter the foreign key constraints until you have created the table to which that constraint refers.

B. Syntax

1. Create a foreign key in a new table:

    <fieldname> data type CONSTRAINT (<fieldname> REFERENCES <tablename of referenced table> (fieldname of referenced attribute)

Create a new table called admin_office with the following attributes. Make the city attribute in the admin_office table a foreign key to the city_id attribute in the city table.	Attribute	Data Type	Size	CREATE TABLE Admin_Office
	Admin_ Office_ID	Number	5	(
				Admin_Office NUMBER(5),
	Add1	VarChar2	30	Add1 VARCHAR2(30),
	City	Number	4	City Number(4) REFERENCES city (city_id) ,
	Sate	Char	2	State CHAR(2) ,
	Zip	Char	5	Zip CHAR(5)
				);

2. Create a foreign key to an existing table

    ALTER TABLE <tablename of table with foreign key>

    ADD FOREIGN KEY <field name which is foreign key>

    REFERENCES <tablename of table with primary key to be referenced>

    (<fieldname of primary key to be reference>);

Make admin_office.state a foreign key to state.stateid. Note, the state table already exists.	ALTER TABLE admin_office ADD FOREIGN KEY (state) REFERENCES state(stateid);

IV. Null Value Constraint

SQL allows you to specify whether a field can be left blank (null) or must be populated (not null). Typically you want fields to be populated (filled in) but sometimes it is appropriate for a field to be left blank.

Null is an unknown value. When a particular row has a null value for a column it means that no value has been entered. A null is not equal to zero. If a column is defined as not null the user must enter data into that column for each row.

For instance, not everyone has a middle name. If you have a field for middle name you would not want to require the user to populate the field if he does not have middle name. Accordingly, you would not impose a not null constraint on that attribute meaning the user can leave it blank.

A. Null Constraint Rules:

1. If you impose a not null constraint, the user **must** populate (enter data into) the field. Since a primary key cannot be null, you do not need to specify not null for the primary key.

2. You cannot add a new column to an EXISTING table with a NOT NULL constraint imposed on it. This is because the table already exists with data and by adding a column with such a constraint we would automatically have null values for all rows that already exist in the table. This makes it impossible for the constraint to be enforced by the DBMS.

B. Syntax

1. Create a column that allows null values:

<fieldname> data type NULL;

2. Create not null constraint: - CAUTION, only use in new tables.

<fieldname> data type NOT NULL;

Create a null and not null constraints in new table called Manager	Attribute	Data Type	Size	PK	Null	CREATE TABLE Manager (Manager_ID NUMBER(5) CONSTRAINT Manager_id PRIMARY KEY, Manager_LName VARCHAR2(30) NOT NULL , Manager_FName VARCHAR2(30) NOT NULL, Manager_MI CHAR(1) NULL);
	Manager _ID	Number	5	Y	N	
	Manager _LName	VarChar2	30			
	Manager _FName	VarChar2	30		N	
	Manager _MI	Char	1		Y	

V. Default Value Constraint

SQL allows you to specify a default value for an attribute. A default value is a value that the system will automatically enter for the value of an attribute unless the user decides to select another value.

When you enter the default value, it MUST match the data type and size for that field. Accordingly, if the field is state description and the data type is Varchar2 (30), the value must be a string and must be entered in quotes indicating it is a string. If the data type is a number, the default value must be entered as a number without quotes.

For instance, if a bank is in Jenkintown, PA, most of the customers will be coming from PA. To expedite data entry, we can specify that when a new customer is added to the customer table, fill 'PA' into the state column. If the customer isn't from PA, the user can enter a different state.

A. Syntax :

1. Create a default value on an existing table

ALTER TABLE <tablename> modify <fieldname> default <default value>

Add a default value of PA to the Admin_Office.state:	ALTER TABLE Admin_Office MODIFY state DEFAULT 'PA';

2. Create default value on new table.

<fieldname> data type default <default value>

Create a new table called bank_type with the following attributes. Make the default bank_type_description 'MALL'	Attribute	Data Type	Size	Primary Key	Null	CREATE TABLE bank_type (Bank_type NUMBER(4) CONSTRAINT bank_type PRIMARY KEY, Bank_type_description VARCHAR2(30) DEFAULT 'MALL' NOT NULL);
	Bank_type	Number	4	Y	N	
	Bank_type_description	VarChar2	30	N	N	

VI. Unique Constraint

A unique constraint constrains the values in that column to be unique i.e. no two rows can have the same value. Of note, the column can have null values.

Remember that primary keys must always be unique but you do not need to specifically include this constraint. The unique constraint is automatically assumed when an attribute is designated as a primary key.

A. Syntax:

1. Create a unique constraint on existing table:

   <fieldname> data type unique

Let's say you want to enforce that a social security number is unique.	ss_number CHAR(5) UNIQUE

2. Create a unique constraint on new table:

A new table called staff and the position code must be unique since there can only be 1 person in the firm with that position.	Attribute	Data Type	Size	PK	Null	CREATE TABLE staff (staff_ID NUMBER(5) CONSTRAINT staff_id PRIMARY KEY, staff_LName VARCHAR2(30) NOT NULL , staff_FName VARCHAR2(30) NOT NULL, staff_position_code CHAR(5) NULL UNIQUE);
	staff_ID	Number	5	Y	N	
	staff_LName	VarChar2	30		N	
	staff_FName	VarChar2	30		N	
	Staff_position_code	Char	5		Y	

VII. Check Constraint

Constraints can also be defined for the values that can be entered into an attribute. This type of constraint is known as a check constraint.

A check constraint is basically a list of the possible values for an attribute. The user must enter one of these values to enter information into the field.

A. Syntax:

1. Syntax to create a new check constraint:

   <fieldname> data type check (<fieldname> = value 1) or (<fieldname> = value 2) or (<fieldname> = value 3), etc.

2. Create check constraint to new table:

Let's say the Jenkintown Bank only allows customers from specific states.	CHECK ((state = 'PA') OR (state = 'NJ') OR (state = 'DE') OR (state = 'NY'));

Create a new table called animal and the species must be a cat, dog, or bird.	Attribute	Data Type	Size	PK	Null	CREATE TABLE animal (animal_ID NUMBER(5) CONSTRAINT animal_id PRIMARY KEY, animal_Name VARCHAR2(30) NOT NULL , species VARCHAR2(15) NOT NULL CHECK ((species = 'cat') OR (species = 'dog') OR (species = 'bird')));
	animal_ID	Number	5	Y	N	
	animal_Name	VarChar2	30		N	
	species	VarChar2	15		N	

3. Create a check constraint on existing table:

Alter table <tablename> add check <fieldname> = value);

Add a check constraint to the animal table to verify that the animal_name can only be 'George', 'Paul', 'Ringo', 'John', 'Bruce', or 'Sting'.	ALTER TABLE animal ADD (CHECK (animal_name IN ('George', 'Paul', 'Ringo', 'John', 'Bruce', 'Sting')));

Chapter 17: DML - SELECT

I. Creating a query using SQL in Access

A. Open Access

B. In the Ribbon, click on Create -> Query Design

1. A dialog box will appear listing the tables in the database

2. Click on the Close button

3. In the Design tab select the SQL view

4. A select will appear. Type the SQL statements directly in the top window.

5. To run the query, click the exclamation point

6. The results of the query will appear.

II. Select Query Background

To retrieve information from a table, use the Select Statement.

The SQL select statement is very English-like. We SELECT the columns that we wish to view, FROM the table that contains the columns. Optionally, we can add criteria through a WHERE clause and sort it in some ORDER. For now, we will only worry about selecting all the rows from a table.

We use a SELECT clause to retrieve information from the database. The simple SELECT has three clauses: SELECT, FROM, and WHERE.

A. SELECT:

The SELECT clause tells which attributes should be displayed in the output.

1. The order of the attributes in the select clause corresponds with the order the attributes will appear in the output.

2. The SELECT clause is required.

B. FROM:

The FROM clause lists the tables where the date is stored and from which the data should be retrieved.

1. The order of the table names is irrelevant to the output.

2. The FROM clause is required.

C. WHERE:

The WHERE clause is used when the user wants to filter the rows returned based on specific criteria. As we'll learn shortly, the WHERE clause is also needed when there are multiple tables in the query and we need to join the tables.

1. The order of the criteria or joins in the where clause is not significant.

2. The WHERE clause is optional and is only required if the rows are filtered based on a specific criteria AND/OR there is a join.

SELECT [distinct] <expression> {, <expression>}

FROM <tablename> [<alias>] {, <tablename> [<alias>]}

[WHERE <search_condition>]

III. Simple SELECT

The simple SELECT includes:

- the SELECT clause which shows the attributes to appear on the output and

- the FROM clause which shows from which tables the attributes appear.:

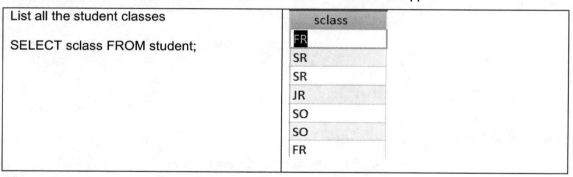

List all the student classes SELECT sclass FROM student;	sclass
	FR
	SR
	SR
	JR
	SO
	SO
	FR

IV. The Asterisk (*) Wildcard

As described earlier, the asterisk is a wild card in SQL*Plus.

The asterisk in a SELECT clause says that all the attributes (columns) in the table should appear in the output. The order of the columns in the output will correspond to the order of the columns in the table as shown here.

	SID	SLNAME	SFNAME	SN	SADD	SCITY	SSTATE	SZIP	SPHONE	SCLASS	SDOB	SPIN	FID
List all the locations in the student table	2	Banderas	Antonio	J	1444 Gorgeous Way	Hunk	PA	33333	1331333313	FR	5/14/1964	1873	
	100	Pitt	Brad	M	144 Windridge Blvd.	Cherry Hill	NJ	54703	7155559876	SR	7/14/1979	8891	2
	101	Jolie	Angelina	D	454 St. John's Street	Wilmington	DE	54702	7155552345	SR	8/19/1979	1230	1
	102	Damon	Matt		8921 Circle Drive	Philadelphia	PA	54715	7155553907	JR	########	1613	1
	103	Clooney	George	J	1716 Summit St.	Eau Claire	NJ	54703	7155556902	SO	9/24/1978	1841	5
	104	Bloom	Orlando	R	1780 Broad Street	Philadelphia	ID	54701	7155558899	SO	########	4420	4
	105	Depp	Johnny	S	1818 Silver Street	Elk Mound	ID	54712	7155554944	FR	12/4/1977	9188	3

SELECT *
FROM student;

V. Filtering in Select Statement (Projection) to Specific Columns:

Up until this point, we have not had the ability to modify the order of the columns in the output of our queries. Moreover, all of the attributes were displayed in every instance. However, a user can determine which attributes (columns) appear as well as the order that they appear in the output. By listing the specific columns to appear, the user is projecting (displaying) only certain columns of the table and an order specified by the user.

Let's say I want a report that shows student id, first name and last name for all the students and I want the output in that order. If I use select *, I would retrieve more information than I need. I can determine the exact output I want with the following query:

SELECT sid, sfname, slname
FROM student;

sid	sfname	slname
2	Antonio	Banderas
100	Brad	Pitt
101	Angelina	Jolie
102	Matt	Damon
103	George	Clooney
104	Orlando	Bloom
105	Johnny	Depp

VI. Order of Attributes in Select

The order you list the attributes in the SELECT clause determines the order of the columns in your output. Each attribute is separated by a comma.

List the last name and then the first name of the faculty

SELECT flname, ffname FROM faculty;

flname	ffname
Knightly	Keira
Streep	Meryl
Redford	Robert
Newman	Paul
Dench	Judith
Binoche	Juliette

To show the first name first and the last name last, revise the query as follows:

SELECT ffname, flname FROM faculty;

ffname	flname
Keira	Knightly
Meryl	Streep
Robert	Redford
Paul	Newman
Judith	Dench
Juliette	Binoche

VII. Distinct

The following query displays the sclass from the student table. You will note SR (for senior) appears twice and SO (for sophomore) appears twice as well. There are a total of 6 rows selected.

SELECT sclass FROM student;	sclass
	FR
	SR
	SR
	JR
	SO
	SO
	FR

This makes sense if you look at the student table:

SID	SLNAME	SFNAME	SMI	SADD	SCITY	SSTATE	SZIP	SPHONE	SCLASS	SDOB	SPIN	FID
100	Pitt	Brad	M	144 Windridge Blvd.	Cherry Hill	NJ	54703	7155559876	SR	7/14/1979	8891	2
101	Jolie	Angelina	D	454 St. John's Street	Wilmington	DE	54702	7155552345	SR	8/19/1979	1230	1
102	Damon	Matt		8921 Circle Drive	Philadelphia	PA	54715	7155553907	JR	10/10/1977	1613	1
103	Clooney	George	J	1716 Summit St.	Eau Claire	NJ	54703	7155556902	SO	9/24/1978	1841	5
104	Bloom	Orlando	R	1780 Broad Street	Philadelphia	ID	54701	7155558899	SO	11/20/1977	4420	4
105	Depp	Johnny	S	1818 Silver Street	Elk Mound	ID	54712	7155554944	FR	12/4/1977	9188	3

It is clear that there are 6 rows which correspond to the row count in the prior query. You can also see that Brad Pitt and Angelina Jolie are the two seniors while George Clooney and Orlando Bloom are the two sophomores.

What if you just want to see the list of states in the table? If you write a query that shows the states, there would be many duplicates and it would be quite lengthy. Fortunately, SQL has a command that solves this problem. To display only the unique values, in other words, to suppress duplication of the values, use the DISTINCT keyword to return unduplicated results.

A. Syntax:

Distinct <fieldname>

Show a listing of the possible types of student class. This will show the values in the sclass attribute but a value will appear only once regardless of how many rows are in the table with that value. SELECT DISTINCT sclass FROM student;	sclass
	FR
	JR
	SO
	SR

VIII. Restrict relational operator – Where Clause

So far we have been able to query all the rows of a table. However, most times we only want to see rows in a table that meet certain criteria.

With a where clause, the user can limit the results to only those rows that satisfy a condition. The condition is indicated in the WHERE clause.

A. Syntax: ... WHERE \<fieldname> = criteria

1. Let's say instead of seeing all the students in the student table we want to see the the first and last names of students whose faculty advisor (FID) is 1. To write this query, we need to start with our SELECT clause. Remember, every select query has to start with a SELECT clause. In this case, we will only select the first and last name and we will put the attributes in that order, as well.

    SELECT fname, lname

2. Next we need to tell SQL which table holds this data. We do that in the FROM clause. Every SELECT query must have a FROM clause.

    FROM student

3. Finally, since we only want the rows in the table with a faculty advisor of 1, we need to restrict the results using a WHERE clause.

    WHERE fid= 1

If we put it all together, the query looks like: SELECT sfname, slname FROM student WHERE fid = 1;	sfname	slname
	Angelina	Jolie
	Matt	Damon

B. It is often advisable to quality check the query by adding the criteria into the SELECT clause to verify it ran correctly. For instance, in this case, we can add fid into the SELECT clause so it appears on the output. Then we can be sure that the rows met our criteria.

SELECT sfname, slname, fid FROM student WHERE fid = 1;	sfname	slname	fid
	Angelina	Jolie	1
	Matt	Damon	1

IX. Searching for rows

A. String Searches:

If you are searching for a string (text or dates), the letters must be entered in single quotes. For instance, suppose you want to identify all students who are sophomores. Since the data in the sclass field is a text data type, when we search for a specific value, the value must be entered in quotes.

SELECT sfname, slname FROM student WHERE SCLASS = 'SO';	sfname	slname
	George	Clooney
	Orlando	Bloom

B. The criteria entered in the where clause must match exactly to the way the value is stored in the database. Accordingly, the values are case sensitive! As you'll note, attribute names and SQL keywords and operators (such as select, where, and, etc.) are NOT case sensitive.

Let's say we want to find all the students who are freshman. If we look for "Freshman", we won't return any rows.

	sfname	slname
SELECT sfname, slname FROM student WHERE sclass = 'Freshman';		

Why won't any rows return? Well, let's start by looking at the table. As you can see, sclass is only 2 characters long. It clearly can't hold a string as long as "Freshman".

Field Name	Data Type
SID	Number
SLNAME	Text
SFNAME	Text
SMI	Text
SADD	Text
SCITY	Text
SSTATE	Text
SZIP	Text
SPHONE	Text
SCLASS	Text
SDOB	Date/Time
SPIN	Number
FID	Number

To see what values are stored in this attribute, write the distinct clause as follows:

	sclass
SELECT DISTINCT sclass FROM student;	FR
	JR
	SO
	SR

The distinct clause allows the user to see that sclass stores only a 2 letter abbreviation. Moreover, the abbreviation for "Freshman" is "FR". Of note, Access is a very forgiving language. If the user searches for 'FR' in small case ('fr'), 2 rows will return since Access tries to match as best as possible the query to the actual values. However, in other relational database management systems, no rows would return because to computer 'FR' is quite different than 'fr';

Once the query is corrected to search for all students with a sclass of 'FR', the proper results will return:

	sfname
SELECT sfname, slname FROM student WHERE sclass = 'FR';;	Johnny
	Antonio

Because in most robust database management systems the values of data must match precisely in order to retrieve the desired rows from a database, data quality is critical. If data is entered into an attribute in different cases or with abbreviations or typographical errors, the user will not be able to retrieve all the rows. Accordingly, we typically suggest adding a lookup table whenever an attribute has a discrete number of values rather than permitting the user to enter free text.

X. Wildcard characters:

Sometimes you are searching for a string (word or list of characters) and you can't locate it. In such an occasion the use of a wildcard can be tremendously helpful. Wildcards can be used in query expressions to expand word searches into pattern searches.

Typically, instead of using the equal sign (=), we use the like operator to indicate that we are doing a string search.

The wildcard characters are:

Wildcard Character	Description
%	The percent wildcard specifies that any characters can appear in multiple positions represented by the wildcard.
?	The question mark wildcard specifies a single position in which any character can occur.

A. Syntax: <fieldname >% OR <fieldname>?

Show the students who have a last name that starts with P. SELECT sfname, slname FROM student WHERE slname LIKE 'P';	**sfname** **slname** Brad / Pitt	
Show all the students with an O in their last name: SELECT sfname, slname FROM student WHERE slname LIKE '%o%';	**sfname** **slname** George / Clooney Orlando / Bloom Johnny / Depp Antonio / Banderas	
I can't recall if Matthew Damon spells his nick name with one t or 2. SELECT sfname, slname FROM student WHERE sfname LIKE 'Mat?';	**sfname** **slname** Matt / Damon	

XI. Comparison Operators

In addition to looking to see if an attribute is equal to a specific value, we might want to know if the attribute is greater than (or greater than or equal to), less than, (or less than or equal to), or not equal to a value. Fortunately, SQL allows for all of these combinations with comparison operators.

The comparison operators are typically used in the WHERE clause to show the relationship between a variable and some value. A comparison operator can be used in combination of with another comparison operator to further filter the records

The comparison operators include:

Symbol	Description
>	Greater Than
>=	Greater than or equal to
<	Less Than
<=	Less than or equal to
<>	Not equal to (in some DBMS can also use !=)
IN	Looks for records with a value which is equal to one of the values in a list
BETWEEN	Looks for records with a value between two different values

Description	Room	capacity
Show the room numbers and capacity of the room of all rooms that have a capacity greater than or equal to 40. SELECT Room, capacity FROM location WHERE capacity >= 40;	101 202 105 211	150 40 42 55
Show the room numbers and capacity of the room of all rooms that have a capacity greater than or equal to 40 and less than or equal to 70. SELECT Room, capacity FROM location WHERE capacity >= 40 and capacity <=70;	202 105 211	40 42 55
Show the building code and capacity of all the buildings except SPK. Show a building code only once. SELECT distinct bldg_code, capacity FROM location WHERE bldg_code <> 'SPK';	bldg_code: CONWELL CONWELL CONWELL CONWELL LIB	1 35 42 55 1

A. IN Operator

The IN operator gives you the ability to allow for multiple conditions in one SQL statement. The list of values enclosed in the parentheses is called an *inlist*.

Note: the IN operator assumes that you are always including the OR comparison operator.

1. syntax: variable in (value, value, value,…)

<table>
<tr><td>Select the student's last and first name and state of all the students that live in New Jersey, Pennsylvania, or New York.

If you were to write this query using a typical comparison operator, it would appear as:

SELECT slname, sfname, sstate
FROM student
WHERE sstate = 'NY' or sstate = 'NJ' or sstate = 'PA';

Alternatively, you could use the in operator to write it as follows. This saves quite a bit of typing since you do not need to repeat the attribute name and the OR operator each time. In addition, it adds clarity for others looking at your code.

SELECT slname, sfname, sstate
FROM student
WHERE sstate in ('NY', 'NJ', 'PA');</td><td>

slname	sfname	sstate
Pitt	Brad	NJ
Damon	Matt	PA
Clooney	George	NJ
Banderas	Antonio	PA

</td></tr>
</table>

B. BETWEEN Operator

The BETWEEN operator gives the user the ability to look for something BETWEEN two values. The between can be used in lieu of creating a query the looks for records with a value greater than X and less than Y, inclusive. For instance, earlier in this section we explored how to write this query:

Show the room numbers and capacity of the room of all rooms that have a capacity greater than or equal to 40 and less than or equal to 70.

This same query can be rewritten using the BETWEEN operator as shown below.

1. Syntax: variable between value and value

	Room	capacity
Show the room numbers and capacity of the room of all rooms that have a capacity greater than or equal to 40 and less than or equal to 70.	202	40
	105	42
	211	55

Show the room numbers and capacity of the room of all rooms that have a capacity greater than or equal to 40 and less than or equal to 70.

Earlier we saw that this query could be written as:

SELECT Room, capacity
FROM location
WHERE capacity >= 40 and capacity <=70;

Using the BETWEEN operator, we can write the query as:

SELECT Room, capacity
FROM location
WHERE capacity between 40 and 70;

XII. Logical Operators

Logical operators test for the truth of a condition. You may remember Venn Diagrams. The diagram below shows 2 groups: those people who live in Pennsylvania and those people who attend Temple. The section in the middle, the intersection, represents the population that satisfies BOTH conditions. In other words, that group lives in Pennsylvania AND attends Temple.

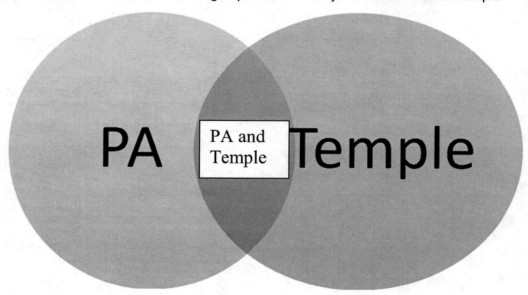

Conversely, the union of PA and Temple is the entire diagram. This means that the person either lives in PA OR attends Temple.

A. With the AND operator, the output displays values that match both conditions in the query. For instance, the condition meets both PA and Temple

Display all the rooms, the building code, and the capacity for rooms with a SPK Building Code which also have a capacity greater than or equal to 40. SELECT room, bldg_code, capacity FROM location WHERE bldg_code = 'SPK' AND capacity >= 40;	room	bldg_code	capacity
	101	SPK	150
	202	SPK	40

As you can see above, both rows have a building code of BUS and have a capacity greater than or equal to 40.

B. With the OR operator only one of the two conditions needs to be true for the entire condition to be true.

Display all the rooms and the building code associated with rooms that have a SPK Building Code OR rooms that have a capacity greater than or equal to 40. SELECT Room, bldg_code, capacity FROM location WHERE bldg_code = 'SPK' OR capacity >= 40;	Room	bldg_code	capacity
	101	SPK	150
	202	SPK	40
	103	SPK	35
	105	SPK	35
	105	CONWELL	42
	211	CONWELL	55

Here you can see that because only one condition needed to be satisfied, more rows met the criteria including rows that were in SP if the capacity was at least 40.

C. Multiple logical operators

A query can include multiple logical conditions. In each case, the syntax must appear as:

Variable comparison operator value logical operator....

List the ids, names, and student class of students who are freshman, junior or sophomores. Select sid, slname, sfname, sclass From student WHERE sclass = 'FR' OR sclass = 'JR' OR sclass = 'SO';	sid	slname	sfname	sclass
	102	Damon	Matt	JR
	103	Clooney	George	SO
	104	Bloom	Orlando	SO
	105	Depp	Johnny	FR
	2	Banderas	Antonio	FR

	sid	sfname	slname	sclass	sstate
List the ids, names, and student class of students who are sophomores or freshman and live in Idaho. An explanation of why I've added the parentheses is coming up next – stay tuned…	104	Orlando	Bloom	SO	ID
	105	Johnny	Depp	FR	ID

SELECT sid, sfname, slname, sclass, sstate
FROM student
WHERE (sclass = 'SO' or sclass = 'FR') AND sstate ='ID';

XIII.   NOT operator

Sometimes when we write a query we are trying to find values that do NOT satisfy a condition. For instance, you might want to write a query that looks for all students who attend Temple with the exception of those students living in 19111. Rather than try to figure out all of the possible zip codes that could exist with the exception of 19111, you can use the NOT operator. The not operator allows you to apply a condition to each row and the NOT essentially reverses (i.e. converts a true to false and vice versa) the outcome thus selecting only those rows that do not satisfy the condition.

A. Syntax: not (<fieldname> operator value

	sfname	slname	sclass
List the first and last name and class of every student who is not a senior.	Matt	Damon	JR
	George	Clooney	SO
SELECT sfname, slname, sclass FROM student WHERE NOT (sclass = 'SR');	Orlando	Bloom	SO
	Johnny	Depp	FR
	Antonio	Banderas	FR

As you can see, only the rows for those students who are not seniors returned.

XIV.   IS NULL and IS NOT NULL Operator

A. IS NULL Operator

There are times when we need to find if a field has not been populated, in other words when the user left the field blank. To do this, we use the null operator. This operator checks to see if there is some entry stored in the field. It is important to note that a null value is not the same as a 0 (zero) or a space. A zero implies that someone actually typed in the number zero. Similarly, a space indicates someone entered hit the space key in the field and stored that as the value.

1. Syntax: <fieldname> IS NULL

NOTE: the syntax for null includes the word is. No other operator such as <> will work.

	SID	CSECID	GRADE	NUMBER_GF
Show all enrollment rows where a grade has not been entered.				0
Select * FROM enrollment WHERE grade IS NULL;				

In this case, every row in the enrollment table has a grade so no rows will return.

B. IS NOT NULL

The converse of the null operator is the not null operator. This operator looks to see that a field has been populated. Any field that has a zero, spaces, or any other value will return with this operator.

1. Syntax: <fieldname> IS NOT NULL

Show all enrollment rows where a grade has not been entered. Select * FROM enrollment WHERE grade IS NOT NULL;	SID	CSECID	GRA	NUMBER_GRADI
	100	1000	A	95
	100	1003	A	96
	100	1005	B	87
	100	1008	B	88
	101	1000	C	76
	101	1004	B	84
	101	1005	A	93
	101	1008	B	85
	102	1000	C	75
	102	1011	D	66
	102	1012	F	55
	103	1010	B	89
	103	1011	A	99
	104	1000	B	87
	104	1004	C	78
	104	1008	C	77
	104	1012	D	69
	104	1010	F	32
	105	1010	A	94
	105	1011	B	89
				0

XV. Precedence

You might have noticed in the prior example that parentheses were added to the statement. Just as you learned in grade school mathematics, you can add parentheses to ensure that an equation is evaluated in the order you wish as opposed to the order of precedence.

Precedence is the order in which the equation is evaluated by default or in this case, how Oracle evaluates different operators in the same expression. When evaluating an expression containing multiple operators, Oracle evaluates operators with higher precedence before evaluating those with lower precedence. Oracle evaluates operators with equal precedence from left to right within a SQL statement. The table shows the operators from highest precedence to lowest. Conditions listed on the same line have the same precedence. As the table indicates, Oracle evaluates operators before conditions.

A. Conditional Precedence

Type of Condition	Purpose
SQL operators are evaluated before SQL conditions	See "Operator Precedence"
=, <, >, <=, >=,	comparison
IS [NOT] NULL, LIKE, [NOT] BETWEEN, [NOT] IN, EXISTS, IS OF type	comparison
NOT	exponentiation, logical negation
AND	conjunction
OR	disjunction

<table>
<tr><td>Select all of rows in the location table for every room in the SPK or LIB building with a capacity greater than 35:

SELECT * FROM location
WHERE bldg_code = 'SPK' OR
bldg_code = 'LIB' AND capacity> 35;</td><td>

LOCID	BLDG_CODE	ROOM	CAPACITY
11	SPK	101	150
12	SPK	202	40
13	SPK	103	35
14	SPK	105	35

</td></tr>
</table>

Is the output to the right the correct response to the query? Why are rooms with capacity less than 35 present in the output? SQL first evaluates the AND condition (i.e. the condition BLDG_CODE = 'CR' and CAPACITY > 35). What will be the result of these two conditions applied to the LOCATION table?

B. Parentheses

As you saw earlier, you can use parentheses in an expression to override operator precedence. Oracle evaluates expressions inside parentheses before evaluating those outside.

<table>
<tr><td>To ensure the previous query (Select all of rows in the location table for every room in the SPK or LIB building with a capacity greater than 35:) is evaluated properly, add parentheses.

SELECT * FROM location
WHERE (bldg_code= 'SPK'
     OR bldg_code= 'LIB'')
     AND CAPACITY > 35;</td><td>

LOCID	BLDG_CODE	ROOM	CAPACITY
11	SPK	101	1
12	SPK	202	

</td></tr>
</table>

XVI. Sorting the Output – Order by

By now you might have noticed that there doesn't seem to be any order to the results of the above queries. That's because we haven't told SQL in what order we want the rows to be returned. However, a user can specify exactly how the rows should be sorted using the ORDER BY operator.

A. Syntax : Order by <fieldname> ASC (default) or DESC

<table>
<tr><td>Create a report of the building code, room number, and capacity for every room with a capacity greater than equal to 40, sorted in ascending order by capacity.

SELECT bldg_code, room, capacity
FROM location
WHERE capacity >= 40
ORDER BY capacity ASC;</td><td>

bldg_code	room	capacity
SPK	202	40
CONWELL	105	42
CONWELL	211	55
SPK	101	150

</td></tr>
</table>

B. The default order is ascending (ASC) so this does not need to be specified. You can change the order to descending by adding the keyword DESC after the column name in the ORDER by clause. You can sort the output on the basis of multiple columns which is called nesting the order by clause. There is no limit to the number of nests you can request.

1. Syntax:

   ORDER BY <fieldname> ASC (default) or DESC, <fieldname> ASC (default) or DESC, <fieldname> ASC (default) or DESC…

Change the prior example to sort the results in descending order by capacity and then ascending order by building code. SELECT bldg_code, room, capacity FROM location WHERE capacity >= 40 ORDER BY capacity DESC, bldg_code ASC ;	bldg_code	room	capacity
	SPK	101	150
	CONWELL	211	55
	CONWELL	105	42
	SPK	202	40

XVII. Alias Operator

A. Alias for attribute names:

By default, SQL will return an attribute's name as the column heading for that attribute. For example, in the query above, the output shows the first column as BLDG_CODE. Although that is indeed the name of the attribute, it isn't particularly user friendly on a report. We'd probably prefer to see something a bit more English-like, such as the word "Building Code". Essentially, we'd like to make an alias for the attribute's name.

To create the alias, enter the column name followed by AS and then the alias you wish to assign to the column in quotes.

Syntax: <fieldname> as "alias name"

List all of the students' first and last names with the column heading of Student First Name and Student Last Name. SELECT sfname AS "Student First Name", slname AS "Student Last Name" FROM student;	'Student First Name'	'Student Last Name'
	Antonio	Banderas
	Brad	Pitt
	Angelina	Jolie
	Matt	Damon
	George	Clooney
	Orlando	Bloom
	Johnny	Depp

B. Alias for table name

We've seen that you can create an alias for a field. You can also create an alias for a table. But why would you want to do that? Some table names are really long. If we need to write the table name repeatedly in a query, it can get a little tiresome and also opens the doors for typos in our query. When you being joining tables and there are a number of tables, sometimes aliases save a bit of time.

Syntax: When aliases are used for table names, we do not include the AS like we do with aliases for attribute names. Just type the alias you want to use after the table's actual name, separated by a space.

1. Syntax: \<tablename\> alias

	bldg_code	room	capacity
Give the location table the alias of loc. For now, this won't seem too useful but soon it will prove most helpful. SELECT loc.bldg_code, loc.room, loc.capacity FROM location loc WHERE capacity >= 40;	SPK	101	150
	SPK	202	40
	CONWELL	105	42
	CONWELL	211	55

2. Aliases are only valid within the query in which they are defined. In other words, you cannot refer to the location table as "loc" in another query unless you add the alias again.

XVIII. Math in SQL

There are a wide range of math functions included in SQL ranging from basic mathematical functions to highly complex statistical functions. The most basic mathematical operations are: Addition (+), Subtraction (-), Multiplication (*), and Division. To write a query, use the fieldnames in lieu of the values.

In a prior example, we saw that you can double the capacity in a room by multiplying capacity by 2. Let's say administration decides to redesign the rooms in Speakman Hall and increase the capacity of each room 4 fold. However, 10% of the room is dedicated to smart technology so that will reduce the capacity.

	room	capacity	Expr1002
Show the current and new capacity for each room. Take the current capacity * 4. Take that total and multiply it by 90% since only 90% of the room capacity is available. SELECT room, capacity, (capacity * 4)* .90 FROM location WHERE bldg_code= 'SPK';	101	150	540
	202	40	144
	103	35	126
	105	35	126

You'll notice that Access gives the newly created field Expr1002.   Since every column (attribute) in a relational database must have a unique name, Access just automatically assigns a the column a name starting with the letters Expr. It will then sequentially assign each subsequent attribute the next number in the series. For instance, if I were to revise the query to determine the capacity * 2 in the last column, it would be assigned the column name of Expr1003.

	room	capacity	Expr1002	Expr1003
Show the current and new capacity (multiplied by 4 and then by 90%) and another column which displays the capacity * 2. SELECT room, capacity, (capacity * 4)* .90, (capacity * 2) FROM location WHERE bldg_code= 'SPK';	101	150	540	300
	202	40	144	80
	103	35	126	70
	105	35	126	70

We could improve the appearance of the output with some aliases.

	room	"Original Capacity"	"New Capacity"	"Final Capacity"
Show the current and new capacity (multiplied by 4 and then by 90%) and another column which displays the capacity * 2. Make the column heading for the columns as original capacity, revised capacity, and final capacity	101	150	540	300
	202	40	144	80
	103	35	126	70
	105	35	126	70

SELECT room, capacity AS "Original Capacity", (capacity * 4)* .90 AS "New Capacity", (capacity * 2) AS "Final Capacity"
FROM location
WHERE bldg_code= 'SPK';

A. SQL Operator Precedence

SQL is a powerful language that allows the user to make exceptionally complex queries which include mathematical computations. When you were in grade school, you learned the Please Excuse My Dear Aunt Sally mnemonic aid which helped you to learn the order of precedence of mathematical functions if parentheses are not used. These same rules apply here with SQL

The levels of precedence among SQL operators are shown below from high to low.

- Parentheses
- Exponents
- Multiplication and Division
- Addition and Subtraction

***Operators listed on the same line have the same precedence.

Take the building capacity of room 101 in Speakman Hall and then divide by 2 + 3. The result of the calculation will be different according to where you use parentheses. If we don't use If we don't use any parentheses, the query will look as follows: SELECT capacity/2 +3 FROM location WHERE bldg_code = 'SPK' AND room = '101';	Expr1000 78
If we use parentheses to be sure that the 2+3 gets evaluated first, the output is dramatically different. Addition has a lower order of precedence then multiplication or division. To force that part of the equation to be evaluated first, add parentheses. SELECT CAPACITY/(2+3) FROM LOCATION WHERE (((LOCATION.[BLDG_CODE])='SPK') AND ((LOCATION.[ROOM])='101'));	Expr1000 30

Chapter 18: Set Operators

"Set operators combine the results of two component queries into a single result. Queries containing set operators are called compound queries." [7]

Consider the following tables:

State:		State_Pivot	
STATEID	STATENAME	STATEID	STATENAME
DE	Delaware	DE	Delaware
NJ	New Jersey	NJ	New Jersey
NY	New York	NY	New York
PA	Pennsylvania	PA	Pennsylvania
		ID	Idaho
		VA	Virginia
		NC	North Carolina

I. **Union**

    A. UNION operator:

    The Union operator takes the results of two individual SQL queries and combines them into an output which is displayed as a single table of all matching rows. The two queries must have the same number of columns and compatible data types in order for the union to be successful. Duplicate rows are automatically removed from the results of a union.

    B. Union All

    The UNION ALL operator does not remove the duplicate rows in the output.

Show all the rows in the state and state_pivot tables. Remove duplicates. SELECT * FROM state UNION SELECT * FROM state_pivot;	STATEID	STATENAME
	DE	Delaware
	ID	Idaho
	NC	North Carolina
	NJ	New Jersey
	NY	New York
	PA	Pennsylvania
	VA	Virginia

---

[7] http://www.acs.ilstu.edu/docs/oracle/server.101/b10759/operators005.htm

Show all the rows in the state and state_pivot tables. Do not remove duplicates.

```
SELECT * FROM state
UNION ALL
SELECT * FROM state_pivot;
```

STATEID	STATENAME
DE	Delaware
NJ	New Jersey
NY	New York
PA	Pennsylvania
DE	Delaware
NJ	New Jersey
NY	New York
PA	Pennsylvania
ID	Idaho
VA	Virginia
NC	North Carolina

Chapter 19: DML and Joins

The power of relational databases really comes from the ability to join tables. As we've seen, data is stored in a number of tables which are related to each other through some common piece(s) of information. Specifically an attribute in one table (the primary key) is repeated in another table as a foreign key. So far, we have only had to write queries from one table but that is clearly not the norm in a normalized database (no pun intended).

When we use joins in queries, we take advantage of the 'controlled redundancy' of relational database tables, by using the foreign key references. It should also become apparent why relational databases require referential integrity. If referential integrity is not enforced, we will not be able to join tables properly. In most instances, when we make a join between two tables, we join the foreign key from one table and the primary key of the corresponding table.

I.   Inner Joins

An inner join is also known as an equijoin.

The general format of a SELECT statement with a join operation is:

```
SELECT <table1.column1,…table2.column,…>
FROM <table1>
INNER JOIN  <table2> ON <table1.column> = <table2.column> … ;
```

A. Rules for joins:

- the attributes must have the same data type.

- the attributes must be of the same size.

- the attributes do NOT need to have the same attribute name.

1. Join Condition

The join condition specifies attributes which are common between two tables. Essentially, the join condition will contain the foreign key reference in one table, and the corresponding primary key in the other table. So what does this mean? Let's take a look at the data entered into our student and faculty tables.

Student Table:

SID	SLNAME	SFNAME	SMI	SADD	SCITY	SSTATE	SZIP	SPHONE	SCLASS	SDOB	SPIN	FID
100	Pitt	Brad	M	144 Windridge Blvd.	Cherry Hill	NJ	54703	7155559876	SR	7/14/1979	8891	2
101	Jolie	Angelina	D	454 St. John's Street	Wilmington	DE	54702	7155552345	SR	8/19/1979	1230	1
102	Damon	Matt		8921 Circle Drive	Philadelphia	PA	54715	7155553907	JR	10/10/1977	1613	1
103	Clooney	George	J	1716 Summit St.	Eau Claire	NJ	54703	7155556902	SO	9/24/1978	1841	5
104	Bloom	Orlando	R	1780 Broad Street	Philadelphia	ID	54701	7155558899	SO	11/20/1977	4420	4
105	Depp	Johnny	S	1818 Silver Street	Elk Mound	ID	54712	7155554944	FR	12/4/1977	9188	3

Faculty Table:

FID	FLNAME	FFNAME	FMI	LOCID	FPHONE	FRANK	FPIN
1	Knightly	Keira	J	12	7155551234	ASSO	1181
2	Streep	Meryl	R	11	7155559087	FULL	1075
3	Redford	Robert	F	13	7155555412	ASST	8531
4	Newman	Paul	M	18	7155556409	INST	1690
5	Dench	Judith	E	22	7155556082	ASSO	9899

Brad Pitt's faculty advisor (fid) is 2. As you can see, fid 2 in the faculty table corresponds to Meryl Streep. This means that the value of Student.fidis equal to Faculty.FID. When we write a join, we are literally saying to SQL that the value of one attribute is equal to the value of another attribute (foreign key = primary key).

List the student's first, last name, and last name of the student's faculty advisor. In this query, we need to find information from two tables: the student table and the faculty table. To make the join, find an attribute that is common between the two tables. Since FID in the student key is a foreign key to the primary key of FID in the faculty table, we can join the tables. SELECT student.SFNAME, student.SLNAME, faculty.FLNAME FROM faculty INNER JOIN student ON (faculty.FID = student.FID);		

sfname	slname	flname
Brad	Pitt	Streep
Angelina	Jolie	Knightly
Matt	Damon	Knightly
George	Clooney	Dench
Orlando	Bloom	Newman
Johnny	Depp	Redford

2. There is no limit to the number of tables that can be added to a query.

3. <u>Rule of Thumb</u> - number of joins per query

   There is typically 1 less join than there are tables. If you are including 3 tables in your query, you will probably have 2 joins.

4. Qualifying columns

   We learned earlier that in order to accurately specify the column to which the table belongs the table name should be qualified though tablename.attribute name notation. For instance, if you want to add the student's last name to a select query, you would write:

   SELECT Student.slname

   While this is the proper notation, we typically just refer to the attribute name without the table name as a short cut. This has worked for us so far. Now however, we are going to learn to write queries that involve more than one table in a database. Accordingly, we will begin to encounter situations where an attribute name may appear in multiple tables. Remember, while an attribute name must be unique within a table, an attribute name can appear in different tables within the same database.

   Why would we do that? Let's consider the attribute First_Name. In our database we could have an attribute in the faculty table called First_Name which refers to the first name of the faculty member. Similarly, we could also have an attribute of First_Name in the student table for the student's first name. If we write a query which includes both the student and faculty tables and we add First_Name in the SELECT clause, how would SQL know we want to include the first name of the student or the faculty member? This situation actually has a special name – natural join.

   So when do you need to qualify an attribute? You need to qualify the attribute with its table name when:

   - You are writing a query that includes more than one table
   - The attribute name you are using is not unique in the tables used in the query

5. If you forget a join in a multi-table query, you will return every possible combination of rows in the tables included in the query. Whenever you return many more rows than you expect in a query which includes more than one table, check to see if you forgot a join.

6. Use of aliases for table names

   It is an extremely common convention to create aliases for table names when creating joins. Unlike with attribute name aliases, you do not need an AS operator.

   a. To create the alias just add the alias' name after the table name. For instance, in the example below, add an f after the table name faculty in the from clause. To create an alias for student table, add an "s" after the word student in the from clause.

   b. You refer to all of the attribute names with the alias table name that was created. For instance, student.sfname becomes s.sfname

List the student's first, last name, and last name of the student's faculty advisor. SELECT s.SFNAME, s.SLNAME, f.FLNAME FROM faculty f INNER JOIN student s ON (f.FID = s.FID);	sfname	slname	flname
	Brad	Pitt	Streep
	Angelina	Jolie	Knightly
	Matt	Damon	Knightly
	George	Clooney	Dench
	Orlando	Bloom	Newman
	Johnny	Depp	Redford

B. Creating a 3 table query

Let's change the previous query. In this case, we'd like to see the faculty advisor's location added to the query.

To add the location, we need to add another table. Whenever we add a table to a query we need to do a few things:

1. If an attribute in the newly added table needs to appear in the output, add the attribute name in the appropriate location in the select clause. Remember to separate the attributes with commas. In this case, we will add bldg_code to the select clause

2. Add the next "inner join" in the from clause

3. Add the table name after the table name

4. Add a join between the new table and its related table in the query. To add the join, make the foreign key in the first table equal to the primary key in the second table. In this case, we'll add a join between faculty.locid (the foreign key) and location.locid (the primary key)

So to add the location to the above query, we'll modify the query as follows:

SELECT s.SfNAME, s.SlNAME, f.FLNAME, l.BLDG_CODE FROM ((faculty f INNER JOIN student s ON f.FID = s.FID) INNER JOIN location l on f.LOCID = l.LOCID);	sfname	slname	flname	bldg_code
	Brad	Pitt	Streep	SPK
	Angelina	Jolie	Knightly	SPK
	Matt	Damon	Knightly	SPK
	George	Clooney	Dench	LIB
	Orlando	Bloom	Newman	CONWELL
	Johnny	Depp	Redford	SPK

SQL Tutorial

C. Creating a 4 table query

Here's an example with more tables. For each student, we want to list his first and last name as well as the name of courses in which he was enrolled and the grades he received.

In this query, we need information from 4 tables. Why 4?

- We need to retrieve the student's first and last name from the student table.
- We find the student's grade from the enrollment table. As we can see in the ERD, enrollment.sid is a foreign key to student.sid so we can join the student and the enrollment table.
- We get the name of the course in the course table. When we make a join, it must be between two tables that have a common value. But, there is no common attribute between the course table and the enrollment table. Why? Because there is a M:N relationship between course and enrollment which is resolved with the bridge entity called course_section.

NOTE: Often times you will need to navigate through a few tables to connect two that have the information you want. In this case, we need to navigate through the bridge entity to connect the enrollment and the course table.

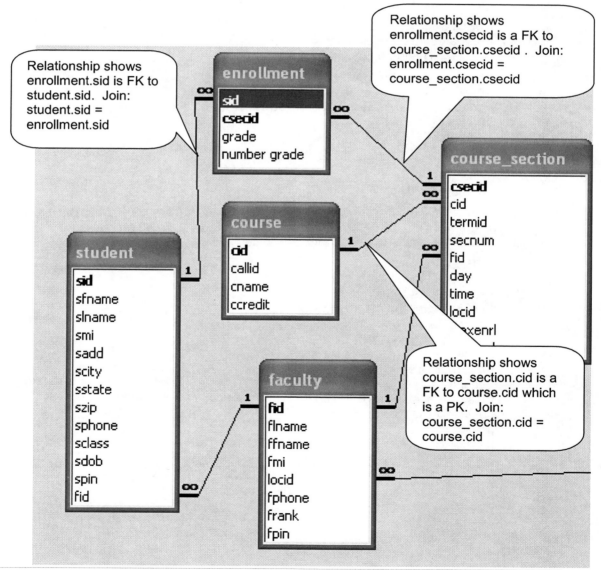

If we follow the relationships between the foreign keys and the primary keys in the ERD below, it is easy to see how to make the joins.

SELECT s.sfname, s.slname, c.cname, e.grade
FROM ((student s INNER JOIN enrollment e on (s.sid = e.sid)) INNER JOIN course_section cs on (cs.csecid = e.csecid)) INNER JOIN course c on (cs.cid = c.cid)

sfname	slname	cname	grade
Brad	Pitt	DBMS	A
Angelina	Jolie	DBMS	C
Matt	Damon	DBMS	C
Orlando	Bloom	DBMS	B
Brad	Pitt	Principles of MIS	A
Angelina	Jolie	Principles of MIS	B
Orlando	Bloom	Principles of MIS	C
Brad	Pitt	Database Management	B
Angelina	Jolie	Database Management	A
Brad	Pitt	Project Management	B
Angelina	Jolie	Project Management	B
Orlando	Bloom	Project Management	C
George	Clooney	DBMS	B
Orlando	Bloom	DBMS	F
Johnny	Depp	DBMS	A
Matt	Damon	Principles of MIS	D
George	Clooney	Principles of MIS	A
Johnny	Depp	Principles of MIS	B
Matt	Damon	Database Management	F
Orlando	Bloom	Database Management	D

Let's improve this query with some attribute aliases. We create them as we've already learned with the AS operator.

SELECT s.sfname AS "Student First Name", s.slname AS "Student Last Name", c.cname AS "Course Name", e.grade AS "Grade"

FROM ((student s INNER JOIN enrollment e on (s.sid = e.sid)) INNER JOIN course_section cs on (cs.csecid = e.csecid)) INNER JOIN course c on (cs.cid = c.cid)

"Student First Name"	"Student Last Name"	"Course Name"	"Grade"
Brad	Pitt	DBMS	A
Angelina	Jolie	DBMS	C
Matt	Damon	DBMS	C
Orlando	Bloom	DBMS	B
Brad	Pitt	Principles of MIS	A
Angelina	Jolie	Principles of MIS	B
Orlando	Bloom	Principles of MIS	C
Brad	Pitt	Database Management	B
Angelina	Jolie	Database Management	A
Brad	Pitt	Project Management	B
Angelina	Jolie	Project Management	B
Orlando	Bloom	Project Management	C
George	Clooney	DBMS	B
Orlando	Bloom	DBMS	F
Johnny	Depp	DBMS	A
Matt	Damon	Principles of MIS	D
George	Clooney	Principles of MIS	A
Johnny	Depp	Principles of MIS	B
Matt	Damon	Database Management	F
Orlando	Bloom	Database Management	D

D. Adding a condition with a multiple table query

One last example with conditions and joins. Now let's say we want to see the same information but only if the student's grade is a B or an A. All we have to do to write this query is add the condition to the WHERE clause as follows:

SELECT s.sfname AS "Student First Name", s.slname AS "Student Last Name", c.cname AS "Course Name", e.grade AS "Grade" FROM ((student s INNER JOIN enrollment e on (s.sid = e.sid)) INNER JOIN course_section cs on (cs.csecid = e.csecid)) INNER JOIN course c on (cs.cid = c.cid) WHERE grade = 'B' OR grade = 'A';

"Student First Name"	"Student Last Name"	"Course Name"	"Grade"
Brad	Pitt	DBMS	A
Brad	Pitt	Principles of MIS	A
Brad	Pitt	Database Management	B
Brad	Pitt	Project Management	B
Angelina	Jolie	Principles of MIS	B
Angelina	Jolie	Database Management	A
Angelina	Jolie	Project Management	B
George	Clooney	DBMS	B
George	Clooney	Principles of MIS	A
Orlando	Bloom	DBMS	B
Johnny	Depp	DBMS	A
Johnny	Depp	Principles of MIS	B

II.   Outer Joins

Sometimes we want to find rows in one table that do not have corresponding rows in another table. Consider this situation: A student hasn't been assigned an advisor yet. In addition, an advisor is teaching abroad and has no students to advise this semester. If we write an inner join that shows students and their associated advisors, these two rows will be excluded. Fortunately, we have a slick little feature called an outer join which is designed to solve just this dilemma.

The general format of a SELECT statement with an outer join operation is identical to an inner join except that a plus sign in parentheses (+) is placed after the optional attribute in the join. [8]

```
SELECT <table1.column1,…table2.column,…>
FROM <table1>
RIGHT/LEFT JOIN  <table2> ON <table1.column> = <table2.column> … ;
```

Just like in an inner join and outer join must have the following conditions:

- the attributes must have the same data type.
- the attributes must be of the same size.
- the attributes do NOT need to have the same attribute name.

There are 3 different types of outer joins, left outer join, right outer join, and full outer join. Access does not support a full outer join but does support left and right outer joins.

A.   LEFT OUTER JOIN:

In a left outer join, all the records from the leftmost table or query in the JOIN clause are included. Unmatched rows in the rightmost table or query in the JOIN clause do not appear. [9]

List the student's first and last name and the advisor's first and last name regardless if the student has a faculty advisor. SELECT sfname, slname, ffname, flname FROM student left outer join faculty on student.fid = faculty.fid;	sfname	slname	ffname	flname
	Antonio	Banderas		
	Angelina	Jolie	Keira	Knightly
	Matt	Damon	Keira	Knightly
	Brad	Pitt	Meryl	Streep
	Johnny	Depp	Robert	Redford
	Orlando	Bloom	Paul	Newman
	George	Clooney	Judith	Dench
	As you can see, Anthonio Banderas has no faculty advisor.			

B.   RIGHT OUTER JOIN:

In a right outer join, all the records from the rightmost table or query in the JOIN clause are included. Unmatched rows in the leftmost table or query in the JOIN clause do not appear. [10]

---

[8] http://oreilly.com/catalog/orsqlpluspr2/chapter/ch01.html
[9] http://office.microsoft.com/en-us/access/HA010345551033.aspx
[10] http://office.microsoft.com/en-us/access/HA010345551033.aspx

sfname	slname	ffname	flname
Angelina	Jolie	Keira	Knightly
Matt	Damon	Keira	Knightly
Brad	Pitt	Meryl	Streep
Johnny	Depp	Robert	Redford
Orlando	Bloom	Paul	Newman
George	Clooney	Judith	Dench
		Juliette	Binoche

Show faculty members and their associated students.

SELECT sfname, slname, ffname, flname
FROM student right outer join faculty on student.fid = faculty.fid;

You can see here that Juliette Binoche doesn't have any students assigned to her.

C. **FULL OUTER JOIN**

A full outer join displays all the rows of both tables, regardless if it is a left or right outer join. Full outer joins are NOT supported by Access

III. Non-ANSI standard format for Joins

The syntax that we've used to develop joins is ANSI (American National Standard Institute) compliant. However, there is another format which was developed prior to the ANIS standard format which is now referred to as a non-ANSI standard format. This approach is used by many database management systems including Oracle but is not supported by Access.

A. INNER JOIN

If you need to specify the joins more clearly, you can use the following syntax:

```
SELECT <table1.column1,…table2.column,…>
FROM <table1, table2 >
WHERE <table1.joincolumn_name> = <table2.joincolumn_name>;
```

B. Steps for creating Non-ANSI standard inner join.

Whenever we add a table to a query we need to do a few things:

1. If an attribute in the newly added table needs to appear in the output, add the attribute name in the appropriate location in the select clause. Remember to separate the attributes with commas.

2. Add the table name to the FROM clause. Remember to separate the table names with commas. In this case, we will add location to the from clause

3. Add a join between the new table and its related table in the query. To add the join, make the foreign key in the first table equal to the primary key in the second table. Remember to add an AND to separate the joins and the conditions.

Comparison of ANSI and Non-ANSI standard Joins				
Query Type	Desired Query	Traditional Join	ANSI Join	Result
Inner Join	Show each student's name, grade and course section number.	SELECT sfname, slname, flname, grade, csecid FROM student, faculty, enrollment WHERE faculty.fid = student.fid AND enrollment.sid = student.sid AND student.sid = enrollment.sid;	SELECT sfname, slname, flname, grade, csecid FROM student INNER JOIN faculty ON faculty.fid = student.fid INNER JOIN enrollment ON enrollment.sid = student.sid;	**SFNAME SLNAME FLNAME GRADE CSECID** Brad Pitt Streep A 1000 Brad Pitt Streep A 1003 Brad Pitt Streep B 1005 Brad Pitt Streep B 1008 Angelina Jolie Knightly C 1000 Angelina Jolie Knightly B 1004 Angelina Jolie Knightly A 1005 Angelina Jolie Knightly B 1008 Matt Damon Knightly C 1000 Matt Damon Knightly D 1011 Matt Damon Knightly F 1012 George Clooney Dench B 1010 George Clooney Dench A 1011 Orlando Bloom Newman B 1000 Orlando Bloom Newman C 1004 Orlando Bloom Newman C 1008 Orlando Bloom Newman D 1012 Orlando Bloom Newman F 1010 Johnny Depp Redford A 1010 Johnny Depp Redford B 1011
Inner Join	Show each student's name, grade and course section number if the student received an A.	SELECT sfname, slname, flname, grade, csecid FROM student, faculty, enrollment WHERE faculty.fid = student.fid AND enrollment.sid = student.sid AND student.sid = enrollment.sid AND grade = 'A';	SELECT sfname, slname, flname, grade, csecid FROM student INNER JOIN faculty ON faculty.fid = student.fid INNER JOIN enrollment ON enrollment.sid = student.sid WHERE grade = 'A';	**SFNAME SLNAME FLNAME GRADE CSECID** Brad Pitt Streep A 1000 Brad Pitt Streep A 1003 Angelina Jolie Knightly A 1005 George Clooney Dench A 1011 Johnny Depp Redford A 1010

Comparison of ANSI and Non-ANSI standard Joins				
Query Type	**Desired Query**	**Traditional Join**	**ANSI Join**	**Result**
Left Outer Join	List the student's first and last name and the advisor's first and last name regardless if the student has a faculty advisor	SELECT sfname, slname, ffname, flname FROM student, faculty WHERE student.fid = faculty.fid(+);	SELECT sfname, slname, ffname, flname FROM student LEFT OUTER JOIN faculty ON (student.fid = faculty.fid);	See table below
Right Outer Join	:Show faculty members and their associated students.	SELECT ffname, flname, sfname, slname FROM student, faculty WHERE student.fid(+) = faculty.fid;	SELECT sfname, slname, ffname, flname FROM student RIGHT OUTER JOIN faculty ON (student.fid = faculty.fid);	See table below

Left Outer Join Result:

SFNAME	SLNAME	FFNAME	FLNAME
Matt	Damon	Keira	Knightly
Angelina	Jolie	Keira	Knightly
Brad	Pitt	Meryl	Streep
Johnny	Depp	Robert	Redford
Orlando	Bloom	Paul	Newman
George	Clooney	Judith	Dench
Antonio	Banderas		

Right Outer Join Result:

SFNAME	SLNAME	FFNAME	FLNAME
Brad	Pitt	Meryl	Streep
Angelina	Jolie	Keira	Knightly
Matt	Damon	Keira	Knightly
George	Clooney	Judith	Dench
Orlando	Bloom	Paul	Newman
Johnny	Depp	Robert	Redford
		Juliette	Binoche

Notice Antonio Banderas does not appear as this output since he has no faculty member which whom he matches. Similarly, Juliette Binoche does not appear on the example above as she has no student with whom she matches.

Comparison of ANSI and Non-ANSI standard Joins						
Query Type	**Desired Query**	**Traditional Join**	**ANSI Join**	**Result**		
Full Outer Join	List the student's first and last name and the advisor's first and last name regardless if the student has a faculty advisor or the faculty has students assigned.	There is no way to do this with a traditional join except with a UNION. SELECT sfname, slname, ffname, flname FROM student, faculty WHERE student.fid = faculty.fid(+) UNION SELECT sfname, slname, ffname, flname FROM student, faculty WHERE student.fid(+) = faculty.fid;	In other relational database management systems you can perform a full outer join as follows. However, Access does NOT support full outer joins. SELECT sfname, slname, ffname, flname FROM student FULL OUTER JOIN faculty ON (student.fid = faculty.fid);	**SFNAME** **SLNAME** **FFNAME** **FLNAME**		

SFNAME	SLNAME	FFNAME	FLNAME
Angelina	Jolie	Keira	Knightly
Antonio	Banderas		
Brad	Pitt	Meryl	Streep
George	Clooney	Judith	Dench
Johnny	Depp	Robert	Redford
Matt	Damon	Keira	Knightly
Orlando	Bloom	Paul	Newman
		Juliette	Binoche

Chapter 20: DML - Update and Delete Records

I. Update Statement

We've seen that we can change a table's structure using the alter statement in DDL. But what if we want to change the data entered into a row? The UPDATE statement allows you to modify the data which was entered into a field.

An UPDATE statement changes the data while the ALTER statement changes the structure of the table. The UPDATE statement changes the values of single rows, groups of rows, or all the rows in a table.

A. Syntax:

```
UPDATE tablename
SET attribute = X
WHERE attribute = X;
```

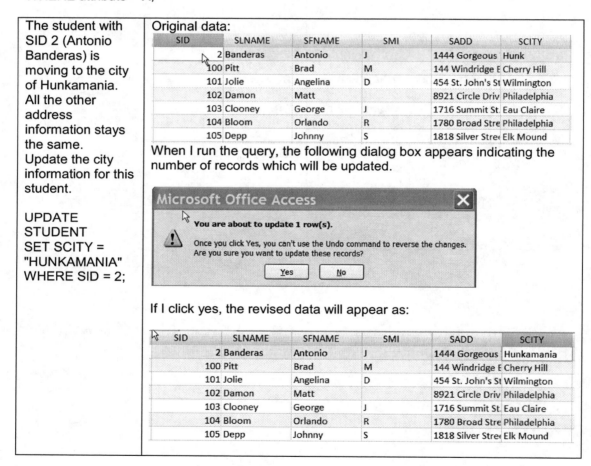

The student with SID 2 (Antonio Banderas) is moving to the city of Hunkamania. All the other address information stays the same. Update the city information for this student.

```
UPDATE
STUDENT
SET SCITY =
"HUNKAMANIA"
WHERE SID = 2;
```

Original data:

SID	SLNAME	SFNAME	SMI	SADD	SCITY
2	Banderas	Antonio	J	1444 Gorgeous	Hunk
100	Pitt	Brad	M	144 Windridge E	Cherry Hill
101	Jolie	Angelina	D	454 St. John's St	Wilmington
102	Damon	Matt		8921 Circle Driv	Philadelphia
103	Clooney	George	J	1716 Summit St.	Eau Claire
104	Bloom	Orlando	R	1780 Broad Stre	Philadelphia
105	Depp	Johnny	S	1818 Silver Stre	Elk Mound

When I run the query, the following dialog box appears indicating the number of records which will be updated.

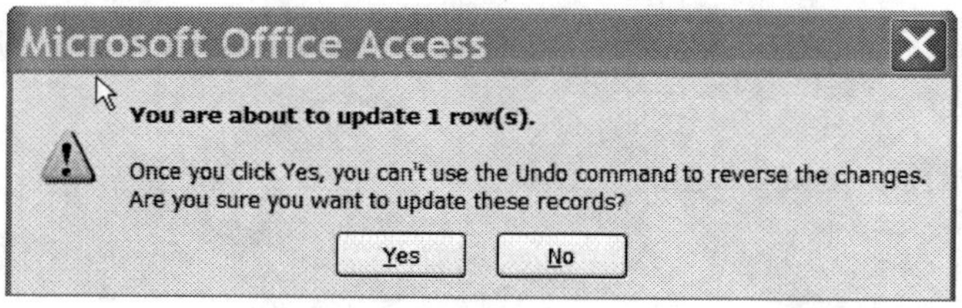

If I click yes, the revised data will appear as:

SID	SLNAME	SFNAME	SMI	SADD	SCITY
2	Banderas	Antonio	J	1444 Gorgeous	Hunkamania
100	Pitt	Brad	M	144 Windridge E	Cherry Hill
101	Jolie	Angelina	D	454 St. John's St	Wilmington
102	Damon	Matt		8921 Circle Driv	Philadelphia
103	Clooney	George	J	1716 Summit St.	Eau Claire
104	Bloom	Orlando	R	1780 Broad Stre	Philadelphia
105	Depp	Johnny	S	1818 Silver Stre	Elk Mound

B. An UPDATE statement with no WHERE clause

If you have an UPDATE statement with no where clause, the update will affect all rows in the table being modified. Accordingly, unless you truly want to modify the entire table it is essential to consider the condition or filter. The WHERE clause specifies which rows are to be updated.

Change the University city to be blank for all universities. UPDATE student SET scity = NULL	**Original Data:** 	SID	SLNAME	SFNAME	SMI	SADD	SCITY
---	---	---	---	---	---
2	Banderas	Antonio	J	1444 Gorgeous	Hunk
100	Pitt	Brad	M	144 Windridge E	Cherry Hill
101	Jolie	Angelina	D	454 St. John's St	Wilmington
102	Damon	Matt		8921 Circle Driv	Philadelphia
103	Clooney	George	J	1716 Summit St	Eau Claire
104	Bloom	Orlando	R	1780 Broad Stre	Philadelphia
105	Depp	Johnny	S	1818 Silver Stre	Elk Mound | **Revised data:** | SID	SLNAME	SFNAME	SMI	SADD	SCITY
---	---	---	---	---	---
2	Banderas	Antonio	J	1444 Gorgeous	
100	Pitt	Brad	M	144 Windridge E	
101	Jolie	Angelina	D	454 St. John's St	
102	Damon	Matt		8921 Circle Driv	
103	Clooney	George	J	1716 Summit St.	
104	Bloom	Orlando	R	1780 Broad Stre	
105	Depp	Johnny	S	1818 Silver Stre		
You can also use computed column values in an update. This example doubles all prices in the titles table: UPDATE product SET price = price * 2	**Original data:** 	SKU	PRODUCT_D	PRICE
---	---	---
13133	Cordless phone	$21.99
15135	Merkury boom I	$45.87
145566	Sony Trinitron 3	$345.76
968767	Iron tiki torch	$7.99
26666	Colonial black c	$58.99	 **Revised data:** 	SKU	PRODUCT_D	PRICE
---	---	---
13133	Cordless phone	$43.98
15135	Merkury boom I	$91.74
145566	Sony Trinitron 3	$691.52
968767	Iron tiki torch	$15.98
26666	Colonial black c	$117.98	

II. DELETE Statement

We've seen that we can delete a table using the DROP table statement in DDL. But what if we want to delete a row in a table? The DROP table statement removes the entire table from the database. Conversely, the DELETE statement removes rows from a table. The DELETE statement may delete single rows, groups of rows, or all the rows in a table. .

A. Syntax:

```
DELETE
FROM <tablename>
WHERE attribute = X;
```

Delete the Willow Grove row from the city table DELETE FROM student WHERE smi = 'J';	Original data: 	SID	SLNAME	SFNAME	SMI
2	Banderas	Antonio	J
100	Pitt	Brad	M
101	Jolie	Angelina	D
102	Damon	Matt	
103	Clooney	George	J
104	Bloom	Orlando	R
105	Depp	Johnny	S | Revised data: | SID	SLNAME	SFNAME	SMI
100	Pitt	Brad	M
101	Jolie	Angelina	D
102	Damon	Matt	
104	Bloom	Orlando	R
105	Depp	Johnny	S	

B. DELETE statement with no WHERE clause

Just like in the update statement, if you have a DELETE statement with no WHERE clause, you will delete all rows in the table. Accordingly, unless you truly want to delete all the rows in the table, it is essential to consider the condition or filter. The WHERE clause specifies which rows are to be deleted
.

Remember a DELETE statement only affects the rows in a table. Even if you delete all the rows, the table structure still exists. In other words, the table is still there but there will be no rows in the table. To delete the table structure, you must use the DROP TABLE DDL command.

Delete the rows from the city table DELETE FROM city;	Original data: | CITY_ID	CITY_NAME
PH	Philadelphia
HV	Huntingdon Valley
WG	Willow Grove
NY	New York | Revised data: | CITY_ID	CITY_NAME
Delete the entire city table: DROP TABLE city CASCADE CONSTRAINTS.	

C. Deleting Foreign Primary Key with Foreign Key

There may be an occasion when the following error will appear when attempting to delete a row.

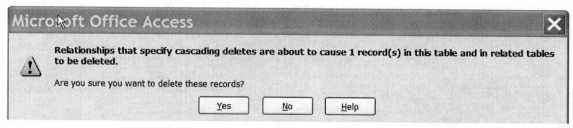

This message is indicating that the row cannot be deleted as it is a foreign key to a row in another table.   SQL will not allow the rows to be deleted as it will result in an integrity error.

In order to delete the rows, you must first delete the corresponding row in the associated table.   Then you can delete the original row.

Chapter 21: DML- Date Functions

I. Date Background Information:

The date data type in most computer system comes with a powerful set of operators and functions to manipulate the date field. Within the database, the date data is stored in a special format that includes date (day, month, and year) and the time (hours, minutes and seconds). In fact the date value is stored in seven bytes, one each for century, year, month, day, hours, minutes, and seconds. Some of the commonly used format masks are described below:

Format	Description	Example
MM	Month number	3
MON	3-letter abbreviation of month	JAN
MONTH	Fully spelled out month	MARCH
D	Number of days in the week	3
DD	Number of days in the month	16
DDD	Number of days in the year	234
DY	3-letter abbreviation of day of week	WED
DAY	Fully spelled-out day of the week	FRIDAY
Y	Last digit of year	8
YY	Last two digits of year	00
YYY	Last three digits of year	000
YYYY	Full four-digit year	2000
HH12	Hours of the day (1 to 12)	9
HH24	Hours of the day (0-23)	18
MI	Minutes of the hour	34
SS	Seconds of minute	29
AM	Display AM or PM depending on time	PM

II. How do Computers Understand Time?

Sometimes, the easiest way to understand time with computers is to consider how dates are handled in Microsoft Excel. Microsoft selected an arbitrary start date. Essentially this is just a point in time which happens to be January 1, 1900. This date is assigned number 1. Each day after the start date is assigned a sequential number in increments of 1. In other words, 1/2/1900 is equal to 2, 1/3/1900 is equal to 3, 1/4/1900 is equal to 4, etc

This may seem complicated but it makes perfect sense when you consider that computers can be really handy at calculating the difference between two numbers. If you can assign each date a number, you can calculate how much time has elapsed between dates. For instance, let's say I bought something on July 12, 2008 (which corresponds to 39641) and the company wants to invoice me in 30 days. The developer can easily write some code that says invoice date = purchase date + 30. In this case, I should be invoiced on 39671 (8/11/2008).

The dates that we store, such as May 1, 2008, really don't mean anything to the computer until we convert them into something that is meaningful such as this start date in Excel. Frankly, the computer sees May 1, 2008 or 5/1/2008 as just another list of characters, or string. This is similar to any other word we might write such as a first name, city, or company name. As you know, you can't do math on strings. For instance, I can't add 30 to my name or the city I live in or to Temple University. How then can we do math with a date like May 1, 2008 so we can tell when it is time to invoice someone? The good folks who brought us SQL have thought up nifty ways so that we can tell the computer that this string is actually a date.

III. **NOW()**

NOW is a function which comes predefined in Access. NOW tells the current date and time stored in the computer. If you know the current date is stored in the NOW function, you can use it to calculate the amount of time that has elapsed between a given date and the current date.

A. Calculations using NOW().

Since you are now a database guru, you are well aware that in good database design we avoid storing attributes that are derived or calculated fields. As such, we don't store a person's age in a database since this should actually be calculated based on the person's date of birth. So how do we actually do this?

If someone tells you his birth date you could quickly calculate how old he is by subtracting the date from today's date. That is precisely how we do it in Access. We can always tell what the current date and time is with now. So, if we subtract the person's birthdate from NOW(), it will return the person's age.

Show each student's first and last name and age. SELECT sfname, slname, NOW() - sdob FROM student;	sfname	slname	Expr1002
	Antonio	Banderas	16471.536724537
	Brad	Pitt	10932.536724537
	Angelina	Jolie	10896.536724537
	Matt	Damon	11574.536724537
	George	Clooney	11225.536724537
	Orlando	Bloom	11533.536724537
	Johnny	Depp	11519.536724537

What the heck? Is Brad Pitt really 10,932 plus years old? Something must be wrong. Let's add some attributes to our query to try and understand what's going on. Let's add the student's date of birth and NOW to the query. I'm going to add some aliases to make the output a little more clear

SELECT sfname, slname,NOW() AS "Current Date", NOW() - sdob AS "Age" FROM student;	sfname	slname	"Current Date"	"Age"
	Antonio	Banderas	6/18/2009 12:58:11 PM	16471.5404050926
	Brad	Pitt	6/18/2009 12:58:11 PM	10932.5404050926
	Angelina	Jolie	6/18/2009 12:58:11 PM	10896.5404050926
	Matt	Damon	6/18/2009 12:58:11 PM	11574.5404050926
	George	Clooney	6/18/2009 12:58:11 PM	11225.5404050926
	Orlando	Bloom	6/18/2009 12:58:11 PM	11533.5404050926
	Johnny	Depp	6/18/2009 12:58:11 PM	11519.5404050926

OK so those dates of birth seem reasonable and the system date looks valid so why is the calculation so screwy? The default result in Access in a date calculation is in days. Basically Access is returning how hold the students are in days. We can easily convert days to years by dividing the number by 365.25 (for leap year) days/years as follows.   Remember, because of My Dear Aunt Sally order of precedence, you really need to make sure to add the parentheses or the student's age will be really weird.

SELECT sfname, slname,NOW() AS "Current Date", ((NOW() - sdob)/365.25)AS "Age" FROM student;			

sfname	slname	"Current Date"	"Age"
Antonio	Banderas	6/18/2009 1:00:10 PM	45.0966236342434
Brad	Pitt	6/18/2009 1:00:10 PM	29.9316681243187
Angelina	Jolie	6/18/2009 1:00:10 PM	29.833105495982
Matt	Damon	6/18/2009 1:00:10 PM	31.6893683296575
George	Clooney	6/18/2009 1:00:10 PM	30.7338584049484
Orlando	Bloom	6/18/2009 1:00:10 PM	31.5771164473851
Johnny	Depp	6/18/2009 1:00:10 PM	31.5387865363653

Chapter 22: Functions in SQL

I. Basics of functions

SQL has a wide range of built in functions that help database folks do our daily jobs. If a function isn't immediately available, it is always advisable to surf the net. Developers are a generous sort and typically like to share useful functions they have created. This makes your life much easier. If you can't find a function, you can always write one yourself and post it for others!

In terms of the last example with age, the output looked much better when we gave the column heading an alias and presented age in years as opposed to days. But, but do we really want all those decimal places after the number of years? Honestly, don't we want to round down rather than up when it comes to age?!!! Lucky for us, SQL has a number of useful mathematical functions.

There are a few things to understand when working with functions.

- A function typically takes an argument. An argument is a piece of information you "pass" to the function. This will make more sense with our first example

- The parameters passed to the function are enclosed in parentheses.

II. Mathematical Functions

A. ROUND (n, precision)

The round function takes a number and the desired level of precision (digits after the decimal point) as arguments and returns the number rounded up or down. The default for Round is 0 spaces after the decimal point.

<table>
<tr><td rowspan="2">Show the student's last name with the column heading of "Student Last Name" and the student's age with the column heading of age. Round age to 2 decimal places

SELECT sfname AS "Student First Name", slname AS "Student Last Name",NOW() AS "Current Date", Round ((NOW() - sdob)/365.25) AS "Age"
FROM student</td>
<td>"Student First Name"</td><td>"Student Last Name"</td><td>"Current Date"</td><td>"Age"</td></tr>
<tr><td>Antonio</td><td>Banderas</td><td>6/18/2009 1:20:58 PM</td><td>45</td></tr>
<tr><td colspan="4">
<table>
<tr><td>Brad</td><td>Pitt</td><td>6/18/2009 1:20:58 PM</td><td>30</td></tr>
<tr><td>Angelina</td><td>Jolie</td><td>6/18/2009 1:20:58 PM</td><td>30</td></tr>
<tr><td>Matt</td><td>Damon</td><td>6/18/2009 1:20:58 PM</td><td>32</td></tr>
<tr><td>George</td><td>Clooney</td><td>6/18/2009 1:20:58 PM</td><td>31</td></tr>
<tr><td>Orlando</td><td>Bloom</td><td>6/18/2009 1:20:58 PM</td><td>32</td></tr>
<tr><td>Johnny</td><td>Depp</td><td>6/18/2009 1:20:58 PM</td><td>32</td></tr>
</table>
</td></tr>
</table>

"Student First Name"	"Student Last Name"	"Current Date"	"Age"
Antonio	Banderas	6/18/2009 1:08:13 PM	45.1
Brad	Pitt	6/18/2009 1:08:13 PM	29.93
Angelina	Jolie	6/18/2009 1:08:13 PM	29.83
Matt	Damon	6/18/2009 1:08:13 PM	31.69
George	Clooney	6/18/2009 1:08:13 PM	30.73
Orlando	Bloom	6/18/2009 1:08:13 PM	31.58
Johnny	Depp	6/18/2009 1:08:13 PM	31.54

Show the student's last name with the column heading of "Student Last Name" and the student's age with the column heading of age. Round age to 2 decimal places

```
SELECT sfname AS
"Student First Name",
slname AS "Student
Last Name",NOW() AS
"Current Date", Round ((
(NOW() - sdob
)/365.25),2) AS "Age"
FROM student;
```

III. String Functions

This is just a subset of some of the common string functions in SQL. These functions do not actually change the way that the value is stored in the field. Rather, the functions just change the way that the value is displayed for the purposes of the query.

A. lcase

This function converts all the characters of the string input to lowercase.

Syntax: lcase(attribute)

With this function, we pass the argument of the attribute which is to be converted to lower case.

Change the faculty member's last name to appear in small case. SELECT lcase(flname) FROM faculty;	Expr1000
	knightly
	streep
	redford
	newman
	dench
	binoche

B. ucase

This function converts all the characters of the string input to lowercase.

Syntax: ucase(attribute)

With this function, we pass the argument of the attribute which is to be converted to upper case.

Change the faculty member's last name to appear in upper case. SELECT ucase(flname) FROM faculty;	Expr1000
	KNIGHTLY
	STREEP
	REDFORD
	NEWMAN
	DENCH
	BINOCHE

C. LEN(string)

The LEN function takes a string as an argument and returns the number of characters in the string.

Syntax: LEN(string)

With this function, we pass the string whose length is to be counted. Returns the length of the string input

SELECT student.SLNAME, len([student]![SLNAME]) AS "Name Length" FROM student;	SLNAME	"Name Length"
	Banderas	8
	Pitt	4
	Jolie	5
	Damon	5
	Clooney	7
	Bloom	5
	Depp	4

Chapter 23: Aggregation

I. Introduction to Aggregation

Although detail level data is great, many times we actually want to see aggregated or summarized data. The result of an aggregate function is just one row of data. Oracle's SQL supports five aggregate functions: count, sum, avg, max, and min.

For example, let's say you have a product table and one of the attributes is price. What if you want to know what is the average price of the products in the table. Or, perhaps you want to know what are the highest (max) and lowest (min) priced products sold. Maybe you want to know how many (count) products we sell. Finally, you might want to add up (sum) the value of all the products.   All of this can be accomplished with aggregation functions.

To help illustrate some of the concepts in aggregation, we'll introduce a new table called the product table. Here is the table structure:

SKU	Text
PRODUCT_DESCRIPTION	Text
PRICE	Currency
QOH	Number
PRODUCTTYPE	Text
MANUFACTURER	Text

II. COUNT

A. The COUNT function lets you count the values (or rows) in a table.

B. COUNT (*) vs. COUNT (field name)

COUNT is quite useful when considering if a table has data in it or not. If you write a query using COUNT (*) and it returns 0 rows, it means that there are no rows but the table exists.

The following is very important to note:

1. COUNT (*) counts rows that contain null values

2. COUNT (fieldname) only counts rows that contain values so it excludes rows with null values.

C. Syntax: COUNT (fieldname)

COUNT is unique from some of the other aggregate functions as it accepts a column in a table of any data type and can even accept an * (asterisk) wildcard.

Show how many products are in the product table. Add an alias to make the output more legible. SELECT COUNT(sku) AS "Count of SKUS" FROM product;	"Count of SKUS"
	17

III. **SUM**

The sum function allows you to add up the values in an attribute. As we'll note, SUM is different than COUNT. COUNT literally counts how many rows exist in a table. SUM performs addition on the values of a field to come up with a total. Accordingly, SUM only works on a field that has a data type of a number. Also, SUM will ignore values which are null.

A. Syntax: SUM (fieldname)

What is the total value of all of the products in the product table? SELECT SUM(price) AS "Total Value of Inventoy " FROM product;	"Total Value of Inventory' $1,889.03

While this query works, it actually isn't really accurate as it assumes that there is only 1 of each item. What we really want to do is figure out what is the value of all the items in inventory.

To do this, we need to do some basic math. We know how many of each item is in inventory through the QOH (Quantity on Hand) attribute. If we multiply the quantity on hand of each item by its price and THEN sum it all up, we will find the value of the inventory.

SELECT SUM(price * QOH) AS "Total Value of Inventory" FROM product;	"Total Value of Inventory' $19,589.41

IV. **AVERAGE**

The AVERAGE function allows you to calculate the average of the values in an attribute. Just like SUM, AVERAGE only works on a field that has a data type of a number and will ignore values which are null.

A. Syntax: AVERAGE(fieldname)

What is the average price of the products in the product table? Add an alias to improve the readability of the output. SELECT AVG(price) AS "Average Price" FROM product;	"Average Price" $111.12

Since price is a data type of currency, Access knows that the output needs to only have 2 decimal places. Let's say we want to round it to the whole dollar.

SELECT ROUND(AVG(price),2) AS "Average Price" FROM product;	"Average Price" $111.12

V. MIN and MAX

The minimum and maximum functions show the smallest value and largest value, respectively, in a set of rows. MIN and MAX work with numeric data types as well as text.

A. ASCII character set

When you are using the MIN and MAX functions with character strings it is important to remember that SQL considers characters according to the ASCII character set. ASCII converts characters into number equivalents. Capital letter "A" is equal to ASCII 65, "B" is 66, etc. Lower letters start at 97 for "a" and work up sequentially. Accordingly, if you look for the minimum value in a field, something with a capital "C" will be show up before a small case "a".

B. Syntax:

MIN(fieldname)

MAX(fieldname)

Show the cheapest price of the products. SELECT MIN(price) AS "Least Expensive Item" FROM product;	"Least Expensive Item" $6.99
Show the most expensive price of the products SELECT MAX(price) AS "Most Expensive Item" FROM product;	"Most Expensive Item" $899.99
Show the first alphabetic value of the products SELECT MIN(product_description) AS "First item" FROM product	"First item" Boy Friend Jeans
Show the last alphabetic value of the products SELECT max(product_description) as "First item" FROM product;	"First item" Union Bay Tiki Flower Shorts

VI. GROUP BY

So far when we've written a query with an aggregation function we have just retrieved one row of data that shows the aggregation for that field's value across the entire table. For instance, we retrieved the average price of all of the products in the product table. But what if we want to break down the output? Let's say we want to see the average price of the products in the product table by product type. Here are the distinct product types in the product type table:

PRODUCTTYPE
China
Electronics
Housewares
Lawn and Garden
Men's Clothes
Women's Clothes

With a GROUP BY, we can find out what is the average price for all of the china items versus the average price of all of the electronic items. If we don't use the GROUP BY, we'll just return the average price for all of the items lumped together in the product table. SQL allows you to see aggregated results "GROUPED BY" some attribute using a GROUP BY clause.

The GROUP BY clause literally tells SQL to group the output by something. It might help to think of it in this way - a GROUP BY clause tells SQL to create a distribution or a little table. Conceptually, this is basically how it works. First SQL reads through all the rows and groups them into categories based on the attribute in the group by clause. Then, once the grouping has occurred, it calculates the summary function (MIN, MAX, SUM, COUNT, OR AVERAGE).

A. Syntax: GROUP BY <fieldname>

- SELECT
- FROM
- WHERE
- GROUP BY
- ORDER BY

Show the average price of items in the product table by product type SELECT AVG(price) as "Average Product Price" FROM product GROUP BY producttype;	**"Average Product Price"** $29.99 $135.90 $34.99 $220.30 $23.99 $32.74
Hmm, we can't tell from this output what the product type is. Let's add product type to the select clause as follows: SELECT producttype, AVG(price) as "Average Product Price" FROM product GROUP BY producttype;	**producttype** / **"Average Product Price"** China — $29.99 Electronics — $135.90 Housewares — $34.99 Lawn and Garde — $220.30 Men's Clothes — $23.99 Women's Cloth — $32.74
Let's add an alias and format the number to the whole dollar: SELECT producttype AS "Product", round(AVG(price),2) as "Average Product Price" FROM product GROUP BY producttype;	**"Product"** / **"Average Product Price"** China — 29.99 Electronics — 135.9 Housewares — 34.99 Lawn and Garden — 220.3 Men's Clothes — 23.99 Women's Clothes — 32.74

SQL Tutorial

B. Multiple forms of aggregation in one query.

SQL allows you to put multiple forms of summary data in one query.

<table>
<tr><td>Show the count of the products, the maximum price, and the minimum price as well as the average price by product type

SELECT producttype,
COUNT(SKU) AS "Number of Items",
ROUND(AVG(price),2) AS "Average Price",
MIN(price) AS "Cheapest Item",
MAX(price) AS "Most Expensive Item"
FROM product
GROUP BY producttype;</td>
<td>

PRODUCTTYPE	Number of Items	Average Price	Cheapest Item	Most Expensive Item
China	1	29.99	29.99	29.99
Electronics	4	135.9	21.99	345.76
Housewares	1	34.99	34.99	34.99
Lawn and Garden	5	220.3	6.99	899.99
Men's Clothes	2	23.99	12.99	34.99
Women's Clothes	4	32.74	24.99	46.99

</td></tr>
</table>

C. Adding more than one attribute (nest) the GROUP BY clause

You can nest the attributes in your GROUP BY clause.

You can use up to 10 fields to group rows, with the order of field names determining the group levels from highest to lowest.

<table>
<tr><td>Show the manufacturer_id and number of items for that manufacturer for each product type.

SELECT producttype, manufacturer,
COUNT(SKU) AS "Number of Items"
FROM product
GROUP BY producttype, manufacturer;</td>
<td>

producttype	manufacture	"Number of Items"
China	2	1
Electronics	11	1
Electronics	13	1
Electronics	8	2
Housewares	1	1
Lawn and Garden	10	1
Lawn and Garden	4	1
Lawn and Garden	5	2
Lawn and Garden	9	1
Men's Clothes	12	1
Men's Clothes	3	1
Women's Clothes	6	1
Women's Clothes	7	3

</td></tr>
</table>

D. Adding criteria with GROUP BY clause

You can add joins and criteria to your query.

In the first query, we'll just show the average product price by product type

<table>
<tr><td>SELECT producttype AS "Product Type",
ROUND(AVG(price),2) AS "Average Product Price"
FROM product
GROUP BY producttype;</td>
<td>

"Product Type"	"Average Product Price"
China	29.99
Electronics	135.9
Housewares	34.99
Lawn and Garden	220.3
Men's Clothes	23.99
Women's Clothes	32.74

</td></tr>
</table>

Now consider if I restrict the output to SKUs > 400000 , we can see that the average amount of some product types has changed (i.e Lawn and Garden's average price went from $220.30 to $47.51) and some product types are completely excluded from the output (i.e. Electronics) since a number of items have been excluded. Show the average price of items in the product table by product type if the quantity on hand is greater than 32. SELECT producttype AS "Product Type", AVG(price) AS "Average Product Price" FROM product where qoh > 32 GROUP BY producttype;	**"Product Type"** — **"Average Product Price"** China — $29.99 Lawn and Garden — $7.99

E. Sorting the results of the GROUP BY clause

Normally, the output of an aggregation query is sorted in ascending order by the attribute in the group by clause. For instance, you'll note in the above example that the output is alphabetically arranged in ascending order by product type. You can override this by an ORDER BY clause.

Sort the example output above by descending product type. SELECT producttype AS "Product Type", AVG(price) AS "Average Product Price" FROM product where qoh > 32 GROUP BY producttype Order by producttype DESC;	**"Product Type"** — **"Average Product Price"** Lawn and Garden — $7.99 China — $29.99
List the number of items, average price, minimum price, maximum prices of all the products grouped by producttype. List the output by maximum price ascending. SELECT producttype, COUNT(SKU) AS "Number of Items", ROUND(AVG(price),2) AS "Average Price", MIN(price) AS "Cheapest Item", MAX(price) AS "Most Expensive Item" FROM product GROUP BY producttype ORDER BY MAX(price) ASC;	See table below

producttype	"Number of Items"	"Average Price"	"Cheapest Item"	"Most Expensive Item"
China	1	29.99	$29.99	$29.99
Men's Clothes	2	23.99	$12.99	$34.99
Housewares	1	34.99	$34.99	$34.99
Women's Clothes	4	32.74	$24.99	$46.99
Electronics	4	135.9	$21.99	$345.76
Lawn and Garden	5	220.3	$6.99	$899.99

F. Displaying non-aggregate attributes in aggregation query

Let's say we want to add the SKU to this output:

SELECT SKU, producttype AS "Product Type", ROUND(AVG(price),2) AS "Average Product Price"

FROM product

GROUP BY producttype;

Wait – we get this error. Why?

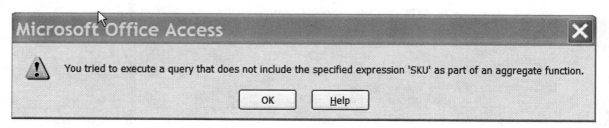

1. Remember that in aggregation you are showing summary data, not row level data. If you try and show row level data such as each individual SKU, SQL will tell you it isn't a aggregate function by. You can only show attributes in the select statement that are being summarized OR are the attribute on which you are grouping your data through a group by clause. For instance, let's revisit one of our queries from the prior section.

SELECT AVG(price) AS "Average Price"

FROM product;

2. If we try to add producttype to this query as shown, we'll get the error below. This is SQL's way of saying you are trying to show single level data but you aren't grouping your output in any way. You either have to add the producttype to a group by clause or take it out of the select clause.

SELECT producttype, AVG(price) AS "Average Price"

FROM product;

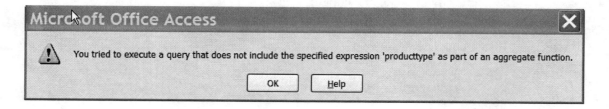

G. Rules of thumb:

1. Put all of the grouping columns in the SELECT list.

2. Only columns may be used for grouping, not expressions.

3. Don't use GROUP BY to get multiple levels of summary value.

4. Don't use GROUP BY without aggregates-DISTINCT gives the same effect and the meaning is clearer.

VII. **HAVING**

We have seen that you can place criteria or filters on queries using a WHERE clause. But SQL has another feature that really is useful. You can filter on aggregation.   Previously we wrote a query that displayed the average product price by product type.

SELECT producttype AS "Product Type", ROUND(AVG(price),2) AS "Average Product Price" FROM product GROUP BY producttype;	"Product Type"	"Average Product Price"
	China	29.99
	Electronics	135.9
	Housewares	34.99
	Lawn and Garden	220.3
	Men's Clothes	23.99
	Women's Clothes	32.74

What if a client asked us to write the same query for those product types where the average is above $33. Look what happens if we try do this with a WHERE clause.

```
SELECT producttype AS "Product Type", round(avg(price),2) AS "Average Product Price"
FROM product
WHERE avg(price) > 33
GROUP BYproducttype;
```

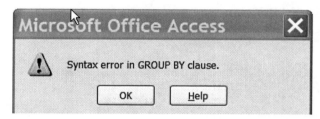

Microsoft Office Access

⚠ Syntax error in GROUP BY clause.

OK   Help

So what do we do? SQL has a special feature called a HAVING clause. HAVING is used to restrict an output based on an aggregated condition.

A. Syntax: HAVING aggregate function(condition)

Show the average product price by product for all products with an average price greater than $33 SELECT producttype AS "Product Type", ROUND(AVG(price),2) AS "Average Product Price" FROM product GROUP BY producttype HAVING AVG(price) > 33;	"Product Type"	"Average Product Price"
	Electronics	135.9
	Housewares	34.99
	Lawn and Garden	220.3

B. HAVING and WHERE Clause

1. Filtering on Aggregated and Unaggregated Data in the Same Query:

There are times when you will want to filter on aggregated data AND un-aggregated date. In these situations you will have both a WHERE and a HAVING clause

For example, let's say we want to know the average product price by product for all products with a minimum price greater than $20 and the manufacturer is more than 2. Since we are looking for a minimum price which is an aggregate function, we will need to use a having for this piece of the query. We are also looking to filter on un-aggregated data since we want to restrict to manufacturers with a code > 2. We will use a WHERE clause to filter on this condition. The query will look as follows:

SELECT producttype, AVG(price) AS "Average Price" FROM product WHERE manufacturer > '2' GROUP BY producttype HAVING MIN(price) > 20;	producttype	"Average Price"
	Electronics	$33.93
	Women's Clothes	$32.74

2. Filtering on Aggregated Data and a Join in the Same Query:

If you want to filter on aggregated data and your query includes more than one table, you will have both a WHERE and a HAVING clause.

For instance, we want to show the average product price by manufacturer for all products with a minimum price greater than $20. In this case, we want to include the manufacturer's name, not the id. This is stored in a table called manufacturer which looks like this:

MANUFACTURER_ID	MANUFACTURERNAME
1	Goebel
2	Mikasa
3	Champion
4	Sunbeam
5	Tiki
6	Lucky Brand
7	Union Bay
8	Intersect
9	Chris and Company
10	Katie and Friends
11	Bogie
12	Denali Brand
13	Sony

a. Since we are looking for an average price which is an aggregate function, we will need to use a having for this piece of the query.

b. Since the manufacturer's name is in the manufacturer table, we need to include 2 tables into this query.

c. Whenever we have more than one table, we need a join. We will use a WHERE clause to join the tables and a HAVING clause to filter on the condition.

SELECT producttype AS "Product Type", ROUND(AVG(price),2) AS "Average Product Price" FROM product Inner Join manufacturer on (product.manufacturer = manufacturer.manufacturer_id) GROUP BY producttype HAVING MIN(price) > 20;	"Product Type"	"Average Product Price"
	China	29.99
	Electronics	135.9
	Housewares	34.99
	Women's Clothes	32.74

3. If you want to filter on aggregated data, your query includes more than one table, AND you want to filter on unaggregated data you will have both a WHERE and a HAVING clause

   For example, show the average product price by manufacturer for all products made by manufacturers with names beginning with D or after in the alphabet AND with a minimum price greater than $20

   a. Since we are looking for a average price which is an aggregate function, we will need to use a HAVING for this piece of the query.

   b. Since the manufacturer's name is in the manufacturer table, we need to include 2 tables into this query. Whenever we have more than one table, we need a join.

   c. We also are filtering on aggregated data as we are limiting the output to just those Manufacturer's with names >D. We will use a WHERE clause to join the tables and a HAVING clause to filter on the condition.

SELECT manufacturername AS "Manufacturer Name", ROUND(AVG(price),2) AS "Average Product Price" FROM product Inner Join manufacturer on (product.manufacturer = manufacturer.manufacturer_id) where MANUFACTURERNAME > 'D' GROUP BY manufacturername HAVING MIN(price) > 20;	"Manufacturer Name"	"Average Product Price"
	Denali Brand	34.99
	Goebel	34.99
	Intersect	33.93
	Katie and Friends	127.54
	Lucky Brand	46.99
	Mikasa	29.99
	Sony	345.76
	Sunbeam	899.99
	Union Bay	27.99

4. Filtering on Aggregated and a Join in the Same Query with Sort:

   Let's say we want to write the same query as above but this time we want the output to be sorted by descending average product price. All we need to do is add an ORDER BY clause and we are good to go.

SELECT manufacturername AS "Manufacturer Name", ROUND(AVG(price),2) AS "Average Product Price" FROM product Inner Join manufacturer on (product.manufacturer = manufacturer.manufacturer_id) where MANUFACTURERNAME > 'D' GROUP BY manufacturername HAVING MIN(price) > 20 ORDER BY ROUND(AVG(price),2) DESC;	"Manufacturer Name"	"Average Product Price"
	Sunbeam	899.99
	Sony	345.76
	Katie and Friends	127.54
	Lucky Brand	46.99
	Goebel	34.99
	Denali Brand	34.99
	Intersect	33.93
	Mikasa	29.99
	Union Bay	27.99

C. The Difference Between the HAVING and WHERE Clauses in a SQL Query

   Although the HAVING clause specifies a condition that is similar to the purpose of a WHERE clause, the two clauses are not interchangeable. Listed below are some differences to help distinguish between the two:

1. The WHERE clause specifies the criteria which individual rows must meet to be selected by a query. It can be used without the GROUP BY clause. The HAVING clause cannot be used without the GROUP BY clause.

2. The WHERE clause selects rows before grouping. The HAVING clause selects rows after grouping.

3. The WHERE clause cannot contain aggregate functions. The HAVING clause can contain aggregate functions.

Paragon Corporation created this output which has a nice summary of the components of an aggregate query.[11]

Clause	Purpose	Example
SELECT	Used to specify what fields will be included in the query result. This clause is always found in SQL query statements.	SELECT AVERAGE(Price) AS "Average Price"
FROM	Specifies what tables data will come from. This exists in all SQL query statements.	SELECT SUM(Amount) AS Total FROM Sales WHERE CustomerID='ABC'
WHERE	Specifies what subset of the data will be used (always has non-aggregate conditions). This clause is almost always found in SQL query statements.	SELECT Sum(Amount) AS Total FROM Sales WHERE CustomerID='ABC'
JOIN	The join clause is used to link more than one table together. This is often found in more complex queries that require retrieving data from more than one table. There are several formats (INNER JOIN, OUTER JOIN, LEFT JOIN, RIGHT JOIN, ..OUTER is usually optional	SELECT Customers.CustomerName, Sales.CustomerID, Sum(Sales.Amount) AS Total FROM Sales INNER JOIN Customers ON Customers.CustomerID = Sales.CustomerID WHERE Sales.CustomerID='ABC'
GROUP BY	Used to specify about what fields data should be aggregated. In this example, we group by CustomerID so that we get a summary of the total purchases per customer	SELECT CustomerID, SUM(Amount) AS Total FROM Sales GROUP BY CustomerID
HAVING	HAVING is very similar to WHERE except the statements within it are of an aggregate nature. Note in this example - we are only returning summaries for customers who have purchased more than 60,000 worth of items	SELECT CustomerID, SUM(Amount) AS Total FROM Sales GROUP BY CustomerID HAVING Sum(Amount) > 60000
Aggregation Functions SUM, COUNT, AVG	Aggregate functions are used to summarize data by rolling up a set of data items into a single item. There are a few basic ones that exist in most systems that support SQL, and many are specific to certain DBMS. An important thing to note is that if a column in the resultset is not an aggregate field, then it must be included in the GROUP BY clause.	SELECT CustomerID, SUM(Amount) AS Total , COUNT(*) As SaleCount, AVG(Amount) AS AverageOrder FROM Sales GROUP BY CustomerID

---

[11] http://www.paragoncorporation.com/ArticleDetail.aspx?ArticleID=6

Chapter 26: Nested Query/SubQuery

I.   Introduction to Nested or Sub Queries

A nested query, also known as a sub-query, is a query within a query. Nested queries can be used to accomplish a number of things. For instance, you can use a nested query to write queries with multiple tables and avoid writing joins. One of the really great things about a nested query is that it allows you to write aggregate queries which include non-aggregated data.

As we saw in the prior section, you cannot have aggregated and non-aggregated data in the same query. But a nested query is really a query within a query. This allows you to write one query, the inner query, which calculates the aggregated part of the query. The second query uses the output of the inner query as an input to the outer query, the un-aggregated query. Sufficiently confused?! Hold on, it will make sense!

II.   Examples with Nested Queries

A. Let's say you have a product table. You want to display the product information for those products which cost less than the average price of all the products. If we tried to write the query as follows you will get an error message as shown below.

SELECT SKU, product_description, price, QOH, producttype, manufacturer FROM product WHERE price > AVG(price);	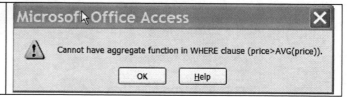

B. To generate the desired output, we essentially need to write 2 queries.

Query 1:

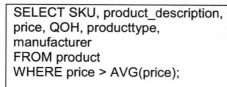

SELECT AVG(price) FROM product;	Expr1000
	$111.12

Now that we know what the average price is, we can write another query that retrieves the un-aggregated information as follows:

QUERY 2:

SELECT sku, product_description, price, QOH, producttype, manufacturer FROM product WHERE price > 111.12;	sku	product_desc	price	QOH	producttype	manufacture
	145566	Sony Trinitron 3	$345.76	14	Electronics	13
	269686	Ear Force game	$129.99	15	Electronics	11
	4653446	Extra Large Win	$127.54	3	Lawn and Garden	10
	276655	Deluxe Patio Se	$899.99	5	Lawn and Garden	4

1. We can see that all of the items' prices were greater than the average price of all of the products. But this means you need to write two queries each time. Because you need to type the information from the first query, there is always room for error. That's where the nesting part comes in. Let's take the two queries and make them into one.

2. We already learned that anything inside a parenthesis is evaluated first so we need to make sure that the inner query (or nested query) is the aggregated part. This will look identical to the aggregated query we already wrote – Query 1. The outer query or the un-aggregated part will look the same as Query 2 except that the numeric output of query 1 is actually replaced with the query.

sku	product_description	price	QOH	producttype	manufacturer
145566	Sony Trinitron 30" TV	$345.76	14	Electronics	13
269686	Ear Force gamer head set	$129.99	15	Electronics	11
4653446	Extra Large Wind Chimes	$127.54	3	Lawn and Garden	10
276655	Deluxe Patio Set - 6 chairs + umbrella	$899.99	5	Lawn and Garden	4

```
SELECT sku,
product_description, price,
QOH, producttype,
manufacturer
FROM product
WHERE price >
(SELECT AVG(price)
FROM product);
```

C. Adding a join to a nested query

The prior query is great but the manufacturer id isn't all that useful. We'd like to see the manufacturer's name. Let's add a join here to get the information from the manufacturer table.

sku	product_description	price	QOH	producttype	manufacturern
145566	Sony Trinitron 30" TV	$345.76	14	Electronics	Sony
269686	Ear Force gamer head set	$129.99	15	Electronics	Bogie
4653446	Extra Large Wind Chimes	$127.54	3	Lawn and Garden	Katie and Friends
276655	Deluxe Patio Set - 6 chairs + umbrella	$899.99	5	Lawn and Garden	Sunbeam

```
SELECT sku,
product_description,
price, QOH,
producttype,
manufacturername
FROM product
inner join manufacturer
on
(product.manufacturer
=
manufacturer.manufac
turer_id)
WHERE price >
(SELECT AVG(price)
FROM product);
```

D. Adding multiple criteria to a query

sku	product_description	price	QOH	producttype	manufa
145566	Sony Trinitron 30" TV	$345.76	14	Electronics	Sony
269686	Ear Force gamer head set	$129.99	15	Electronics	Bogie

Limit the above query to so that it only displays electronic products

```
SELECT sku,
product_description,
price, QOH,
producttype,
manufacturername
FROM product
inner join
manufacturer on
(product.manufactur
er =
manufacturer.manuf
acturer_id)
WHERE producttype
= 'Electronics'  and
price >
(SELECT
AVG(price)
FROM product);
```

E. Mathematical functions and nested queries

	sku	product_description	price	QOH	"Inventory Value'	producttype	manufact
Let's add the value of the inventory (QOH * Price) to the query and improve the headings	145566	Sony Trinitron 30" TV	$345.76	14	$4,840.64	Electronics	Sony
	269686	Ear Force gamer head set	$129.99	15	$1,949.85	Electronics	Bogie
SELECT sku, product_description, price, QOH, (price * QOH) AS "Inventory Value", producttype, manufacturername FROM product inner join manufacturer on (product.manufacturer = manufacturer.manufacturer_id) WHERE producttype = 'Electronics' and price > (SELECT AVG(price) FROM product);							

F. Sort the output

	sku	product_description	price	QOH	"Inventory Value'	producttype	manufacturer
Sort the output by ascending manufacturer's name	269686	Ear Force gamer head set	$129.99	15	$1,949.85	Electronics	Bogie
	145566	Sony Trinitron 30" TV	$345.76	14	$4,840.64	Electronics	Sony
SELECT sku, product_description, price, QOH, (price * QOH) AS "Inventory Value", producttype, manufacturername FROM product inner join manufacturer on (product.manufacturer = manufacturer.manufacturer_id) WHERE producttype = 'Electronics' and price > (SELECT AVG(price) FROM product) ORDER BY manufacturername ASC;							

Index

1.1 DATA VS. INFORMATION

To understand what drives database design, you must understand the difference between data and information. **Data** are raw facts. The word *raw* indicates that the facts have not yet been processed to reveal their meaning. For example, suppose that you want to know what the users of a computer lab think of its services. Typically, you would begin by surveying users to assess the computer lab's performance. Figure 1.1, Panel A, shows the Web survey form that enables users to respond to your questions. When the survey form has been completed, the form's raw data are saved to a data repository, such as the one shown in Figure 1.1, Panel B. Although you now have the facts in hand, they are not particularly useful in this format—reading page after page of zeros and ones is not likely to provide much insight. Therefore, you transform the raw data into a data summary like the one shown in Figure 1.1, Panel C. Now it's possible to get quick answers to questions such as "What is the composition of our lab's customer base?" In this case, you can quickly determine that most of your customers are juniors (24.59%) and seniors (53.01%). Because graphics can enhance your ability to quickly extract meaning from data, you show the data summary bar graph in Figure 1.1, Panel D.

FIGURE 1.1   Transforming raw data into information

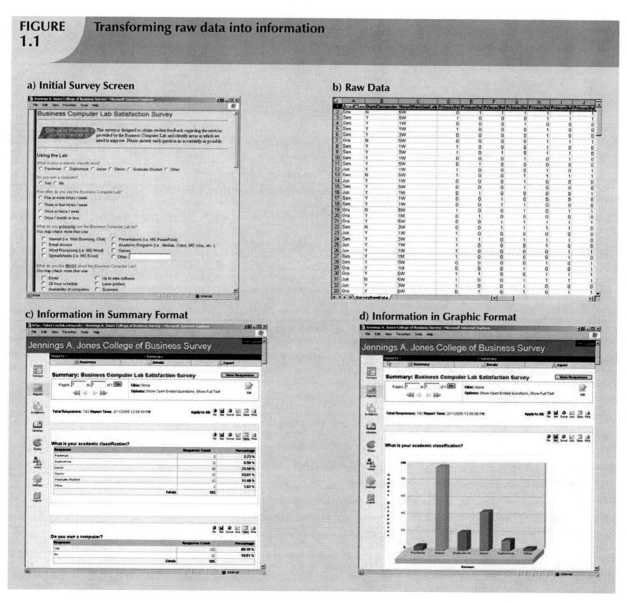

a) Initial Survey Screen

b) Raw Data

c) Information in Summary Format

d) Information in Graphic Format

Information is the result of processing raw data to reveal its meaning. Data processing can be as simple as organizing data to reveal patterns or as complex as making forecasts or drawing inferences using statistical modeling. To reveal meaning, information requires *context*. For example, an average temperature reading of 105 degrees does not mean much unless you also know its context: Is this in degrees Fahrenheit or Celsius? Is this a machine temperature, a body temperature, or an outside air temperature? Information can be used as the foundation for decision making. For example, the data summary for each question on the survey form can point out the lab's strengths and weaknesses, helping you to make informed decisions to better meet the needs of lab customers.

Keep in mind that raw data must be properly *formatted* for storage, processing, and presentation. For example, in Panel C of Figure 1.1, the student classification is formatted to show the results based on the classifications Freshman, Sophomore, Junior, Senior, and Graduate Student. The respondents' yes/no responses might need to be converted to a Y/N format for data storage. More complex formatting is required when working with complex data types, such as sounds, videos, or images.

In this "information age," production of accurate, relevant, and timely information is the key to good decision making. In turn, good decision making is the key to business survival in a global market. We are now said to be entering the "knowledge age."[1] Data are the foundation of information, which is the bedrock of **knowledge**—that is, the body of information and facts about a specific subject. Knowledge implies familiarity, awareness, and understanding of information as it applies to an environment. A key characteristic of knowledge is that "new" knowledge can be derived from "old" knowledge.

Let's summarize some key points:

- Data constitute the building blocks of information.
- Information is produced by processing data.
- Information is used to reveal the meaning of data.
- Accurate, relevant, and timely information is the key to good decision making.
- Good decision making is the key to organizational survival in a global environment.

Timely and useful information requires accurate data. Such data must be generated properly, and it must be stored in a format that is easy to access and process. And, like any basic resource, the data environment must be managed carefully. **Data management** is a discipline that focuses on the proper generation, storage, and retrieval of data. Given the crucial role that data plays, it should not surprise you that data management is a core activity for any business, government agency, service organization, or charity.

1.2 INTRODUCING THE DATABASE AND THE DBMS

Efficient data management typically requires the use of a computer database. A **database** is a shared, integrated computer structure that stores a collection of:

- End-user data, that is, raw facts of interest to the end user.
- **Metadata**, or data about data, through which the end-user data are integrated and managed.

The metadata provide a description of the data characteristics and the set of relationships that link the data found within the database. For example, the metadata component stores information such as the name of each data element, the type of values (numeric, dates or text) stored on each data element, whether or not the data element can be left empty, and so on. Therefore, the metadata provide information that complements and expands the value and use of the data. In short, metadata present a more complete picture of the data in the database. Given the characteristics of metadata, you might hear a database described as a "collection of *self-describing* data."

---

[1] Peter Drucker coined the phrase "knowledge worker" in 1959 in his book *Landmarks of Tomorrow*. In 1994, Ms. Esther Dyson, Mr. George Gilder, Dr. George Keyworth, and Dr. Alvin Toffler introduced the concept of the "knowledge age."

A **database management system (DBMS)** is a collection of programs that manages the database structure and controls access to the data stored in the database. In a sense, a database resembles a very well-organized electronic filing cabinet in which powerful software, known as a *database management system*, helps manage the cabinet's contents.

1.2.1 ROLE AND ADVANTAGES OF THE DBMS

The DBMS serves as the intermediary between the user and the database. The database structure itself is stored as a collection of files, and the only way to access the data in those files is through the DBMS. Figure 1.2 emphasizes the point that the DBMS presents the end user (or application program) with a single, integrated view of the data in the database. The DBMS receives all application requests and translates them into the complex operations required to fulfill those requests. The DBMS hides much of the database's internal complexity from the application programs and users. The application program might be written by a programmer using a programming language such as Visual Basic.NET, Java, or C++, or it might be created through a DBMS utility program.

FIGURE 1.2	The DBMS manages the interaction between the end user and the database

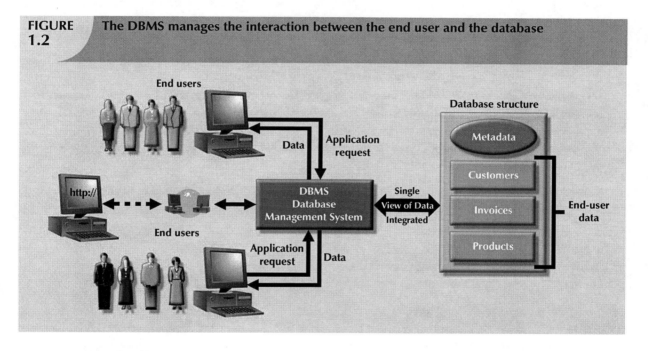

Having a DBMS between the end user's applications and the database offers some important advantages. First, the DBMS enables the data in the database *to be shared* among multiple applications or users. Second, the DBMS *integrates* the many different users' views of the data into a single all-encompassing data repository.

Because data are the crucial raw material from which information is derived, you must have a good method to manage such data. As you will discover in this book, the DBMS helps make data management more efficient and effective. In particular, a DBMS provides advantages such as:

- *Improved data sharing.* The DBMS helps create an environment in which end users have better access to more data and better-managed data. Such access makes it possible for end users to respond quickly to changes in their environment.
- *Improved data security.* The more users access the data, the greater the risks of data security breaches. Corporations invest considerable amounts of time, effort, and money to ensure that corporate data are used properly. A DBMS provides a framework for better enforcement of data privacy and security policies.

- *Better data integration*. Wider access to well-managed data promotes an integrated view of the organization's operations and a clearer view of the big picture. It becomes much easier to see how actions in one segment of the company affect other segments.

- *Minimized data inconsistency*. **Data inconsistency** exists when different versions of the same data appear in different places. For example, data inconsistency exists when a company's sales department stores a sales representative's name as "Bill Brown" and the company's personnel department stores that same person's name as "William G. Brown" or when the company's regional sales office shows the price of a product as $45.95 and its national sales office shows the same product's price as $43.95. The probability of data inconsistency is greatly reduced in a properly designed database.

- *Improved data access*. The DBMS makes it possible to produce quick answers to ad hoc queries. From a database perspective, a **query** is a specific request issued to the DBMS for data manipulation—for example, to read or update the data. Simply put, a query is a question, and an **ad hoc query** is a spur-of-the-moment question. The DBMS sends back an answer (called the **query result set**) to the application. For example, end users, when dealing with large amounts of sales data, might want quick answers to questions (ad hoc queries) such as:

  - What was the dollar volume of sales by product during the past six months?
  - What is the sales bonus figure for each of our salespeople during the past three months?
  - How many of our customers have credit balances of $3,000 or more?

- *Improved decision making*. Better-managed data and improved data access make it possible to generate better quality information, on which better decisions are based.

- *Increased end-user productivity*. The availability of data, combined with the tools that transform data into usable information, empowers end users to make quick, informed decisions that can make the difference between success and failure in the global economy.

The advantages of using a DBMS are not limited to the few just listed. In fact, you will discover many more advantages as you learn more about the technical details of databases and their proper design.

1.2.2 TYPES OF DATABASES

A DBMS can support many different types of databases. Databases can be classified according to the number of users, the database location(s), and the expected type and extent of use.

The number of users determines whether the database is classified as single-user or multiuser. A **single-user database** supports only one user at a time. In other words, if user A is using the database, users B and C must wait until user A is done. A single-user database that runs on a personal computer is called a **desktop database**. In contrast, a **multiuser database** supports multiple users at the same time. When the multiuser database supports a relatively small number of users (usually fewer than 50) or a specific department within an organization, it is called a **workgroup database**. When the database is used by the entire organization and supports many users (more than 50, usually hundreds) across many departments, the database is known as an **enterprise database**.

Location might also be used to classify the database. For example, a database that supports data located at a single site is called a **centralized database**. A database that supports data distributed across several different sites is called a **distributed database**. The extent to which a database can be distributed and the way in which such distribution is managed is addressed in detail in Chapter 12, Distributed Database Management Systems.

The most popular way of classifying databases today, however, is based on how they will be used and on the time sensitivity of the information gathered from them. For example, transactions such as product or service sales, payments, and supply purchases reflect critical day-to-day operations. Such transactions must be recorded accurately and immediately. A database that is designed primarily to support a company's day-to-day operations is classified as an **operational database** (sometimes referred to as a **transactional** or **production database**). In contrast, a **data warehouse** focuses primarily on storing data used to generate information required to make tactical or strategic decisions. Such decisions typically require extensive "data massaging" (data manipulation) to extract information to formulate pricing decisions, sales forecasts, market positioning, and so on. Most decision-support data are based on historical data obtained from operational databases. Additionally, the data warehouse can store data derived from many sources. To make it easier to retrieve such data, the data warehouse structure is quite different from that of an operational or transactional database. The design, implementation, and use of data warehouses are covered in detail in Chapter 13, Business Intelligence and Data Warehouses.

Databases can also be classified to reflect the degree to which the data are structured. **Unstructured data** are data that exist in their original (raw) state, that is, in the format in which they were collected. Therefore, unstructured data exist in a format that does not lend itself to the processing that yields information. **Structured data** are the result of taking unstructured data and formatting (structuring) such data to facilitate storage, use, and the generation of information. You apply structure (format) based on the type of processing that you intend to perform on the data. Some data might be not ready (unstructured) for some types of processing, but they might be ready (structured) for other types of processing. For example, the data value 37890 might refer to a zip code, a sales value, or a product code. If this value represents a zip code or a product code and is stored as text, you cannot perform mathematical computations with it. On the other hand, if this value represents a sales transaction, it is necessary to format it as numeric.

To further illustrate the structure concept, imagine a stack of printed paper invoices. If you want to merely store these invoices as images for future retrieval and display, you can scan them and save them in a graphic format. On the other hand, if you want to derive information such as monthly totals and average sales, such graphic storage would not be useful. Instead, you could store the invoice data in a (structured) spreadsheet format so that you can perform the requisite computations. Actually, most data you encounter is best classified as semistructured. **Semistructured data** are data that have already been processed to some extent. For example, if you look at a typical Web page, the data are presented to you in a prearranged format to convey some information.

The database types mentioned thus far focus on the storage and management of highly structured data. However, corporations are not limited to the use of structured data. They also use semistructured and unstructured data. Just think of the very valuable information that can be found on company e-mails, memos, documents such as procedures and rules, Web page contents, and so on. Unstructured and semistructured data storage and management needs are being addressed through a new generation of databases known as XML databases. **Extensible Markup Language (XML)** is a special language used to represent and manipulate data elements in a textual format. An **XML database** supports the storage and management of semistructured XML data.

Table 1.1 compares features of several well-known database management systems.

TABLE 1.1	Types of Databases							
PRODUCT	NUMBER OF USERS			DATA LOCATION		DATA USAGE		XML
	SINGLE USER	MULTIUSER		CENTRALIZED	DISTRIBUTED	OPERATIONAL	DATA WAREHOUSE	
		WORK-GROUP	ENTER-PRISE					
MS Access	X	X		X		X		
MS SQL Server	X^2	X	X	X	X	X	X	X
IBM DB2	X^2	X	X	X	X	X	X	X
MySQL	X	X	X	X	X	X	X	X*
Oracle RDBMS	X^2	X	X	X	X	X	X	X
* Supports XML functions only. XML data is stored in large text objects.								

[2] Vendor offers single-user/personal DBMS version.

Most of the database design, implementation, and management issues addressed in this book are based on production (transaction) databases. The focus on production databases is based on two considerations. First, production databases are the databases most frequently encountered in common activities such as enrolling in a class, registering a car, buying a product, or making a bank deposit or withdrawal. Second, data warehouse databases derive most of their data from production databases, and if production databases are poorly designed, the data warehouse databases based on them will lose their reliability and value as well.

1.3 WHY DATABASE DESIGN IS IMPORTANT

Database design refers to the activities that focus on the design of the database structure that will be used to store and manage end-user data. A database that meets all user requirements does not just happen; its structure must be designed carefully. In fact, database design is such a crucial aspect of working with databases that most of this book is dedicated to the development of good database design techniques. Even a good DBMS will perform poorly with a badly designed database.

Proper database design requires the designer to identify precisely the database's expected use. Designing a transactional database emphasizes accurate and consistent data and operational speed. The design of a data warehouse database recognizes the use of historical and aggregated data. Designing a database to be used in a centralized, single-user environment requires a different approach from that used in the design of a distributed, multiuser database. This book emphasizes the design of transactional, centralized, single-user, and multiuser databases. Chapters 12 and 13 also examine critical issues confronting the designer of distributed and data warehouse databases.

A well-designed database facilitates data management and generates accurate and valuable information. A poorly designed database is likely to become a breeding ground for difficult-to-trace errors that may lead to bad decision making—and bad decision making can lead to the failure of an organization. Database design is simply too important to be left to luck. That's why college students study database design, why organizations of all types and sizes send personnel to database design seminars, and why database design consultants often make an excellent living.

1.4 HISTORICAL ROOTS: FILES AND FILE SYSTEMS

Although managing data through the use of file systems is now largely obsolete, there are several good reasons for studying them in some detail:

- An understanding of the relatively simple characteristics of file systems makes the complexity of database design easier to understand.
- An awareness of the problems that plagued file systems can help you avoid those same pitfalls with DBMS software.
- If you intend to convert an obsolete file system to a database system, knowledge of the file system's basic limitations will be useful.

In the recent past, a manager of almost any small organization was (and sometimes still is) able to keep track of necessary data by using a manual file system. Such a file system was traditionally composed of a collection of file folders, each properly tagged and kept in a filing cabinet. Organization of the data within the file folders was determined by the data's expected use. Ideally, the contents of each file folder were logically related. For example, a file folder in a doctor's office might contain patient data, one file folder for each patient. All of the data in that file folder would describe only that particular patient's medical history. Similarly, a personnel manager might organize personnel data by category of employment (for example, clerical, technical, sales, and administrative). Therefore, a file folder labeled "Technical" would contain data pertaining to only those people whose duties were properly classified as technical.

As long as a data collection was relatively small and an organization's managers had few reporting requirements, the manual system served its role well as a data repository. However, as organizations grew and as reporting requirements became more complex, keeping track of data in a manual file system became more difficult. In fact, finding and using data in growing collections of file folders turned into such a time-consuming and cumbersome task that it became unlikely that such data could generate useful information. Consider just these few questions to which a retail business owner might want answers:

- What products sold well during the past week, month, quarter, or year?
- What is the current daily, weekly, monthly, quarterly, or yearly sales dollar volume?
- How do the current period's sales compare to those of last week, last month, or last year?
- Did the various cost categories increase, decrease, or remain stable during the past week, month, quarter, or year?
- Did sales show trends that could change the inventory requirements?

The list of questions such as these tends to be long and to increase in number as an organization grows.

Unfortunately, generating reports from a manual file system can be slow and cumbersome. In fact, some business managers faced government-imposed reporting requirements that required weeks of intensive effort each quarter, even when a well-designed manual system was used. Consequently, necessity called for the design of a computer-based system that would track data and produce required reports.

The conversion from a manual file system to a matching computer file system could be technically complex. (Because people are accustomed to today's relatively user-friendly computer interfaces, they have forgotten how painfully hostile computers used to be!) Consequently, a new kind of professional, known as a **data processing (DP) specialist**, had to be hired or "grown" from the current staff. The DP specialist created the necessary computer file structures, often wrote the software that managed the data within those structures, and designed the application programs that produced reports based on the file data. Thus, numerous homegrown computerized file systems were born.

Initially, the computer files within the file system were similar to the manual files. A simple example of a customer data file for a small insurance company is shown in Figure 1.3. (You will discover later that the file structure shown in Figure 1.3, although typically found in early file systems, is unsatisfactory for a database.)

FIGURE 1.3   **Contents of the CUSTOMER file**

C_NAME	C_PHONE	C_ADDRESS	C_ZIP	A_NAME	A_PHONE	TP	AMT	REN
Alfred A. Ramas	615-844-2573	218 Fork Rd., Babs, TN	36123	Leah F. Hahn	615-882-1244	T1	100.00	05-Apr-2008
Leona K. Dunne	713-894-1238	Box 12A, Fox, KY	25246	Alex B. Alby	713-228-1249	T1	250.00	16-Jun-2008
Kathy W. Smith	615-894-2285	125 Oak Ln, Babs, TN	36123	Leah F. Hahn	615-882-2144	S2	150.00	29-Jan-2009
Paul F. Olowski	615-894-2180	217 Lee Ln., Babs, TN	36123	Leah F. Hahn	615-882-1244	S1	300.00	14-Oct-2008
Myron Orlando	615-222-1672	Box 111, New, TN	36155	Alex B. Alby	713-228-1249	T1	100.00	28-Dec-2008
Amy B. O'Brian	713-442-3381	387 Troll Dr., Fox, KY	25246	John T. Okon	615-123-5589	T2	850.00	22-Sep-2008
James G. Brown	615-297-1228	21 Tye Rd., Nash, TN	37118	Leah F. Hahn	615-882-1244	S1	120.00	25-Mar-2009
George Williams	615-290-2556	155 Maple, Nash, TN	37119	John T. Okon	615-123-5589	S1	250.00	17-Jul-2008
Anne G. Farriss	713-382-7185	2119 Elm, Crew, KY	25432	Alex B. Alby	713-228-1249	T2	100.00	03-Dec-2008
Olette K. Smith	615-297-3809	2782 Main, Nash, TN	37118	John T. Okon	615-123-5589	S2	500.00	14-Mar-2009

C_NAME = Customer name
C_PHONE = Customer phone
C_ADDRESS = Customer address
C_ZIP = Customer zip code

A_NAME = Agent name
A_PHONE = Agent phone
TP = Insurance type
AMT = Insurance policy amount, in thousands of $
REN = Insurance renewal date

ONLINE CONTENT

The databases used in each chapter are available in the Student Online Companion for this book. Throughout the book, Online Content boxes highlight material related to chapter content located in the Student Online Companion.

The description of computer files requires a specialized vocabulary. Every discipline develops its own jargon to enable its practitioners to communicate clearly. The basic file vocabulary shown in Table 1.2 will help you understand subsequent discussions more easily.

TABLE 1.2	Basic File Terminology
TERM	**DEFINITION**
Data	"Raw" facts, such as a telephone number, a birth date, a customer name, and a year-to-date (YTD) sales value. Data have little meaning unless they have been organized in some logical manner. The smallest piece of data that can be "recognized" by the computer is a single character, such as the letter A, the number 5, or a symbol such as /. A single character requires 1 byte of computer storage.
Field	A character or group of characters (alphabetic or numeric) that has a specific meaning. A field is used to define and store data.
Record	A logically connected set of one or more fields that describes a person, place, or thing. For example, the fields that constitute a record for a customer named J. D. Rudd might consist of J. D. Rudd's name, address, phone number, date of birth, credit limit, and unpaid balance.
File	A collection of related records. For example, a file might contain data about vendors of ROBCOR Company, or a file might contain the records for the students currently enrolled at Gigantic University.

Using the proper file terminology given in Table 1.2, you can identify the file components shown in Figure 1.3. The CUSTOMER file shown in Figure 1.3 contains 10 records. Each record is composed of nine fields: C_NAME, C_PHONE, C_ADDRESS, C_ZIP, A_NAME, A_PHONE, TP, AMT, and REN. The 10 records are stored in a named file. Because the file in Figure 1.3 contains customer data for the insurance company, its filename is CUSTOMER.

Using the CUSTOMER file's contents, the DP specialist wrote programs that produced very useful reports for the insurance company's sales department:

- Monthly summaries that showed the types and amounts of insurance sold by each agent. (Such reports might be used to analyze each agent's productivity.)
- Monthly checks to determine which customers must be contacted for renewal.
- Reports that analyzed the ratios of insurance types sold by each agent.
- Periodic customer contact letters designed to summarize coverage and to provide various customer relations bonuses.

As time went on, the insurance company needed additional programs to produce new reports. Although it took some time to specify the report contents and to write the programs that produced the reports, the sales department manager did not miss the old manual system—using the computer saved much time and effort. The reports were impressive, and the ability to perform complex data searches yielded the information needed to make sound decisions.

Then the sales department at the insurance company created a file named SALES, which helped track daily sales efforts. Additional files were created as needed to produce even more useful reports. In fact, the sales department's success was so obvious that the personnel department manager demanded access to the DP specialist to automate payroll processing and other personnel functions. Consequently, the DP specialist was asked to create the AGENT file shown in Figure 1.4. The data in the AGENT file were used to write checks, keep track of taxes paid, and summarize insurance coverage, among other tasks.

FIGURE 1.4   Contents of the AGENT file

A_NAME	A_PHONE	A_ADDRESS	ZIP	HIRED	YTD_PAY	YTD_FIT	YTD_FICA	YTD_SLS	DEP
Alex B. Alby	713-228-1249	123 Toll, Nash, TN	37119	01-Nov-2000	26566.24	6641.56	2125.30	132737.75	3
Leah F. Hahn	615-882-1244	334 Main, Fox, KY	25246	23-May-1986	32213.78	8053.44	2577.10	138967.35	0
John T. Okon	615-123-5589	452 Elm, New, TN	36155	15-Jun-2005	23198.29	5799.57	1855.86	127093.45	2

A_NAME	= Agent name		YTD_PAY	= Year-to-date pay
A_PHONE	= Agent phone		YTD_FIT	= Year-to-date federal income tax paid
A_ADDRESS	= Agent address		YTD_FICA	= Year-to-date Social Security taxes paid
ZIP	= Agent zip code		YTD_SLS	= Year-to-date sales
HIRED	= Agent date of hire		DEP	= Number of dependents

As the number of files increased, a small file system, like the one shown in Figure 1.5, evolved. Each file in the system used its own application program to store, retrieve, and modify data. And each file was owned by the individual or the department that commissioned its creation.

FIGURE 1.5   A simple file system

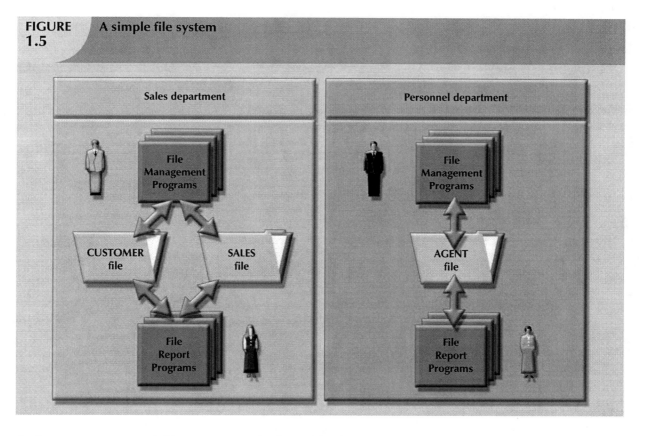

As the insurance company's file system grew, the demand for the DP specialist's programming skills grew even faster, and the DP specialist was authorized to hire additional programmers. The size of the file system also required a larger, more complex computer. The new computer and the additional programming staff caused the DP specialist to spend less time programming and more time managing technical and human resources. Therefore, the DP specialist's job evolved into that of a **data processing (DP) manager**, who supervised a new DP department. In spite of these organizational changes, however, the DP department's primary activity remained programming, and the DP manager inevitably spent much time as a supervising senior programmer and program troubleshooter.

1.5 PROBLEMS WITH FILE SYSTEM DATA MANAGEMENT

The file system method of organizing and managing data was a definite improvement over a manual system, and the file system served a useful purpose in data management for over two decades—a very long time in the computer era. Nonetheless, many problems and limitations became evident in this approach. A critique of the file system method serves two major purposes:

- Understanding the shortcomings of the file system enables you to understand the development of modern databases.

- Many of the problems are not unique to file systems. Failure to understand such problems is likely to lead to their duplication in a database environment, even though database technology makes it easy to avoid them.

The first and most glaring problem with the file system approach is that even the simplest data-retrieval task requires extensive programming. With the older file systems, programmers had to specify what must be done and how it was to be done. As you will learn in upcoming chapters, modern databases use a nonprocedural data manipulation language that allows the user to specify what must be done without specifying how it must be done. Typically, this nonprocedural language is used for data retrieval (such as query by example and report generator tools), is much faster, and can work with different DBMSs.

The need to write programs to produce even the simplest reports makes ad hoc queries impossible. Harried DP specialists and DP managers who work with mature file systems often receive numerous requests for new reports. They are often forced to say that the report will be ready "next week" or even "next month." If you need the information now, getting it next week or next month will not serve your information needs.

Furthermore, making changes in an existing structure can be difficult in a file system environment. For example, changing just one field in the original CUSTOMER file would require a program that:

1. Reads a record from the original file.
2. Transforms the original data to conform to the new structure's storage requirements.
3. Writes the transformed data into the new file structure.
4. Repeats steps 2 to 4 for each record in the original file.

In fact, any change to a file structure, no matter how minor, forces modifications in all of the programs that use the data in that file. Modifications are likely to produce errors (bugs), and additional time is spent using a debugging process to find those errors.

Another problem related to the need for extensive programming is that as the number of files in the system expands, system administration becomes more difficult. Even a simple file system with a few files requires the creation and maintenance of several file management programs (each file must have its own file management programs that allow the user to add, modify, and delete records, to list the file contents, and to generate reports). Because ad hoc queries are not possible, the file reporting programs can multiply quickly. The problem is compounded by the fact that each department in the organization "owns" its data by creating its own files.

Another fault of a file system database is that security features are difficult to program and are, therefore, often omitted in a file system environment. Such features include effective password protection, the ability to lock out parts of files or parts of the system itself, and other measures designed to safeguard data confidentiality. Even when an attempt is made to improve system and data security, the security devices tend to be limited in scope and effectiveness.

To summarize the limitations of file system data management so far:

- It requires extensive programming.
- It can not perform ad hoc queries.
- System administration can be complex and difficult.

- It is difficult to make changes to existing structures.
- Security features are likely to be inadequate.

Those limitations, in turn, lead to problems of structural and data dependency.

1.5.1 STRUCTURAL AND DATA DEPENDENCE

A file system exhibits **structural dependence,** which means that access to a file is dependent on its structure. For example, adding a customer date-of-birth field to the CUSTOMER file shown in Figure 1.3 would require the four steps described in the previous section. Given this change, none of the previous programs will work with the new CUSTOMER file structure. Therefore, all of the file system programs must be modified to conform to the new file structure. In short, because the file system application programs are affected by change in the file structure, they exhibit structural dependence. Conversely, **structural independence** exists when it is possible to make changes in the file structure without affecting the application program's ability to access the data.

Even changes in the characteristics of data, such as changing a field from integer to decimal, require changes in all the programs that access the file. Because all data access programs are subject to change when any of the file's data storage characteristics change (that is, changing the data type), the file system is said to exhibit **data dependence**. Conversely, **data independence** exists when it is possible to make changes in the data storage characteristics without affecting the application program's ability to access the data.

The practical significance of data dependence is the difference between the **logical data format** (how the human being views the data) and the **physical data format** (how the computer must work with the data). Any program that accesses a file system's file must tell the computer not only what to do, but also how to do it. Consequently, each program must contain lines that specify the opening of a specific file type, its record specification, and its field definitions. Data dependence makes the file system extremely cumbersome from the point of view of a programmer and database manager.

1.5.2 FIELD DEFINITIONS AND NAMING CONVENTIONS

At first glance, the CUSTOMER file shown in Figure 1.3 appears to have served its purpose well: requested reports usually could be generated. But suppose you want to create a customer phone directory based on the data stored in the CUSTOMER file. Storing the customer name as a single field turns out to be a liability because the directory must break up the field contents to list the last names, first names, and initials in alphabetical order.

Similarly, producing a listing of customers by city is a more difficult task than is necessary. From the user's point of view, a much better (more flexible) record definition would be one that anticipates reporting requirements by breaking up fields into their component parts. Thus, the revised customer file fields might be listed as shown in Table 1.3. (Note that the revised file is named CUSTOMER_V2 to indicate that this is the second version of the CUSTOMER file.)

TABLE 1.3   Sample Fields in the CUSTOMER_V2 File

FIELD	CONTENTS	SAMPLE ENTRY
CUS_LNAME	Customer last name	Ramas
CUS_FNAME	Customer first name	Alfred
CUS_INITIAL	Customer initial	A
CUS_AREACODE	Customer area code	615
CUS_PHONE	Customer phone	234-5678
CUS_ADDRESS	Customer street address or box number	123 Green Meadow Lane
CUS_CITY	Customer city	Murfreesboro
CUS_STATE	Customer state	TN
CUS_ZIP	Customer zip code	37130
AGENT_CODE	Agent code	502

Selecting proper field names is also important. For example, make sure that the field names are reasonably descriptive. In examining the file structure shown in Figure 1.3, it is not obvious that the field name REN represents the customer's insurance renewal date. Using the field name CUS_RENEW_DATE would be better for two reasons. First, the prefix CUS can be used as an indicator of the field's origin, which is the CUSTOMER_V2 file. Therefore, you know that the field in question yields a customer property. Second, the RENEW_DATE portion of the field name is more descriptive of the field's contents. With proper naming conventions, the file structure becomes *self-documenting*. That is, by simply looking at a field name, you can determine which file the field belongs to and what information the field is likely to contain.

> **NOTE**
>
> You might have noticed the addition of the AGENT_CODE field in Table 1.3. Clearly, you must know what agent represents each customer, so the customer file must include agent data. You will learn in Section 1.5.3 that storing the agent *name*, as was done in the original CUSTOMER file shown in Figure 1.3, will yield some major problems that are eliminated by using a unique code that is assigned to each agent. And you will learn in Chapter 2, Data Models, what other benefits are obtained from storing such a code in the (revised) customer table. In any case, because the agent code is an *agent* characteristic, its prefix is AGENT.

Some software packages place restrictions on the length of field names, so it is wise to be as descriptive as possible within those restrictions. In addition, very long field names make it difficult to fit more than a few fields on a page, thus making output spacing a problem. For example, the field name CUSTOMER_INSURANCE_RENEWAL_DATE, while being self-documenting, is less desirable than CUS_RENEW_DATE.

Another problem in Figure 1.3's CUSTOMER file is the difficulty of finding desired data efficiently. The CUSTOMER file currently does not have a unique record identifier. For example, it is possible to have several customers named John B. Smith. Consequently, the addition of a CUS_ACCOUNT field that contains a unique customer account number would be appropriate.

The criticisms of field definitions and naming conventions shown in the file structure of Figure 1.3 are not unique to file systems. Because such conventions will prove to be important later, they are introduced early. You will revisit field definitions and naming conventions when you learn about database design in Chapter 4, Entity Relationship (ER) Modeling and in Chapter 6, Advanced Data Modeling; when you learn about database implementation issues in Chapter 9, Database Design; and when you see an actual database design implemented in Appendixes B and C (The University Lab design and implementation). Regardless of the data environment, the design—whether it involves a file system or a database—must always reflect the designer's documentation needs and the end user's reporting and processing requirements. Both types of needs are best served by adhering to proper field definitions and naming conventions.

ONLINE CONTENT

Appendixes A through L are available in the Student Online Companion for this book.

No naming convention can fit all requirements for all systems. Some words or phrases are reserved for the DBMSs internal use. For example, the name ORDER generates an error in some DBMSs. Similarly, your DBMS might interpret a hyphen (-) as a command to subtract. Therefore, the field CUS-NAME would be interpreted as a command to subtract the NAME field from the CUS field. Because neither field exists, you would get an error message. On the other hand, CUS_NAME would work fine because it uses an underscore.

1.5.3 DATA REDUNDANCY

The file system's structure makes it difficult to combine data from multiple sources and its lack of security renders the file system vulnerable to security breaches. The organizational structure promotes the storage of the same basic data in different locations. (Database professionals use the term **islands of information** for such scattered data locations.) Because it is unlikely that data stored in different locations will always be updated consistently, the islands of information often contain different versions of the same data. For example, in Figures 1.3 and 1.4, the agent names and phone numbers occur in both the CUSTOMER and the AGENT files. You need only one correct copy of the agent names and phone numbers. Having them occur in more than one place produces data redundancy. **Data redundancy** exists when the same data are stored unnecessarily at different places.

Uncontrolled data redundancy sets the stage for:

- *Data inconsistency.* Data inconsistency exists when different and conflicting versions of the same data appear in different places. For example, suppose you change an agent's phone number or address in the AGENT file. If you forget to make corresponding changes in the CUSTOMER file, the files contain different data for the same agent. Reports will yield inconsistent results depending on which version of the data is used.

NOTE

Data that display data inconsistency are also referred to as data that lack data integrity. **Data integrity** is defined as the condition in which all of the data in the database are consistent with the real-world events and conditions. In other words, data integrity means that:

- Data are *accurate*—there are no data inconsistencies
- Data are *verifiable*—the data will always yield consistent results.

Data entry errors are more likely to occur when complex entries (such as 10-digit phone numbers) are made in several different files and/or recur frequently in one or more files. In fact, the CUSTOMER file shown in Figure 1.3 contains just such an entry error: the third record in the CUSTOMER file has a transposed digit in the agent's phone number (615-882-2144 rather than 615-882-1244).

It is possible to enter a nonexistent sales agent's name and phone number into the CUSTOMER file, but customers are not likely to be impressed if the insurance agency supplies the name and phone number of an agent who does not exist. And should the personnel manager allow a nonexistent agent to accrue bonuses and benefits? In fact, a data entry error such as an incorrectly spelled name or an incorrect phone number yields the same kind of data integrity problems.

- *Data anomalies.* The dictionary defines *anomaly* as "an abnormality." Ideally, a field value change should be made in only a single place. Data redundancy, however, fosters an abnormal condition by forcing field value changes in many different locations. Look at the CUSTOMER file in Figure 1.3. If agent Leah F. Hahn decides to get married and move, the agent name, address, and phone are likely to change. Instead of making just a single name and/or phone/address change in a single file (AGENT), you also must make the change each time that agent's name, phone number, and address occur in the CUSTOMER file. You could be faced with the prospect of making hundreds of corrections, one for each of the customers served by that agent! The same problem occurs when an agent decides to quit. Each customer served by that agent must be assigned a new agent. Any change in any field value must be correctly made in many places to maintain data integrity. A **data anomaly** develops when all of the required changes in the redundant data are not made successfully. The data anomalies found in Figure 1.3 are commonly defined as follows:

- *Update anomalies*. If agent Leah F. Hahn has a new phone number, that number must be entered in each of the CUSTOMER file records in which Ms. Hahn's phone number is shown. In this case, only three changes must be made. In a large file system, such changes might occur in hundreds or even thousands of records. Clearly, the potential for data inconsistencies is great.

- *Insertion anomalies*. If only the CUSTOMER file existed, to add a new agent, you would also add a dummy customer data entry to reflect the new agent's addition. Again, the potential for creating data inconsistencies would be great.

- *Deletion anomalies*. If you delete the customers Amy B. O'Brian, George Williams, and Olette K. Smith, you will also delete John T. Okon's agent data. Clearly, this is not desirable.

1.6 DATABASE SYSTEMS

The problems inherent in file systems make using a database system very desirable. Unlike the file system, with its many separate and unrelated files, the database system consists of logically related data stored in a single logical data repository. (The "logical" label reflects the fact that, although the data repository appears to be a single unit to the end user, its contents may actually be physically distributed among multiple data storage facilities and/or locations.) Because the database's data repository is a single logical unit, the database represents a major change in the way end-user data are stored, accessed, and managed. The database's DBMS, shown in Figure 1.6, provides numerous advantages over file system management, shown in Figure 1.5, by making it possible to eliminate most of the file system's data inconsistency, data anomaly, data dependency, and structural dependency problems. Better yet, the current generation of DBMS software stores not only the data structures, but also the relationships between those structures and the access paths to those structures—all in a central location. The current generation of DBMS software also takes care of defining, storing, and managing all required access paths to those components.

FIGURE
1.6

FIGURE 1.6   Contrasting database and file systems

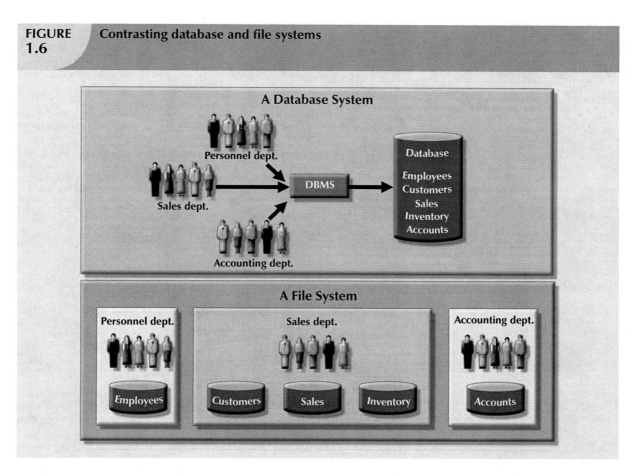

Remember that the DBMS is just one of several crucial components of a database system. The DBMS may even be referred to as the database system's heart. However, just as it takes more than a heart to make a human being function, it takes more than a DBMS to make a database system function. In the sections that follow, you'll learn what a database system is, what its components are, and how the DBMS fits into the database system picture.

1.6.1   THE DATABASE SYSTEM ENVIRONMENT

The term **database system** refers to an organization of components that define and regulate the collection, storage, management, and use of data within a database environment. From a general management point of view, the database system is composed of the five major parts shown in Figure 1.7: hardware, software, people, procedures, and data.

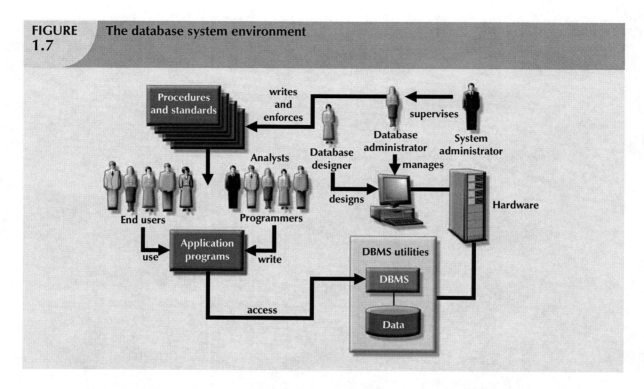

FIGURE 1.7   The database system environment

Let's take a closer look at the five components shown in Figure 1.7:

- *Hardware*. Hardware refers to all of the system's physical devices; for example, computers (microcomputers, workstations, servers, and supercomputers), storage devices, printers, network devices (hubs, switches, routers, fiber optics), and other devices (automated teller machines, ID readers, and so on).

- *Software*. Although the most readily identified software is the DBMS itself, to make the database system function fully, three types of software are needed: operating system software, DBMS software, and application programs and utilities.

  - *Operating system software* manages all hardware components and makes it possible for all other software to run on the computers. Examples of operating system software include Microsoft Windows, Linux, Mac OS, UNIX, and MVS.

  - *DBMS software* manages the database within the database system. Some examples of DBMS software include Microsoft SQL Server, Oracle Corporation's Oracle, MySQL AB's MySQL and IBM's DB2.

  - *Application programs and utility software* are used to access and manipulate data in the DBMS and to manage the computer environment in which data access and manipulation take place. Application programs are most commonly used to access data found within the database to generate reports, tabulations, and other information to facilitate decision making. Utilities are the software tools used to help manage the database system's computer components. For example, all of the major DBMS vendors now provide graphical user interfaces (GUIs) to help create database structures, control database access, and monitor database operations.

- *People*. This component includes all users of the database system. On the basis of primary job functions, five types of users can be identified in a database system: systems administrators, database administrators, database designers, systems analysts and programmers, and end users. Each user type, described below, performs both unique and complementary functions.

  - *System administrators* oversee the database system's general operations.

  - *Database administrators*, also known as DBAs, manage the DBMS and ensure that the database is functioning properly. The DBA's role is sufficiently important to warrant a detailed exploration in Chapter 15, Database Administration and Security.

- *Database designers* design the database structure. They are, in effect, the database architects. If the database design is poor, even the best application programmers and the most dedicated DBAs cannot produce a useful database environment. Because organizations strive to optimize their data resources, the database designer's job description has expanded to cover new dimensions and growing responsibilities.

- *Systems analysts and programmers* design and implement the application programs. They design and create the data entry screens, reports, and procedures through which end users access and manipulate the database's data.

- *End users* are the people who use the application programs to run the organization's daily operations. For example, salesclerks, supervisors, managers, and directors are all classified as end users. High-level end users employ the information obtained from the database to make tactical and strategic business decisions.

- *Procedures.* Procedures are the instructions and rules that govern the design and use of the database system. Procedures are a critical, although occasionally forgotten, component of the system. Procedures play an important role in a company because they enforce the standards by which business is conducted within the organization and with customers. Procedures also are used to ensure that there is an organized way to monitor and audit both the data that enter the database and the information that is generated through the use of that data.

- *Data.* The word *data* covers the collection of facts stored in the database. Because data are the raw material from which information is generated, the determination of what data are to be entered into the database and how that data are to be organized is a vital part of the database designer's job.

A database system adds a new dimension to an organization's management structure. Just how complex this managerial structure is depends on the organization's size, its functions, and its corporate culture. Therefore, database systems can be created and managed at different levels of complexity and with varying adherence to precise standards. For example, compare a local movie rental system with a national insurance claims system. The movie rental system may be managed by two people, the hardware used is probably a single microcomputer, the procedures are probably simple, and the data volume tends to be low. The national insurance claims system is likely to have at least one systems administrator, several full-time DBAs, and many designers and programmers; the hardware probably includes several servers at multiple locations throughout the United States; the procedures are likely to be numerous, complex, and rigorous; and the data volume tends to be high.

In addition to the different levels of database system complexity, managers must also take another important fact into account: database solutions must be cost-effective as well as tactically and strategically effective. Producing a million-dollar solution to a thousand-dollar problem is hardly an example of good database system selection or of good database design and management. Finally, the database technology already in use is likely to affect the selection of a database system.

1.6.2 DBMS FUNCTIONS

A DBMS performs several important functions that guarantee the integrity and consistency of the data in the database. Most of those functions are transparent to end users, and most can be achieved only through the use of a DBMS. They include data dictionary management, data storage management, data transformation and presentation, security management, multiuser access control, backup and recovery management, data integrity management, database access languages and application programming interfaces, and database communication interfaces. Each of these functions is explained below.

- *Data dictionary management.* The DBMS stores definitions of the data elements and their relationships (metadata) in a **data dictionary**. In turn, all programs that access the data in the database work through the DBMS. The DBMS uses the data dictionary to look up the required data component structures and relationships, thus relieving you from having to code such complex relationships in each program. Additionally, any changes made in a database structure are automatically recorded in the data dictionary, thereby freeing you from having to modify all of the programs that access the changed structure. In other words, the DBMS provides data abstraction, and it removes structural and data dependency from the system. For example, Figure 1.8 shows how Microsoft SQL Server Express presents the data definition for the CUSTOMER table.

FIGURE
1.8

Illustrating metadata with Microsoft SQL Server Express

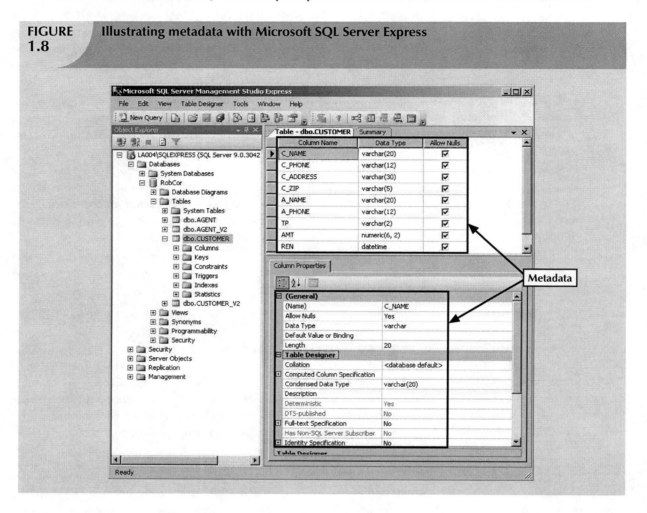

- *Data storage management.* The DBMS creates and manages the complex structures required for data storage, thus relieving you from the difficult task of defining and programming the physical data characteristics. A modern DBMS provides storage not only for the data, but also for related data entry forms or screen definitions, report definitions, data validation rules, procedural code, structures to handle video and picture formats, and so on. Data storage management is also important for database performance tuning. **Performance tuning** relates to the activities that make the database perform more efficiently in terms of storage and access speed. Although the user sees the database as a single data storage unit, the DBMS actually stores the database in multiple physical data files. (See Figure 1.9.) Such data files may even be stored on different storage media. Therefore, the DBMS doesn't have to wait for one disk request to finish before the next one starts. In other words, the DBMS can fulfill database requests concurrently. Data storage management and performance tuning issues are addressed in Chapter 11, Database Performance Tuning and Query Optimization.

FIGURE 1.9   Illustrating data storage management with Oracle

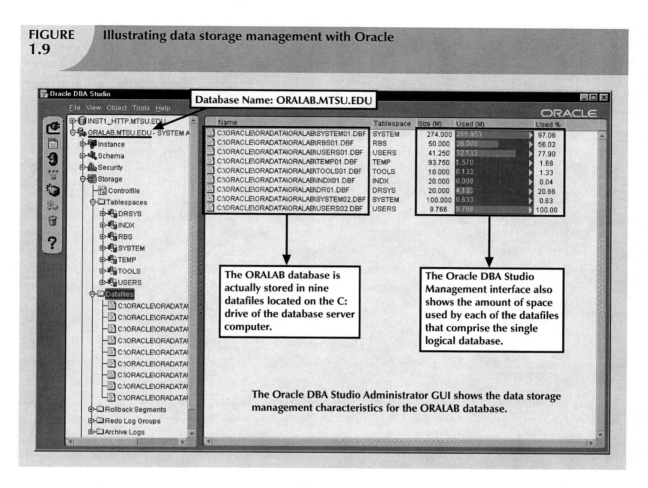

The Oracle DBA Studio Administrator GUI shows the data storage management characteristics for the ORALAB database.

- *Data transformation and presentation.* The DBMS transforms entered data to conform to required data structures. The DBMS relieves you of the chore of making a distinction between the logical data format and the physical data format. That is, the DBMS formats the physically retrieved data to make it conform to the user's logical expectations. For example, imagine an enterprise database used by a multinational company. An end user in England would expect to enter data such as July 11, 2008 as "11/07/2008." In contrast, the same date would be entered in the United States as "07/11/2008." Regardless of the data presentation format, the DBMS must manage the date in the proper format for each country.

- *Security management.* The DBMS creates a security system that enforces user security and data privacy. Security rules determine which users can access the database, which data items each user can access, and which data operations (read, add, delete, or modify) the user can perform. This is especially important in multiuser database systems. Chapter 15, Database Administration and Security, examines data security and privacy issues in greater detail. All database users may be authenticated to the DBMS through a username and password or through biometric authentication such as a fingerprint scan. The DBMS uses this information to assign access privileges to various database components such as queries and reports.

- *Multiuser access control.* To provide data integrity and data consistency, the DBMS uses sophisticated algorithms to ensure that multiple users can access the database concurrently without compromising the integrity of the database. Chapter 10, Transaction Management and Concurrency Control, covers the details of the multiuser access control.

- *Backup and recovery management.* The DBMS provides backup and data recovery to ensure data safety and integrity. Current DBMS systems provide special utilities that allow the DBA to perform routine and special backup and restore procedures. Recovery management deals with the recovery of the database after a failure, such as a bad sector in the disk or a power failure. Such capability is critical to preserving the database's integrity. Chapter 15 covers backup and recovery issues.

- *Data integrity management.* The DBMS promotes and enforces integrity rules, thus minimizing data redundancy and maximizing data consistency. The data relationships stored in the data dictionary are used to enforce data integrity. Ensuring data integrity is especially important in transaction-oriented database systems. Data integrity and transaction management issues are addressed in Chapter 7, Introduction to Structured Query Language (SQL), and Chapter 10, Transaction Management and Concurrency Control.

- *Database access languages and application programming interfaces.* The DBMS provides data access through a query language. A **query language** is a nonprocedural language—one that lets the user specify what must be done without having to specify how it is to be done. **Structured Query Language (SQL)** is the de facto query language and data access standard supported by the majority of DBMS vendors. Chapter 7, Introduction to Structured Query Language (SQL), and Chapter 8, Advanced SQL, address the use of SQL. The DBMS also provides application programming interfaces to procedural languages such as COBOL, C, Java, Visual Basic.NET, and C++. In addition, the DBMS provides administrative utilities used by the DBA and the database designer to create, implement, monitor, and maintain the database.

- *Database communication interfaces.* Current-generation DBMSs accept end-user requests via multiple, different network environments. For example, the DBMS might provide access to the database via the Internet through the use of Web browsers such as Mozilla Firefox or Microsoft Internet Explorer. In this environment, communications can be accomplished in several ways:

  - End users can generate answers to queries by filling in screen forms through their preferred Web browser.
  - The DBMS can automatically publish predefined reports on a Web site.
  - The DBMS can connect to third-party systems to distribute information via e-mail or other productivity applications.

Database communication interfaces are examined in greater detail in Chapter 12, Distributed Database Management Systems, in Chapter 14, Database Connectivity and Web Technologies, and in Appendix I, Databases in Electronic Commerce. (Appendixes are found in the Student Online Companion.)

1.6.3 MANAGING THE DATABASE SYSTEM: A SHIFT IN FOCUS

The introduction of a database system over the file system provides a framework in which strict procedures and standards can be enforced. Consequently, the role of the human component changes from an emphasis on programming (in the file system) to a focus on the broader aspects of managing the organization's data resources and on the administration of the complex database software itself.

The database system makes it possible to tackle far more sophisticated uses of the data resources as long as the database is designed to make use of that available power. The kinds of data structures created within the database and the extent of the relationships among them play a powerful role in determining the effectiveness of the database system.

Although the database system yields considerable advantages over previous data management approaches, database systems do carry significant disadvantages. For example:

- *Increased costs.* Database systems require sophisticated hardware and software and highly skilled personnel. The cost of maintaining the hardware, software, and personnel required to operate and manage a database system can be substantial. Training, licensing, and regulation compliance costs are often overlooked when database systems are implemented.

- *Management complexity.* Database systems interface with many different technologies and have a significant impact on a company's resources and culture. The changes introduced by the adoption of a database system must be properly managed to ensure that they help advance the company's objectives. Given the fact that databases systems hold crucial company data that are accessed from multiple sources, security issues must be assessed constantly.

- *Maintaining currency.* To maximize the efficiency of the database system, you must keep your system current. Therefore, you must perform frequent updates and apply the latest patches and security measures to all components. Because database technology advances rapidly, personnel training costs tend to be significant.

- *Vendor dependence.* Given the heavy investment in technology and personnel training, companies might be reluctant to change database vendors. As a consequence, vendors are less likely to offer pricing point advantages to existing customers, and those customers might be limited in their choice of database system components.

- *Frequent upgrade/replacement cycles.* DBMS vendors frequently upgrade their products by adding new functionality. Such new features often come bundled in new upgrade versions of the software. Some of these versions require hardware upgrades. Not only do the upgrades themselves cost money, but it also costs money to train database users and administrators to properly use and manage the new features.

13.1 THE NEED FOR DATA ANALYSIS

Organizations tend to grow and prosper as they gain a better understanding of their environment. Most managers want to be able to track daily transactions to evaluate how the business is performing. By tapping into the operational database, management can develop strategies to meet organizational goals. In addition, data analysis can provide information about short-term tactical evaluations and strategies such as these: Are our sales promotions working? What market percentage are we controlling? Are we attracting new customers? Tactical and strategic decisions are also shaped by constant pressure from external and internal forces, including globalization, the cultural and legal environment, and (perhaps most importantly) technology.

Given the many and varied competitive pressures, managers are always looking for a competitive advantage through product development and maintenance, service, market positioning, sales promotion, and so on. Managers understand that the business climate is dynamic, and thus, mandates their prompt reaction to change in order to remain competitive. In addition, the modern business climate requires managers to approach increasingly complex problems that involve a rapidly growing number of internal and external variables. It should also come as no surprise that interest is growing in creating support systems dedicated to facilitating quick decision making in a complex environment.

Different managerial levels require different decision support needs. For example, transaction-processing systems, based on operational databases, are tailored to serve the information needs of people who deal with short-term inventory, accounts payable, and purchasing. Middle-level managers, general managers, vice presidents, and presidents focus on strategic and tactical decision making. Those managers require detailed information designed to help them make decisions in a complex data and analysis environment.

Companies and software vendors addressed these multilevel decision support needs by creating independent applications to fit the needs of particular areas (finance, customer management, human resources, product support, etc.). Applications were also tailored to different industry sectors such as education, retail, health care, or financial. This approach worked well for some time, but changes in the business world (globalization, expanding markets, mergers and acquisitions, increased regulation, and more) called for new ways of integrating and managing data across levels and sectors. This more comprehensive and integrated decision support framework within organizations became known as business intelligence.

13.2 BUSINESS INTELLIGENCE

Business intelligence (BI)[1] is a term used to describe a comprehensive, cohesive, and integrated set of tools and processes used to capture, collect, integrate, store, and analyze data with the purpose of generating and presenting information used to support business decision making. As the names implies, BI is about creating intelligence about a business. This intelligence is based on learning and understanding the facts about a business environment. BI is a framework that allows a business to transform data into information, information into knowledge, and knowledge into wisdom. BI has the potential to positively affect a company's culture by creating "business wisdom" and distributing it to all users in an organization. This business wisdom empowers users to make sound business decisions based on the accumulated

---

[1] In 1989, while working at Gartner Inc., Howard Dresner popularized "BI" as an umbrella term to describe a set of concepts and methods to improve business decision making by using fact-based support systems. Source: http://www.computerworld.com/action/article.do?command=viewArticleBasic&articleId=266298

knowledge of the business as reflected on recorded facts (historic operational data). Table 13.1 gives some real-world examples of companies that have implemented BI tools (data warehouse, data mart, OLAP, and/or data mining tools) and shows how the use of such tools benefited the companies.

TABLE 13.1	Solving Business Problems and Adding Value with BI Tools	
COMPANY	**PROBLEM**	**BENEFIT**
MOEN Manufacturer of bathroom and kitchen fixtures and supplies Source: Cognos Corp. *www.cognos.com*	• Information generation very limited and time-consuming. • How to extract data using a 3GL known by only five people. • Response time unacceptable for managers' decision-making purposes.	• Provided quick answers to ad hoc questions for decision making. • Provided access to data for decision-making purposes. • Received in-depth view of product performance and customer margins.
NASDAQ Largest U.S. electronic stock market trading organization Source: Oracle *www.oracle.com*	• Inability to provide real-time ad hoc query and standard reporting to executives, business analysts, and other users. • Excessive storage costs for many terabytes of data.	• Reduced storage cost by moving to a multitier storage solution. • Implemented new data warehouse center with support for ad hoc query and reporting and near real-time data access for end users.
Sega of America, Inc. Interactive entertainment systems and video games Source: Oracle Corp. *www.oracle.com*	• Needed a way to rapidly analyze a great amount of data. • Needed to track advertising, coupons, and rebates associated with effects of pricing changes. • Used to do it with Excel spreadsheets, leading to human-caused errors.	• Eliminated data-entry errors. • Identified successful marketing strategies to dominate interactive entertainment niches. • Used product analysis to identify better markets/product offerings.
Owens and Minor, Inc. Medical and surgical supply distributor Source: *CFO Magazine* *www.cfomagazine.com*	• Lost its largest customer, which represented 10% of its annual revenue ($360 million). • Stock plunged 23%. • Cumbersome process to get information out of antiquated mainframe system.	• Increased earnings per share in just five months. • Gained more business, thanks to opening the data warehouse to its clients. • Managers gained quick access to data for decision-making purposes.
Amazon.com Leading online retailer Source: *PC Week Online* *whitepapers.zdnet.com/ whitepaper.aspx? docid=241748*	• Difficulty in managing a very rapidly growing data environment. • Existing data warehouse solution not capable of supporting extremely rapid growth. • Needed more flexible and reliable data warehouse solution to protect its investment in data and infrastructure.	• Implemented new data warehouse with superior scalability and performance. • Improved business intelligence. • Improved management of product flow through the entire supply chain. • Improved customer experience.

BI is a comprehensive endeavor because it encompasses all business processes within an organization. *Business processes* are the central units of operation in a business. Implementing BI in an organization involves capturing not only business data (internal and external) but also the metadata, or knowledge about the data. In practice, BI is a complex proposition that requires a deep understanding and alignment of the business processes, the internal and external data, and the information needs of users at all levels in an organization.

BI is not a product by itself, but a framework of concepts, practices, tools, and technologies that help a business better understand its core capabilities, provide snapshots of the company situation, and identify key opportunities to create competitive advantage. In practice, BI provides a well-orchestrated framework for the management of data that works across all levels of the organization. BI involves the following general steps:

1. Collecting and storing operational data

2. Aggregating the operational data into decision support data

3. Analyzing decision support data to generate information

4. Presenting such information to the end user to support business decisions

5. Making business decisions, which in turn generate more data that is collected, stored, etc. (restarting the process)

6. Monitoring results to evaluate outcomes of the business decisions (providing more data to be collected, stored, etc.)

To implement all these steps, BI uses varied components and technologies. In the following sections, you will learn about the basic BI architecture and implementations.

13.3 BUSINESS INTELLIGENCE ARCHITECTURE

BI covers a range of technologies and applications to manage the entire data life cycle from acquisition to storage, transformation, integration, analysis, monitoring, presentation, and archiving. BI functionality ranges from simple data gathering and extraction to very complex data analysis and presentation applications. There is no single BI architecture; instead, it ranges from highly integrated applications from a single vendor to a loosely integrated, multivendor environment. However, there are some general types of functionality that all BI implementations share.

Like any critical business IT infrastructure, the BI architecture is composed of data, people, processes, technology, and the management of such components. Figure 13.1 depicts how all those components fit together within the BI framework.

Remember that the main focus of BI is to gather, integrate, and store business data for the purpose of creating information. As depicted in Figure 13.1, BI integrates people and processes using technology in order to add value to the business. Such value is derived from how end users use such information in their daily activities, and in particular, their daily business decision making. Also note that the BI technology components are varied. This chapter will explain those components in greater detail in the following sections.

The focus of traditional information systems was on operational automation and reporting; in contrast, BI tools focus on the strategic and tactical use of information. In order to achieve this goal, BI recognizes that technology alone is not enough. Therefore, BI uses an arrangement of best management practices to manage data as a corporate asset. One of the most recent developments in this area is the use of master data management techniques. **Master data management (MDM)** is a collection of concepts, techniques, and processes for the proper identification, definition, and management of data elements within an organization. MDM's main goal is to provide a comprehensive and consistent definition of all data within an organization. MDM ensures that all company resources (people, procedures, and IT systems) that operate over data have uniform and consistent views of the company's data.

FIGURE 13.1	Business intelligence framework

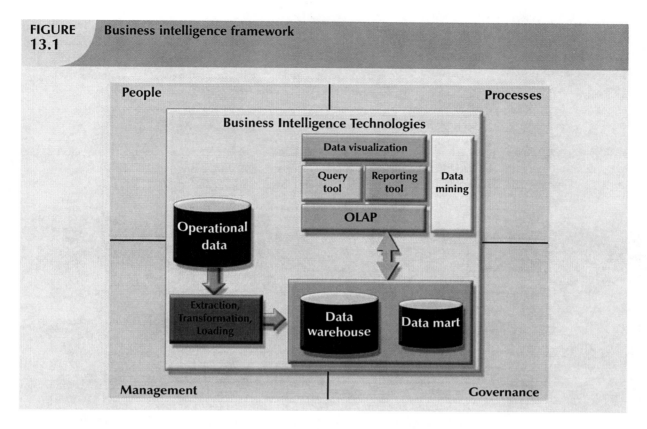

An added benefit of this meticulous approach to data management and decision making is that it provides a framework for business governance. **Governance** is a method or process of government. In this case, BI provides a method for controlling and monitoring business health and for consistent decision making. Furthermore, having such governance creates accountability for business decisions. In the present age of business flux, accountability is increasingly important. Had governance been as pivotal to business operations a few years back, crises precipitated by the likes of Enron, WorldCom, and Arthur Andersen might have been avoided.

Monitoring a business's health is crucial to understanding where the company is and where it is headed. In order to do this, BI makes extensive use of a special type of metrics known as key performance indicators. **Key performance indicators (KPI)** are quantifiable measurements (numeric or scale based) that assess the company's effectiveness or success in reaching its strategic and operational goals. There are many different KPI used by different industries. Some examples of KPI are:

- *General*. Year-to-year measurements of profit by line of business, same store sales, product turnovers, product recalls, sales by promotion, sales by employee, etc.
- *Finance*. Earnings per share, profit margin, revenue per employee, percentage of sales to account receivables, assets to sales, etc.
- *Human resources*. Applicants to job openings, employee turnover, employee longevity, etc.
- *Education*. Graduation rates, number of incoming freshmen, student retention rates, etc.

KPIs are determined after the main strategic, tactical, and operational goals for a business are defined. To tie the KPI to the strategic master plan of an organization, a KPI will be compared to a desired goal within a specific time frame. For example, if you are in an academic environment, you might be interested in ways to measure student satisfaction or retention. In this case, a sample goal would be to "Increase the graduating senior average exit exam grades from 9 to 12 by fall, 2010." Another sample KPI would be: "Increase the returning student rate of freshman year to sophomore year from 60% to 75% by 2012." In this case, such performance indicators would be measured and monitored on a year-to-year basis, and plans to achieve such goals would be set in place.

Another way to understand BI architecture is by describing the basic components that form part of its infrastructure. Some of the components have overlapping functionality; however, there are four basic components that all BI environments should provide. These are described in Table 13.2 and illustrated in Figure 13.2.

TABLE 13.2	Basic BI Architectural Components
COMPONENT	**DESCRIPTION**
Data extraction, transformation, and loading (ETL) tools	This component is in charge of collecting, filtering, integrating, and aggregating operational data to be saved into a data store optimized for decision support. For example, to determine the relative market share by selected product lines, you require data from competitors' products. Such data can be located in external databases provided by industry groups or by companies that market the data. As the name implies, this component extracts the data, filters the extracted data to select the relevant records, and packages the data in the right format to be added to the data store component.
Data store	The data store is optimized for decision support and is generally represented by a data warehouse or a data mart. The data store contains business data extracted from the operational database and from external data sources. The business data are stored in structures that are optimized for data analysis and query speed. The external data sources provide data that cannot be found within the company but that are relevant to the business, such as stock prices, market indicators, marketing information (such as demographics), and competitors' data.
Data query and analysis tools	This component performs data retrieval, data analysis, and data mining tasks using the data in the data store and business data analysis models. This component is used by the data analyst to create the queries that access the database. Depending on the implementation, the query tool accesses either the operational database, or more commonly, the data store. This tool advises the user on which data to select and how to build a reliable business data model. This component is generally represented in the form of an OLAP tool.
Data presentation and visualization tools	This component is in charge of presenting the data to the end user in a variety of ways. This component is used by the data analyst to organize and present the data. This tool helps the end user select the most appropriate presentation format, such as summary report, map, pie or bar graph, or mixed graphs. The query tool and the presentation tool are the front end to the BI environment.

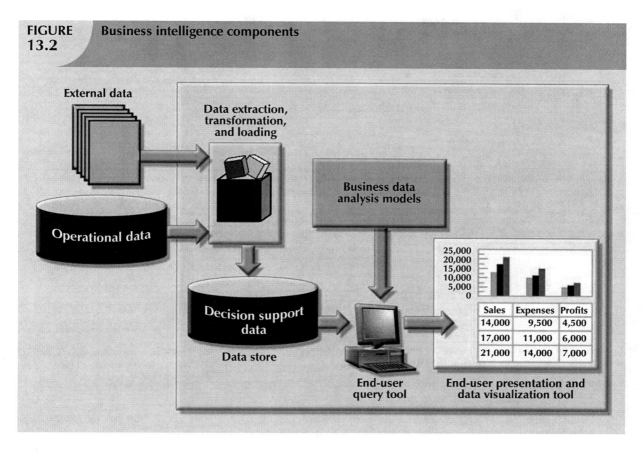

FIGURE 13.2   Business intelligence components

Each BI component shown in Table 13.2 has generated a fast-growing market for specialized tools. And thanks to the advancement of client/server technologies, those components can interact with other components to form a truly open architecture. As a matter of fact, you can integrate multiple tools from different vendors into a single BI framework. Table 13.3 shows a sample of common BI tools and vendors.

TABLE 13.3   Sample of Business Intelligence Tools

TOOL	DESCRIPTION	SAMPLE VENDORS
Decision support systems	A **decision support system (DSS)** is an arrangement of computerized tools used to assist managerial decision making within a business. *Decision support* systems were the precursors of modern BI systems. A DSS typically has a much narrower focus and reach than a BI solution.	SAP Teradata IBM Proclarity
Dashboards and business activity monitoring	**Dashboards** use Web-based technologies to present key business performance indicators or information in a single integrated view, generally using graphics in a clear, concise, and easy to understand manner.	*Salesforce* VisualCalc Cognos BusinessObjects Information Builders Actuate
Portals	**Portals** provide a unified, single point of entry for information distribution. Portals are a Web-based technology that uses a Web browser to integrate data from multiple sources into a single Web page. Many different types of BI functionality can be accessed through a portal.	Oracle Portal Actuate Microsoft

TABLE 13.3	Sample of Business Intelligence Tools (continued)	
TOOL	**DESCRIPTION**	**SAMPLE VENDORS**
Data analysis and reporting tools	Advanced tools used to query multiple diverse data sources to create single integrated reports.	Mircrosoft Reporting Services Information Builders Eclipse BIRT MicroStrategy SAS WebReportStudio
Data mining tools	Tools that provide advanced statistical analysis to uncover problems and opportunities hidden within business data.	MicroStrategy Intelligence Server MS Analytics Services
Data warehouses	The data warehouse is the foundation on which a BI infrastructure is built. Data is captured from the OLTP system and placed on the DW on near-real time basis. BI provides companywide integration of data and the capability to respond to business issues in a timely manner.	Microsoft Oracle IBM MicroStrategy
OLAP tools	Online analytical processing provides multidimensional data analysis.	Cognos BusinessObjects Oracle Microsoft
Data visualization	Tools that provide advanced visual analysis and techniques to enhance understanding of business data.	Advanced Visual Systems Dundas iDashboards

Although BI has an unquestionably important role in modern business operations, keep in mind that the *manager* must initiate the decision support process by asking the appropriate questions. The BI environment exists to support the manager; it does *not* replace the management function. If the manager fails to ask the appropriate questions, problems will not be identified and solved, and opportunities will be missed. In spite of the very powerful BI presence, the human component is still at the center of business technology.

NOTE

> Although the term BI includes a variety of components and tools, this chapter focuses on its data warehouse component.

13.4 DECISION SUPPORT DATA

Although BI is used at strategic and tactical managerial levels within organizations, *its effectiveness depends on the quality of data gathered at the operational level.* Yet operational data are seldom well suited to the decision support tasks. The differences between operational data and decision support data are examined in the next section.

13.4.1 OPERATIONAL DATA VS. DECISION SUPPORT DATA

Operational data and decision support data serve different purposes. Therefore, it is not surprising to learn that their formats and structures differ.

Most operational data are stored in a relational database in which the structures (tables) tend to be highly normalized. Operational data storage is optimized to support transactions that represent daily operations. For example, each time an item is sold, it must be accounted for. Customer data, inventory data, and so on, are in a frequent update mode. To provide effective update performance, operational systems store data in many tables, each with a minimum number of fields. Thus, a simple sales transaction might be represented by five or more different tables (for example, invoice,

invoice line, discount, store, and department). Although such an arrangement is excellent in an operational database, it is not efficient for query processing. For example, to extract a simple invoice, you would have to join several tables. Whereas operational data are useful for capturing daily business transactions, decision support data give tactical and strategic business meaning to the operational data. From the data analyst's point of view, decision support data differ from operational data in three main areas: time span, granularity, and dimensionality.

- *Time span.* Operational data cover a short time frame. In contrast, decision support data tend to cover a longer time frame. Managers are seldom interested in a specific sales invoice to customer X; rather, they tend to focus on sales generated during the last month, the last year, or the last five years.

- *Granularity (level of aggregation).* Decision support data must be presented at different levels of aggregation, from highly summarized to near-atomic. For example, if managers must analyze sales by region, they must be able to access data showing the sales by region, by city within the region, by store within the city within the region, and so on. In that case, summarized data to compare the regions is required, but also data in a structure that enables a manager to **drill down**, or decompose, the data into more atomic components (that is, finer-grained data at lower levels of aggregation). In contrast, when you **roll up** the data, you are aggregating the data to a higher level.

- *Dimensionality.* Operational data focus on representing individual transactions rather than on the effects of the transactions over time. In contrast, data analysts tend to include many data dimensions and are interested in how the data relate over those dimensions. For example, an analyst might want to know how product X fared relative to product Z during the past six months by region, state, city, store, and customer. In that case, both place and time are part of the picture.

Figure 13.3 shows how decision support data can be examined from multiple dimensions (such as product, region, and year), using a variety of filters to produce each dimension. The ability to analyze, extract, and present information in meaningful ways is one of the differences between decision support data and transaction-at-a-time operational data.

From the designer's point of view, the differences between operational and decision support data are as follows:

- Operational data represent transactions as they happen in real time. Decision support data are a snapshot of the operational data at a given point in time. Therefore, decision support data are historic, representing a time slice of the operational data.

- Operational and decision support data are different in terms of transaction *type* and transaction *volume*. Whereas operational data are characterized by update transactions, decision support data are mainly characterized by *query* (read-only) transactions. Decision support data also require *periodic* updates to load new data that are summarized from the operational data. Finally, the concurrent transaction volume in operational data tends to be very high when compared with the low-to-medium levels found in decision support data.

- Operational data are commonly stored in many tables, and the stored data represent the information about a given transaction only. Decision support data are generally stored in a few tables that store data derived from the operational data. The decision support data do not include the details of each operational transaction. Instead, decision support data represent transaction *summaries*; therefore, the decision support database stores data that are integrated, aggregated, and summarized for decision support purposes.

- The degree to which decision support data are summarized is very high when contrasted with operational data. Therefore, you will see a great deal of derived data in decision support databases. For example, rather than storing all 10,000 sales transactions for a given store on a given day, the decision support database might simply store the total number of units sold and the total sales dollars generated during that day. Decision support data might be collected to monitor such aggregates as total sales for each store or for each product. The purpose of the summaries is simple: they are to be used to establish and evaluate sales trends, product sales comparisons, and so on, that serve decision needs. (How well are items selling? Should this product be discontinued? Has the advertising been effective as measured by increased sales?)

- The data models that govern operational data and decision support data are different. The operational database's frequent and rapid data updates make data anomalies a potentially devastating problem. Therefore,

FIGURE 13.3   Transforming operational data into decision support data

Operational Data

	A	B	C	D	E
3	Year	Region	Agent	Product	Value
4	2004	East	Carlos	Erasers	50
5	2004	East	Tere	Erasers	12
6	2004	North	Carlos	Widgets	120
7	2004	North	Tere	Widgets	100
8	2004	North	Carlos	Widgets	30
9	2004	South	Victor	Balls	145
10	2004	South	Victor	Balls	34
11	2004	South	Victor	Balls	80
12	2004	West	Mary	Pencils	89
13	2004	West	Mary	Pencils	56
14	2005	East	Carlos	Pencils	45
15	2005	East	Victor	Balls	55
16	2005	North	Mary	Pencils	60
17	2005	North	Victor	Erasers	20
18	2005	South	Carlos	Widgets	30
19	2005	South	Mary	Widgets	75
20	2005	South	Mary	Widgets	50
21	2005	South	Tere	Balls	70
22	2005	South	Tere	Erasers	90
23	2005	West	Carlos	Widgets	25
24	2005	West	Tere	Balls	100

Decision Support Data

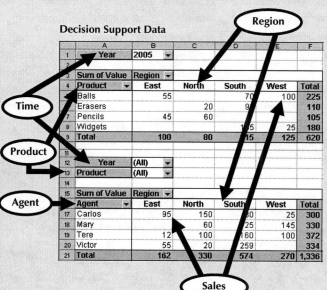

Operational data have a narrow time span, low granularity, and single focus. Such data are usually presented in tabular format, in which each row represents a single transaction. This format often makes it difficult to derive useful information.

Decision support system (DSS) data focus on a broader time span, tend to have high levels of granularity, and can be examined in multiple dimensions. For example, note these possible aggregations:
- Sales by product, region, agent, etc.
- Sales for all years or only a few selected years.
- Sales for all products or only a few selected products.

ONLINE CONTENT

The operational data in Figure 13.3 are found in the Student Online Companion for this book. The decision support data in Figure 13.3 shows the output for the solution to Problem 2 at the end of this chapter.

the data requirements in a typical relational transaction (operational) system generally require normalized structures that yield many tables, each of which contains the minimum number of attributes. In contrast, the decision support database is not subject to such transaction updates, and the focus is on querying capability. Therefore, decision support databases tend to be non-normalized and include few tables, each of which contains a large number of attributes.

- Query activity (frequency and complexity) in the operational database tends to be low to allow additional processing cycles for the more crucial update transactions. Therefore, queries against operational data typically are narrow in scope, low in complexity, and speed-critical. In contrast, decision support data exist for the sole purpose of serving query requirements. Queries against decision support data typically are broad in scope, high in complexity, and less speed-critical.

- Finally, decision support data are characterized by very large amounts of data. The large data volume is the result of two factors. First, data are stored in non-normalized structures that are likely to display many data redundancies and duplications. Second, the same data can be categorized in many different ways to represent different snapshots. For example, sales data might be stored in relation to product, store, customer, region, and manager.

Table 13.4 summarizes the differences between operational and decision support data from the database designer's point of view.

TABLE 13.4

Contrasting Operational and Decision Support Data Characteristics

CHARACTERISTIC	OPERATIONAL DATA	DECISION SUPPORT DATA
Data currency	Current operations Real-time data	Historic data Snapshot of company data Time component (week/month/year)
Granularity	Atomic-detailed data	Summarized data
Summarization level	Low; some aggregate yields	High; many aggregation levels
Data model	Highly normalized Mostly relational DBMS	Non-normalized Complex structures Some relational, but mostly multidimensional DBMS
Transaction type	Mostly updates	Mostly query
Transaction volumes	High update volumes	Periodic loads and summary calculations
Transaction speed	Updates are critical	Retrievals are critical
Query activity	Low to medium	High
Query scope	Narrow range	Broad range
Query complexity	Simple to medium	Very complex
Data volumes	Hundreds of megabytes, up to gigabytes	Hundreds of gigabytes, up to terabytes

The many differences between operational data and decision support data are good indicators of the requirements of the decision support database, described in the next section.

13.4.2 DECISION SUPPORT DATABASE REQUIREMENTS

A decision support database is a specialized DBMS tailored to provide fast answers to complex queries. There are four main requirements for a decision support database: the database schema, data extraction and loading, the end-user analytical interface, and database size.

TABLE 13.5

Ten-Year Sales History for a Single-Department, in Millions of Dollars

YEAR	SALES
1998	8,227
1999	9,109
2000	10,104
2001	11,553
2002	10,018
2003	11,875
2004	12,699
2005	14,875
2006	16,301
2007	19,986

Database Schema

The decision support database schema must support complex (non-normalized) data representations. As noted earlier, the decision support database must contain data that are aggregated and summarized. In addition to meeting those requirements, the queries must be able to extract multidimensional time slices. If you are using an RDBMS, the conditions suggest using non-normalized and even duplicated data. To see why this must be true, take a look at the 10-year sales history for a single store containing a single department. At this point, the data are fully normalized within the single table, as shown in Table 13.5.

This structure works well when you have only one store with only one department. However, it is very unlikely that such a simple environment has much need for a decision support database. One would suppose that a decision support database becomes a factor when dealing with more than one store, each of which has more than one department. To support all of the decision support requirements, the database must contain data for all of the stores and all of their departments—and the database must be able to support multidimensional queries that track sales by stores, by departments, and over time. For simplicity, suppose there are only two stores (A and B) and two departments (1 and 2) within each store. Let's also change the time dimension to include yearly data. Table 13.6 shows the sales figures under the specified conditions. Only 1998, 2002, and 2007 are shown; ellipses (…) are used to indicate that data values were omitted. You can see in Table 13.6 that the number of rows and attributes already multiplies quickly and that the table exhibits multiple redundancies.

TABLE 13.6 Yearly Sales Summaries, Two Stores and Two Departments per Store, in Millions of Dollars

YEAR	STORE	DEPARTMENT	SALES
1998	A	1	1,985
1998	A	2	2,401
1998	B	1	1,879
1998	B	2	1,962
…	…	…	…
2002	A	1	3,912
2002	A	2	4,158
2002	B	1	3,426
2002	B	2	1,203
…	…	…	…
2007	A	1	7,683
2007	A	2	6,912
2007	B	1	3,768
2007	B	2	1,623

Now suppose that the company has 10 departments per store and 20 stores nationwide. And suppose you want to access *yearly* sales summaries. Now you are dealing with 200 rows and 12 monthly sales attributes per row. (Actually, there are 13 attributes per row if you add each store's sales total for each year.)

The decision support database schema must also be optimized for query (read-only) retrievals. To optimize query speed, the DBMS must support features such as bitmap indexes and data partitioning to increase search speed. In addition, the DBMS query optimizer must be enhanced to support the non-normalized and complex structures found in decision support databases.

Data Extraction and Filtering

The decision support database is created largely by extracting data from the operational database and by importing additional data from external sources. Thus, the DBMS must support advanced data extraction and data filtering tools. To minimize the impact on the operational database, the data extraction capabilities should allow batch and scheduled data extraction. The data extraction capabilities should also support different data sources: flat files and hierarchical, network, and relational databases, as well as multiple vendors. Data filtering capabilities must include the ability to check for inconsistent data or data validation rules. Finally, to filter and integrate the operational data into the decision support database, the DBMS must support advanced data integration, aggregation, and classification.

Using data from multiple external sources also usually means having to solve data-formatting conflicts. For example, data such as Social Security numbers and dates can occur in different formats; measurements can be based on different scales, and the same data elements can have different names. In short, data must be filtered and purified to ensure that only the pertinent decision support data are stored in the database and that they are stored in a standard format.

End-User Analytical Interface

The decision support DBMS must support advanced data modeling and data presentation tools. Using those tools makes it easy for data analysts to define the nature and extent of business problems. Once the problems have been defined, the decision support DBMS must generate the necessary queries to retrieve the appropriate data from the decision support database. If necessary, the query results may then be evaluated with data analysis tools supported by the decision support DBMS. Because queries yield crucial information for decision makers, the queries must be optimized for speedy processing. The end-user analytical interface is one of the most critical DBMS components. When properly implemented, an analytical interface permits the user to navigate through the data to simplify and accelerate the decision-making process.

Database Size

Decision support databases tend to be very large; gigabyte and terabyte ranges are not unusual. For example, in 2005, Wal-Mart, the world's largest company, had 260 terabytes of data in its data warehouses. As mentioned earlier, the decision support database typically contains redundant and duplicated data to improve data retrieval and simplify information generation. Therefore, the DBMS must be capable of supporting **very large databases** (**VLDBs**). To support a VLDB adequately, the DBMS might be required to use advanced hardware, such as multiple disk arrays, and even more importantly, to support multiple-processor technologies, such as a symmetric multiprocessor (SMP) or a massively parallel processor (MPP).

The complex information requirements and the ever-growing demand for sophisticated data analysis sparked the creation of a new type of data repository. This repository contains data in formats that facilitate data extraction, data analysis, and decision making. This data repository is known as a data warehouse and has become the foundation for a new generation of decision support systems.

13.5 THE DATA WAREHOUSE

Bill Inmon, the acknowledged "father" of the **data warehouse**, defines the term as "an *integrated, subject-oriented, time-variant, nonvolatile* collection of data (italics added for emphasis) that provides support for decision making."[2] To understand that definition, let's take a more detailed look at its components.

- *Integrated.* The data warehouse is a centralized, consolidated database that integrates data derived from the entire organization and from multiple sources with diverse formats. Data integration implies that all business entities, data elements, data characteristics, and business metrics *are described in the same way throughout the enterprise*. Although this requirement sounds logical, you would be amazed to discover how many different measurements for "sales performance" can exist within an organization; the same scenario holds true for any other business element. For instance, the status of an order might be indicated with text labels such as "open," "received," "cancelled," and "closed" in one department and as "1," "2," "3," and "4" in another department. A student's status might be defined as "freshman," "sophomore," "junior," or "senior" in the accounting department and as "FR," "SO," "JR," or "SR" in the computer information systems department. To avoid the potential format tangle, the data in the data warehouse must conform to a common format acceptable throughout the organization. This integration can be time-consuming, but once accomplished, it enhances decision making and helps managers better understand the company's operations. This understanding can be translated into recognition of strategic business opportunities.

- *Subject-oriented.* Data warehouse data are arranged and optimized to provide answers to questions coming from diverse functional areas within a company. Data warehouse data are organized and summarized by topic, such as sales, marketing, finance, distribution, and transportation. For each topic, the data warehouse contains

---

[2] Inmon, Bill and Chuck Kelley. "The Twelve Rules of Data Warehouse for a Client/Server World," *Data Management Review*, 4(5), May 1994, pp. 6–16.

specific subjects of interest—products, customers, departments, regions, promotions, and so on. This form of data organization is quite different from the more functional or process-oriented organization of typical transaction systems. For example, an invoicing system designer concentrates on designing normalized data structures (relational tables) to support the business process by storing invoice components in two tables: INVOICE and INVLINE. In contrast, the data warehouse has a *subject* orientation. Data warehouse designers focus specifically on the data rather than on the processes that modify the data. (After all, data warehouse data are not subject to numerous real-time data updates!) Therefore, instead of storing an invoice, the data warehouse stores its "sales by product" and "sales by customer" components because decision support activities require the retrieval of sales summaries by product or customer.

- *Time-variant.* In contrast to operational data, which focus on current transactions, warehouse data represent the flow of data through time. The data warehouse can even contain projected data generated through statistical and other models. It is also time-variant in the sense that once data are periodically uploaded to the data warehouse, all time-dependent aggregations are recomputed. For example, when data for previous weekly sales are uploaded to the data warehouse, the weekly, monthly, yearly, and other time-dependent aggregates for products, customers, stores, and other variables are also updated. Because data in a data warehouse constitute a snapshot of the company history as measured by its variables, the time component is crucial. The data warehouse contains a time ID that is used to generate summaries and aggregations by week, month, quarter, year, and so on. Once the data enter the data warehouse, the time ID assigned to the data cannot be changed.

- *Nonvolatile.* Once data enter the data warehouse, they are never removed. Because the data in the warehouse represent the company's history, the operational data, representing the near-term history, are always added to it. Because data are never deleted and new data are continually added, the data warehouse is always growing. That's why the DBMS must be able to support multigigabyte and even multiterabyte databases, operating on multiprocessor hardware. Table 13.7 summarizes the differences between data warehouses and operational databases.

TABLE 13.7 Characteristics of Data Warehouse Data and Operational Database Data

CHARACTERISTIC	OPERATIONAL DATABASE DATA	DATA WAREHOUSE DATA
Integrated	Similar data can have different representations or meanings. For example, Social Security numbers may be stored as ###-##-#### or as #########, and a given condition may be labeled as T/F or 0/1 or Y/N. A sales value may be shown in thousands or in millions.	Provide a unified view of all data elements with a common definition and representation for all business units.
Subject-oriented	Data are stored with a functional, or process, orientation. For example, data may be stored for invoices, payments, and credit amounts.	Data are stored with a subject orientation that facilitates multiple views of the data and facilitates decision making. For example, sales may be recorded by product, by division, by manager, or by region.
Time-variant	Data are recorded as current transactions. For example, the sales data may be the sale of a product on a given date, such as $342.78 on 12-MAY-2008.	Data are recorded with a historical perspective in mind. Therefore, a time dimension is added to facilitate data analysis and various time comparisons.
Nonvolatile	Data updates are frequent and common. For example, an inventory amount changes with each sale. Therefore, the data environment is fluid.	Data cannot be changed. Data are added only periodically from historical systems. Once the data are properly stored, no changes are allowed. Therefore, the data environment is relatively static.

In summary, the data warehouse is usually a read-only database optimized for data analysis and query processing. Typically, data are extracted from various sources and are then transformed and integrated—in other words, passed through a data filter—before being loaded into the data warehouse. Users access the data warehouse via front-end tools and/or end-user application software to extract the data in usable form. Figure 13.4 illustrates how a data warehouse is created from the data contained in an operational database.

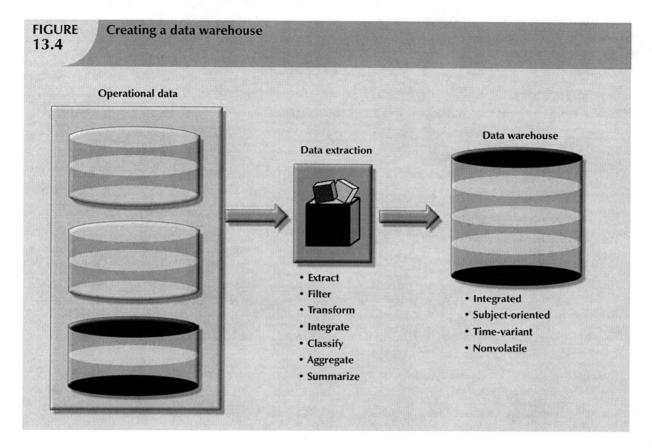

FIGURE 13.4   Creating a data warehouse

Operational data

Data extraction

- Extract
- Filter
- Transform
- Integrate
- Classify
- Aggregate
- Summarize

Data warehouse

- Integrated
- Subject-oriented
- Time-variant
- Nonvolatile

Although the centralized and integrated data warehouse can be a very attractive proposition that yields many benefits, managers may be reluctant to embrace this strategy. Creating a data warehouse requires time, money, and considerable managerial effort. Therefore, it is not surprising that many companies begin their foray into data warehousing by focusing on more manageable data sets that are targeted to meet the special needs of small groups within the organization. These smaller data stores are called data marts. A **data mart** is a small, single-subject data warehouse subset that provides decision support to a small group of people. In addition, a data mart could also be created from data extracted from a larger data warehouse with the specific function to support faster data access to a target group or function. That is, data marts and data warehouses can coexist within a business intelligence environment.

Some organizations choose to implement data marts not only because of the lower cost and shorter implementation time, but also because of the current technological advances and inevitable "people issues" that make data marts attractive. Powerful computers can provide a customized decision support system to small groups in ways that might not be possible with a centralized system. Also, a company's culture may predispose its employees to resist major changes, but they might quickly embrace relatively minor changes that lead to demonstrably improved decision support. In addition, people at different organizational levels are likely to require data with different summarization, aggregation, and presentation formats. Data marts can serve as a test vehicle for companies exploring the potential benefits of data warehouses. By migrating gradually from data marts to data warehouses, a specific department's decision support needs can be addressed within a reasonable time frame (six months to one year), as compared to the longer time frame usually required to implement a data warehouse (one to three years). Information technology (IT) departments also benefit from this approach because their personnel have the opportunity to learn the issues and develop the skills required to create a data warehouse.

The only difference between a data mart and a data warehouse is the size and scope of the problem being solved. Therefore, the problem definitions and data requirements are essentially the same for both. To be useful, the data warehouse must conform to uniform structures and formats to avoid data conflicts and to support decision making. In fact, before a decision support database can be considered a true data warehouse, it must conform to the rules described in the next section.

13.5.1 TWELVE RULES THAT DEFINE A DATA WAREHOUSE

In 1994, William H. Inmon and Chuck Kelley created 12 rules defining a data warehouse, which summarize many of the points made in this chapter about data warehouses.[3]

1. The data warehouse and operational environments are separated.

2. The data warehouse data are integrated.

3. The data warehouse contains historical data over a long time.

4. The data warehouse data are snapshot data captured at a given point in time.

5. The data warehouse data are subject oriented.

6. The data warehouse data are mainly read-only with periodic batch updates from operational data. No online updates are allowed.

7. The data warehouse development life cycle differs from classical systems development. The data warehouse development is data-driven; the classical approach is process-driven.

8. The data warehouse contains data with several levels of detail: current detail data, old detail data, lightly summarized data, and highly summarized data.

9. The data warehouse environment is characterized by read-only transactions to very large data sets. The operational environment is characterized by numerous update transactions to a few data entities at a time.

10. The data warehouse environment has a system that traces data sources, transformations, and storage.

11. The data warehouse's metadata are a critical component of this environment. The metadata identify and define all data elements. The metadata provide the source, transformation, integration, storage, usage, relationships, and history of each data element.

12. The data warehouse contains a chargeback mechanism for resource usage that enforces optimal use of the data by end users.

Note how those 12 rules capture the complete data warehouse life cycle—from its introduction as an entity separate from the operational data store to its components, functionality, and management processes. The next section illustrates the historical progression of decision support architectural styles. This discussion will help you understand how the data store components evolved to produce the data warehouse.

13.5.2 DECISION SUPPORT ARCHITECTURAL STYLES

Several decision support database architectural styles are available. These architectures provide advanced decision support features, and some are capable of providing access to multidimensional data analysis. Table 13.8 summarizes the main architectural styles that you are likely to encounter in the decision support database environment.

[3] Inmon, Bill and Chuck Kelley. "The Twelve Rules of Data Warehouse for a Client/Server World," *Data Management Review*, 4 (5), May 1994, pp. 6–16.

TABLE 13.8 Decision Support Architectural Styles

SYSTEM TYPE	SOURCE DATA	DATA EXTRACTION/ INTEGRATION PROCESS	DECISION SUPPORT DATA STORE	END-USER QUERY TOOL	END USER PRESENTATION TOOL
Traditional mainframe-based online transaction processing (OLTP)	Operational data	None Reports, reads, and summarizes data directly from operational data	None Temporary files used for reporting purposes	Very basic Predefined reporting formats Basic sorting, totaling, and averaging	Very basic Menu-driven, predefined reports, text and numbers only
Managerial information system (MIS) with third-generation language (3GL)	Operational data	Basic extraction and aggregation Reads, filters, and summarizes operational data into intermediate data store	Lightly aggregated data in RDBMS	Same as above, in addition to some ad hoc reporting using SQL	Same as above, in addition to some ad hoc columnar report definitions
First-generation departmental DSS	Operational data	Data extraction and integration process to populate a DSS data store; is run periodically	First DSS database generation Usually RDBMS	Query tool with some analytical capabilities and predefined reports	Advanced presentation tools with plotting and graphics capabilities
First-generation enterprise data warehouse using RDBMS	Operational data External data (census data)	Advanced data extraction and integration tools Features include access to diverse data sources, transformations, filters, aggregations, classifications, scheduling, and conflict resolution	Data warehouse integrated decision support database to support the entire organization Uses RDBMS technology optimized for query purposes Star schema model	Same as above, in addition to support for more advanced queries and analytical functions with extensions	Same as above, in addition to additional multidimensional presentation tools with drill-down capabilities
Second-generation data warehouse using multidimensional database management system (MDBMS)	Operational data External data (Industry group data)	Same as above	Data warehouse stores data by using MDBMS technology based on data structures; referred to as cubes with multiple dimensions	Same as above, but uses different query interface to access MDBMS (proprietary)	Same as above, but uses cubes and multidimensional matrixes Limited in terms of cube size

You might be tempted to think that the data warehouse is just a big summarized database. The previous discussion indicates that a good data warehouse is much more than that. A complete data warehouse architecture includes support for a decision support data store, a data extraction and integration filter, and a specialized presentation interface. In the next section you will learn more about a common decision support architectural style known as Online Analytical Processing (OLAP).

13.6 ONLINE ANALYTICAL PROCESSING

The need for more intensive decision support prompted the introduction of a new generation of tools. Those new tools, called **online analytical processing (OLAP)**, create an advanced data analysis environment that supports decision making, business modeling, and operations research. OLAP systems share four main characteristics:

- They use multidimensional data analysis techniques.
- They provide advanced database support.
- They provide easy-to-use end-user interfaces.
- They support client/server architecture.

Let's examine each of those characteristics.

13.6.1 MULTIDIMENSIONAL DATA ANALYSIS TECHNIQUES

The most distinct characteristic of modern OLAP tools is their capacity for multidimensional analysis. In multidimensional analysis, data are processed and viewed as part of a multidimensional structure. This type of data analysis is particularly attractive to business decision makers because they tend to view business data as data that are related to other business data.

To better understand this view, let's examine how, as a business data analyst, you might investigate sales figures. In this case, you are probably interested in the sales figures as they relate to other business variables such as customers and time. In other words, customers and time are viewed as different dimensions of sales. Figure 13.5 illustrates how the operational (one-dimensional) view differs from the multidimensional view of sales.

Note in Figure 13.5 that the tabular (operational) view of sales data is not well suited to decision support, because the relationship between INVOICE and LINE does not provide a business perspective of the sales data. On the other hand, the end user's view of sales data *from a business perspective* is more closely represented by the multidimensional view of sales than by the tabular view of separate tables. Note also that the multidimensional view allows end users to consolidate or aggregate data at different levels: total sales figures by customers and by date. Finally, the multidimensional view of data allows a business data analyst to easily switch business perspectives (dimensions) from sales by customer to sales by division, by region, and so on.

Multidimensional data analysis techniques are augmented by the following functions:

- *Advanced data presentation functions.* 3-D graphics, pivot tables, crosstabs, data rotation, and three-dimensional cubes. Such facilities are compatible with desktop spreadsheets, statistical packages, and query and report packages.
- *Advanced data aggregation, consolidation, and classification functions.* These allow the data analyst to create multiple data aggregation levels, slice and dice data (see Section 13.6.3), and drill down and roll up data across different dimensions and aggregation levels. For example, aggregating data across the time dimension (by week, month, quarter, and year) allows the data analyst to drill down and roll up across time dimensions.
- *Advanced computational functions.* These include business-oriented variables (market share, period comparisons, sales margins, product margins, and percentage changes), financial and accounting ratios (profitability, overhead, cost allocations, and returns), and statistical and forecasting functions. These functions are provided automatically, and the end user does not need to redefine their components each time they are accessed.
- *Advanced data modeling functions.* These provide support for what-if scenarios, variable assessment, variable contributions to outcome, linear programming, and other modeling tools.

FIGURE 13.5   Operational vs. multidimensional view of sales

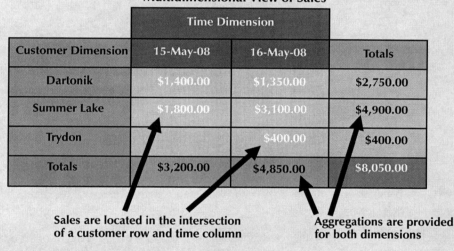

Database name: Ch13_Text

Table name: DW_INVOICE

INV_NUM	INV_DATE	CUS_NAME	INV_TOTAL
2034	15-May-08	Dartonik	1400.00
2035	15-May-08	Summer Lake	1200.00
2036	16-May-08	Dartonik	1350.00
2037	16-May-08	Summer lake	3100.00
2038	16-May-08	Trydon	400.00

Table name: DW_LINE

INV_NUM	LINE_NUM	PROD_DESCRIPTION	LINE_PRICE	LINE_QUANTITY	LINE_AMOUNT
2034	1	Optical Mouse	45.00	20	900.00
2034	2	Wireless RF remote and laser pointer	50.00	10	500.00
2035	1	Everlast Hard Drive, 60 GB	200.00	6	1200.00
2036	1	Optical Mouse	45.00	30	1350.00
2037	1	Optical Mouse	45.00	10	450.00
2037	2	Roadster 56KB Ext. Modem	120.00	5	600.00
2037	3	Everlast Hard Drive, 60 GB	205.00	10	2050.00
2038	1	NoTech Speaker Set	50.00	8	400.00

Multidimensional View of Sales

Customer Dimension	Time Dimension		Totals
	15-May-08	16-May-08	
Dartonik	$1,400.00	$1,350.00	$2,750.00
Summer Lake	$1,800.00	$3,100.00	$4,900.00
Trydon		$400.00	$400.00
Totals	$3,200.00	$4,850.00	$8,050.00

Sales are located in the intersection of a customer row and time column

Aggregations are provided for both dimensions

Because many analysis and presentation functions are common to desktop spreadsheet packages, most OLAP vendors have closely integrated their systems with spreadsheets such as Microsoft Excel and IBM Lotus 1-2-3. Using the features available in graphical end-user interfaces such as Windows, the OLAP menu option simply becomes another option within the spreadsheet menu bar, as shown in Figure 13.6. This seamless integration is an advantage for OLAP systems and for spreadsheet vendors because end users gain access to advanced data analysis features by using familiar programs and interfaces. Therefore, additional training and development costs are minimized.

13.6.2 ADVANCED DATABASE SUPPORT

To deliver efficient decision support, OLAP tools must have advanced data access features. Such features include:

- Access to many different kinds of DBMSs, flat files, and internal and external data sources.
- Access to aggregated data warehouse data as well as to the detail data found in operational databases.
- Advanced data navigation features such as drill-down and roll-up.
- Rapid and consistent query response times.

FIGURE 13.6   Integration of OLAP with a spreadsheet program

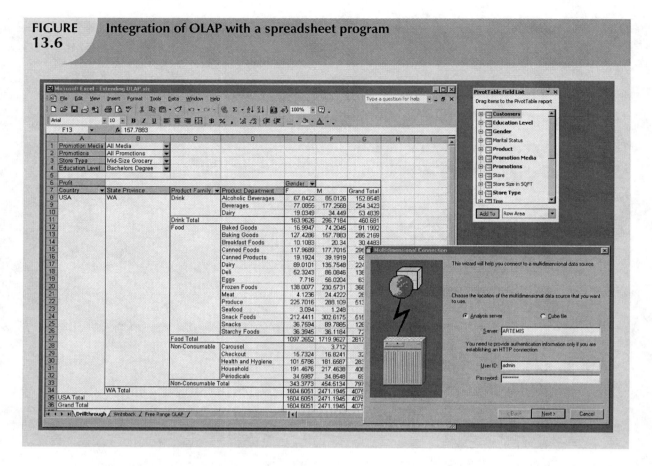

- The ability to map end-user requests, expressed in either business or model terms, to the appropriate data source and then to the proper data access language (usually SQL). The query code must be optimized to match the data source, regardless of whether the source is operational or data warehouse data.
- Support for very large databases. As already explained, the data warehouse can easily and quickly grow to multiple gigabytes and even terabytes.

To provide a seamless interface, OLAP tools map the data elements from the data warehouse and from the operational database to their own data dictionaries. These metadata are used to translate end-user data analysis requests into the proper (optimized) query codes, which are then directed to the appropriate data source(s).

13.6.3 EASY-TO-USE END-USER INTERFACE

Advanced OLAP features become more useful when access to them is kept simple. OLAP tool vendors learned this lesson early and have equipped their sophisticated data extraction and analysis tools with easy-to-use graphical interfaces. Many of the interface features are "borrowed" from previous generations of data analysis tools that are already familiar to end users. This familiarity makes OLAP easily accepted and readily used.

13.6.4 CLIENT/SERVER ARCHITECTURE

Client/server architecture provides a framework within which new systems can be designed, developed, and implemented. The client/server environment enables an OLAP system to be divided into several components that define its architecture. Those components can then be placed on the same computer, or they can be distributed among several computers. Thus, OLAP is designed to meet ease-of-use requirements while keeping the system flexible.

13.6.5 OLAP ARCHITECTURE

OLAP operational characteristics can be divided into three main modules:

- Graphical user interface (GUI).
- Analytical processing logic.
- Data-processing logic.

In the client/server environment, those three OLAP modules make the defining features of OLAP possible: multidimensional data analysis, advanced database support, and an easy-to-use interface. Figure 13.7 illustrates OLAP's client/server components and attributes.

FIGURE 13.7   OLAP client/server architecture

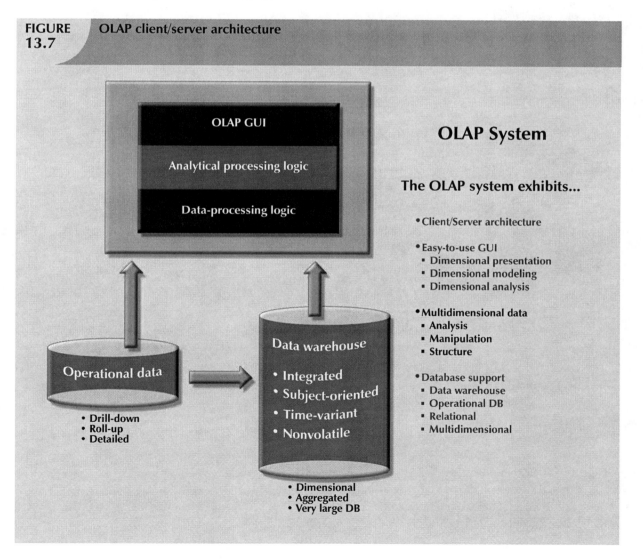

As Figure 13.7 illustrates, OLAP systems are designed to use both operational and data warehouse data. Figure 13.7 shows the OLAP system components located on a single computer, but this single-user scenario is only one of many. In fact, one problem with the installation shown here is that each data analyst must have a powerful computer to store the OLAP system and perform all data processing locally. In addition, each analyst uses a separate copy of the data. Therefore, the data copies must be synchronized to ensure that analysts are working with the same data. In other words, each end user must have his/her own "private" copy (extract) of the data and programs, thus returning to the *islands of information* problems discussed in Chapter 1, Database Systems. This approach does not provide the benefits of a single business image shared among all users.

A more common and practical architecture is one in which the OLAP GUI runs on client workstations, while the OLAP engine, or server, composed of the OLAP analytical processing logic and OLAP data-processing logic, runs on a shared computer. In that case, the OLAP server will be a front end to the data warehouse's decision support data. This front end or middle layer (because it sits between the data warehouse and the end-user GUI) accepts and processes the data-processing requests generated by the many end-user analytical tools. The end-user GUI might be a custom-made program or, more likely, a plug-in module that is integrated with Lotus 1-2-3, Microsoft Excel, or a third-party data analysis and query tool. Figure 13.8 illustrates such an arrangement.

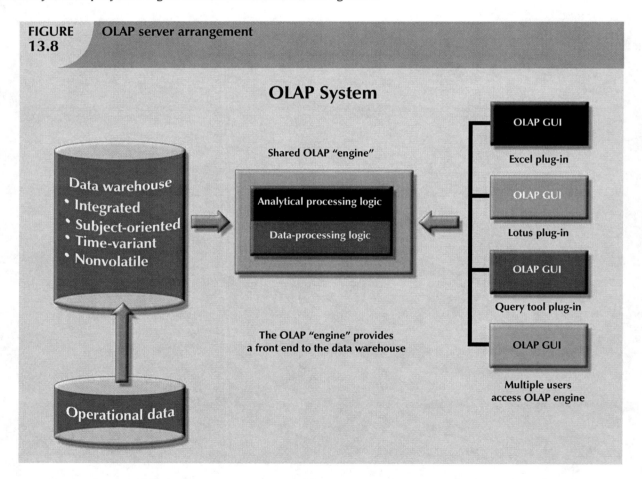

FIGURE 13.8   OLAP server arrangement

Note in Figure 13.8 that the data warehouse is created and maintained by a process or software tool that is independent of the OLAP system. This independent software performs the data extraction, filtering, and integration necessary to transform operational data into data warehouse data. This scenario reflects the fact that in most cases, the data warehousing and data analysis activities are handled separately.

At this point, you might ask why you need a data warehouse if OLAP provides the necessary multidimensional data analysis of operational data. The answer lies in the definition of OLAP. OLAP is defined as an "advanced data analysis environment that supports decision making, business modeling, and research activities." The keyword here is *environment*, which includes client/server technology. Environment is defined as "surroundings or atmosphere." And an atmosphere surrounds a nucleus. *In this case, the nucleus is composed of all business activities within an organization as represented by the operational data.* Just as there are several layers within the atmosphere, there are several layers of data processing, each outer layer representing a more aggregated data analysis. The fact is that an OLAP system might access both data storage types (operational or data warehouse) or only one; it depends on the vendor's implementation of the product selected. In any case, multidimensional data analysis requires some type of multidimensional data representation, which is normally provided by the OLAP engine.

In most implementations, the data warehouse and OLAP are interrelated, complementary environments. While the data warehouse holds integrated, subject-oriented, time-variant, and nonvolatile decision support data, the OLAP system provides the front end through which end users access and analyze such data. Yet an OLAP system can also directly access operational data, transforming it and storing it in a multidimensional structure. In other words, the OLAP system can provide a multidimensional data store component, as shown in Figure 13.9.

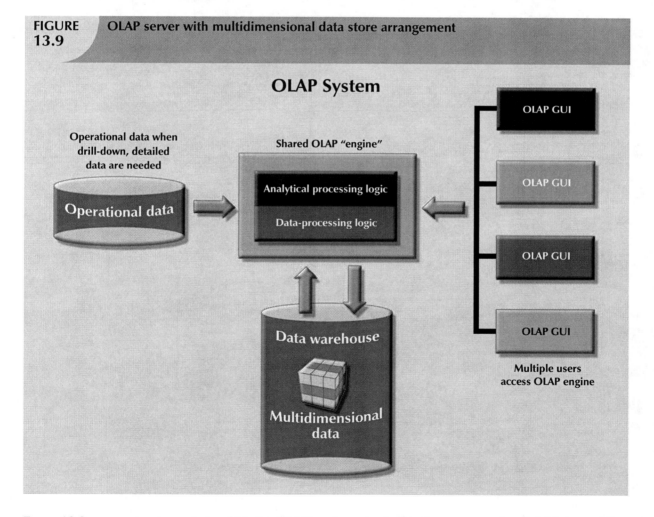

FIGURE 13.9   OLAP server with multidimensional data store arrangement

Figure 13.9 represents a scenario in which the OLAP engine extracts data from an operational database and then stores it in a multidimensional structure for further data analysis. The extraction process follows the same conventions used with data warehouses. Therefore, the OLAP provides a mini data-warehouse component that looks remarkably like the data mart mentioned in previous sections. In this scenario, the OLAP engine has to perform all of the data extraction, filtering, integration, classification, and aggregation functions that the data warehouse normally provides. In fact, when properly implemented, the data warehouse performs all data preparation functions instead of letting OLAP perform those chores; as a result, there is no duplication of functions. Better yet, the data warehouse handles the data component more efficiently than OLAP does; so you can appreciate the benefits of having a central data warehouse serve as the large enterprise decision support database.

To provide better performance, some OLAP systems merge the data warehouse and data mart approaches by storing small extracts of the data warehouse at end-user workstations. The objective is to increase the speed of data access and data visualization (the graphic representations of data trends and characteristics). The logic behind that approach is the assumption that most end users usually work with fairly small, stable data warehouse data subsets. For example, a sales analyst is most likely to work with sales data, whereas a customer representative is likely to work with customer data. Figure 13.10 illustrates that scenario.

FIGURE 13.10   OLAP server with local mini data marts

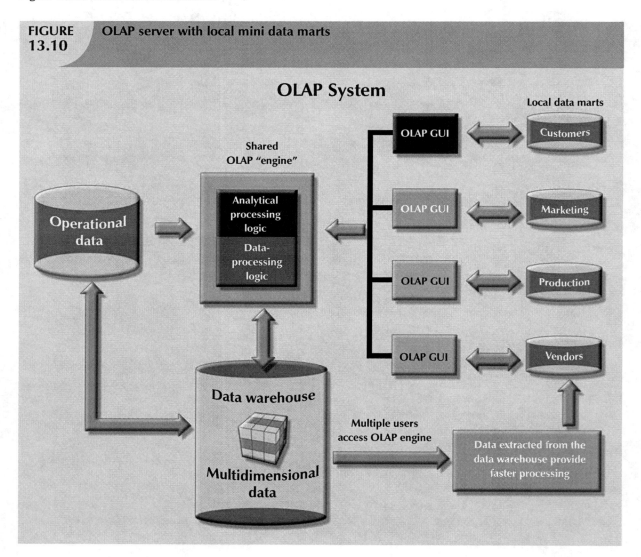

Whatever the arrangement of the OLAP components, one thing is certain: multidimensional data must be used. But how are multidimensional data best stored and managed? OLAP proponents are sharply divided. Some favor the use of relational databases to store the multidimensional data; others argue for the superiority of specialized multidimensional databases to store multidimensional data. The basic characteristics of each approach are examined next.

13.6.6 RELATIONAL OLAP

Relational online analytical processing (ROLAP) provides OLAP functionality by using relational databases and familiar relational query tools to store and analyze multidimensional data. That approach builds on existing relational technologies and represents a natural extension to all of the companies that already use relational database management systems within their organizations. ROLAP adds the following extensions to traditional RDBMS technology:

- Multidimensional data schema support within the RDBMS.
- Data access language and query performance optimized for multidimensional data.
- Support for very large databases (VLDBs).

Multidimensional Data Schema Support within the RDBMS

Relational technology uses normalized tables to store data. The reliance on normalization as the design methodology for relational databases is seen as a stumbling block to its use in OLAP systems. Normalization divides business entities into smaller pieces to produce the normalized tables. For example, sales data components might be stored in four or five different tables. The reason for using normalized tables is to reduce redundancies, thereby eliminating data anomalies, and to facilitate data updates. Unfortunately, for decision support purposes, it is easier to understand data when they are seen with respect to other data. (See the example in Figure 13.5.) Given that view of the data environment, this book has stressed that decision support data tend to be non-normalized, duplicated, and pre-aggregated. Those characteristics seem to preclude the use of standard relational design techniques and RDBMSs as the foundation for multidimensional data.

Fortunately for those heavily invested in relational technology, ROLAP uses a special design technique to enable RDBMS technology to support multidimensional data representations. This special design technique is known as a star schema, which is covered in detail in Section 13.7.

The star schema is designed to optimize data query operations rather than data update operations. Naturally, changing the data design foundation means that the tools used to access such data will have to change. End users who are familiar with the traditional relational query tools will discover that those tools do not work efficiently with the new star schema. However, ROLAP saves the day by adding support for the star schema when familiar query tools are used. ROLAP provides advanced data analysis functions and improves query optimization and data visualization methods.

Data Access Language and Query Performance Optimized for Multidimensional Data

Another criticism of relational databases is that SQL is not suited for performing advanced data analysis. Most decision support data requests require the use of multiple-pass SQL queries or multiple nested SQL statements. To answer this criticism, ROLAP extends SQL so that it can differentiate between access requirements for data warehouse data (based on the star schema) and operational data (normalized tables). In that way, a ROLAP system is able to generate the SQL code required to access the star schema data.

Query performance is also improved because the query optimizer is modified to identify the SQL code's intended query targets. For example, if the query target is the data warehouse, the optimizer passes the requests to the data warehouse. However, if the end user performs drill-down queries against operational data, the query optimizer identifies that operation and properly optimizes the SQL requests before passing them through to the operational DBMS.

Another source of improved query performance is the use of advanced indexing techniques such as bitmapped indexes within relational databases. As the name suggests, a bitmapped index is based on 0 and 1 bits to represent a given condition. For example, if the REGION attribute in Figure 13.3 has only four outcomes—North, South, East, and West—those outcomes may be represented as shown in Table 13.9. (Only the first 10 rows from Figure 13.3 are represented in Table 13.9. The "1" represents "bit on," and the "0" represents "bit off." For example, to represent a row with a REGION attribute = "East," only the "East" bit would be on. Note that each row must be represented in the index table.)

TABLE 13.9	Bitmap Representation of Region Values		
NORTH	SOUTH	EAST	WEST
0	0	1	0
0	0	1	0
1	0	0	0
1	0	0	0
1	0	0	0
0	1	0	0
0	1	0	0
0	1	0	0
0	0	0	1
0	0	0	1

Note that the index in Table 13.9 takes a minimum amount of space. Therefore, bitmapped indexes are more efficient at handling large amounts of data than are the indexes typically found in many relational databases. But do keep in mind that bitmapped indexes are primarily used in situations where the number of possible values for an attribute (in other words, the attribute domain) is fairly small. For example, REGION has only four outcomes in this example. Marital status—married, single, widowed, divorced—would be another good bitmapped index candidate, as would gender—M or F.

ROLAP tools are mainly client/server products in which the end-user interface, the analytical processing, and the data processing take place on different computers. Figure 13.11 shows the interaction of the client/server ROLAP components.

FIGURE 13.11   Typical ROLAP client/server architecture

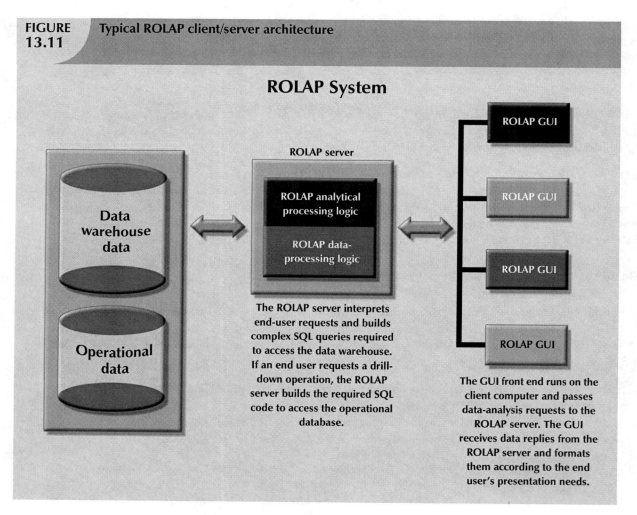

ROLAP System

Data warehouse data

Operational data

ROLAP server

ROLAP analytical processing logic

ROLAP data-processing logic

The ROLAP server interprets end-user requests and builds complex SQL queries required to access the data warehouse. If an end user requests a drill-down operation, the ROLAP server builds the required SQL code to access the operational database.

ROLAP GUI

ROLAP GUI

ROLAP GUI

ROLAP GUI

The GUI front end runs on the client computer and passes data-analysis requests to the ROLAP server. The GUI receives data replies from the ROLAP server and formats them according to the end user's presentation needs.

Support for Very Large Databases

Recall that support for VLDBs is a requirement for decision support databases. Therefore, when the relational database is used in a decision support role, it also must be able to store very large amounts of data. Both the storage capability and the process of loading data into the database are crucial. Therefore, the RDBMS must have the proper tools to import, integrate, and populate the data warehouse with data. Decision support data are normally loaded in bulk (batch) mode from the operational data. However, batch operations require that both the source and the destination databases be reserved (locked). The speed of the data-loading operations is important, especially when you realize that most operational systems run 24 hours a day, 7 days a week, 52 weeks a year. Therefore, the window of opportunity for maintenance and batch loading is open only briefly, typically during slack periods.

With an open client/server architecture, ROLAP provides advanced decision support capabilities that are scalable to the entire enterprise. Clearly, ROLAP is a logical choice for companies that already use relational databases for their operational data. Given the size of the relational database market, it is hardly surprising that most current RDBMS vendors have extended their products to support data warehouses.

13.6.7 MULTIDIMENSIONAL OLAP

Multidimensional online analytical processing (MOLAP) extends OLAP functionality to **multidimensional database management systems (MDBMSs)**. (An MDBMS uses special proprietary techniques to store data in matrix-like n-dimensional arrays.) MOLAP's premise is that multidimensional databases are best suited to manage, store, and analyze multidimensional data. Most of the proprietary techniques used in MDBMSs are derived from engineering fields such as computer-aided design/computer-aided manufacturing (CAD/CAM) and geographic information systems (GIS).

Conceptually, MDBMS end users visualize the stored data as a three-dimensional cube known as a **data cube**. The location of each data value in the data cube is a function of the x-, y-, and z-axes in a three-dimensional space. The x-, y-, and z-axes represent the dimensions of the data value. The data cubes can grow to n number of dimensions, thus becoming *hypercubes*. Data cubes are created by extracting data from the operational databases or from the data warehouse. One important characteristic of data cubes is that they are static; that is, they are not subject to change and must be created before they can be used. Data cubes cannot be created by ad hoc queries. Instead, you query pre-created cubes with defined axes; for example, a cube for sales will have the product, location, and time dimensions, and you can query only those dimensions. Therefore, the data cube creation process is critical and requires in-depth front-end design work. The front-end design work may be well justified because MOLAP databases are known to be much faster than their ROLAP counterparts, especially when dealing with small to medium data sets. To speed data access, data cubes are normally held in memory in what is called the **cube cache**. (A data cube is only a window to a predefined subset of data in the database. A *data cube* and a *database* are not the same thing.) Because MOLAP also benefits from a client/server infrastructure, the cube cache can be located at the MOLAP server, at the MOLAP client, or in both locations. Figure 13.12 shows the basic MOLAP architecture.

Because the data cube is predefined with a set number of dimensions, the addition of a new dimension requires that the entire data cube be re-created. This re-creation process is time consuming. Therefore, when data cubes are created too often, the MDBMS loses some of its speed advantage over the relational database. And although MDBMSs have performance advantages over relational databases, the MDBMS is best suited to small and medium data sets. Scalability is somewhat limited because the size of the data cube is restricted to avoid lengthy data access times caused by having less work space (memory) available for the operating system and the application programs. In addition, the MDBMS makes use of proprietary data storage techniques that, in turn, require proprietary data access methods using a multidimensional query language.

Multidimensional data analysis is also affected by how the database system handles sparsity. **Sparsity** is a measurement of the density of the data held in the data cube and is computed by dividing the total number of actual values in the cube by the total number of cells in the cube. Because the data cube's dimensions are predefined, not all cells are populated. In other words, some cells are empty. Returning to the sales example, there may be many products

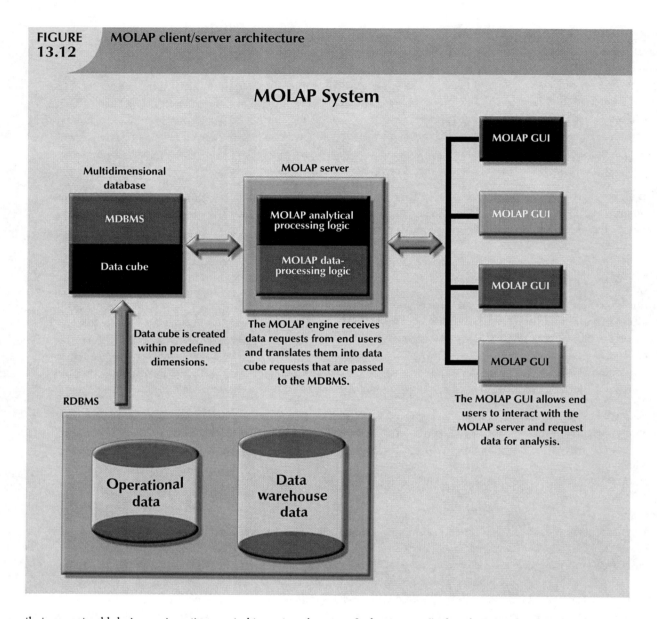

FIGURE 13.12   MOLAP client/server architecture

MOLAP System

MOLAP GUI

MOLAP GUI

MOLAP GUI

MOLAP GUI

Multidimensional database

MDBMS

Data cube

MOLAP server

MOLAP analytical processing logic

MOLAP data-processing logic

Data cube is created within predefined dimensions.

RDBMS

The MOLAP engine receives data requests from end users and translates them into data cube requests that are passed to the MDBMS.

The MOLAP GUI allows end users to interact with the MOLAP server and request data for analysis.

Operational data

Data warehouse data

that are not sold during a given time period in a given location. In fact, you will often find that fewer than 50 percent of the data cube's cells are populated. In any case, multidimensional databases must handle sparsity effectively to reduce processing overhead and resource requirements.

Relational proponents also argue that using proprietary solutions makes it difficult to integrate the MDBMS with other data sources and tools used within the enterprise. Although it takes a substantial investment of time and effort to integrate the new technology and the existing information systems architecture, MOLAP may be a good solution for those situations in which small- to medium-sized databases are the norm and application software speed is critical.

13.6.8   RELATIONAL VS. MULTIDIMENSIONAL OLAP

Table 13.10 summarizes some OLAP and MOLAP pros and cons. Keep in mind, too, that the selection of one or the other often depends on the evaluator's vantage point. For example, a proper evaluation of OLAP must include price, supported hardware platforms, compatibility with the existing DBMS, programming requirements, performance, and availability of administrative tools. The summary in Table 13.10 provides a useful starting point for comparison.

TABLE 13.10	Relational vs. Multidimensional OLAP	
CHARACTERISTIC	ROLAP	MOLAP
Schema	Uses star schema Additional dimensions can be added dynamically	Uses data cubes Additional dimensions require re-creation of the data cube
Database size	Medium to large	Small to medium
Architecture	Client/server Standards-based Open	Client/server Proprietary
Access	Supports ad hoc requests Unlimited dimensions	Limited to predefined dimensions
Resources	High	Very high
Flexibility	High	Low
Scalability	High	Low
Speed	Good with small data sets; average for medium to large data sets	Faster for small to medium data sets; average for large data sets

ROLAP and MOLAP vendors are working toward the integration of their respective solutions within a unified decision support framework. Many OLAP products are able to handle tabular and multidimensional data with the same ease. For example, if you are using Excel OLAP functionality, as shown earlier in Figure 13.6, you can access relational OLAP data in a SQL server as well as cube (multidimensional data) in the local computer. In the meantime, relational databases successfully use the star schema design to handle multidimensional data, and their market share makes it unlikely that their popularity will fade anytime soon.

13.7 STAR SCHEMAS

The **star schema** is a data modeling technique used to map multidimensional decision support data into a relational database. In effect, the star schema creates the near equivalent of a multidimensional database schema from the existing relational database. The star schema was developed because existing relational modeling techniques, ER, and normalization did not yield a database structure that served advanced data analysis requirements well.

Star schemas yield an easily implemented model for multidimensional data analysis while still preserving the relational structures on which the operational database is built. The basic star schema has four components: facts, dimensions, attributes, and attribute hierarchies.

13.7.1 FACTS

Facts are numeric measurements (values) that represent a specific business aspect or activity. For example, sales figures are numeric measurements that represent product and/or service sales. Facts commonly used in business data analysis are units, costs, prices, and revenues. Facts are normally stored in a fact table that is the center of the star schema. The **fact table** contains facts that are linked through their dimensions, which are explained in the next section.

Facts can also be computed or derived at run time. Such computed or derived facts are sometimes called **metrics** to differentiate them from stored facts. The fact table is updated periodically (daily, weekly, monthly, and so on) with data from operational databases.

13.7.2 DIMENSIONS

Dimensions are qualifying characteristics that provide additional perspectives to a given fact. Recall that dimensions are of interest because *decision support data are almost always viewed in relation to other data.* For instance, sales might be compared by product from region to region and from one time period to the next. The kind of problem typically addressed by a BI system might be to make a comparison of the sales of unit X by region for the first quarters of 1998 through 2007. In that example, sales have product, location, and time dimensions. In effect, dimensions are the magnifying glass through which you study the facts. Such dimensions are normally stored in **dimension tables**. Figure 13.13 depicts a star schema for sales with product, location, and time dimensions.

FIGURE 13.13   Simple star schema

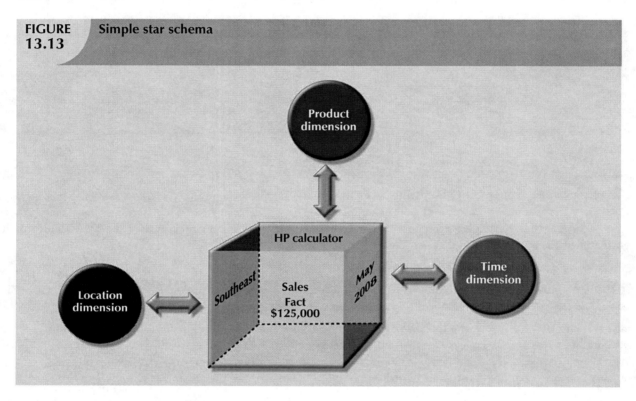

13.7.3 ATTRIBUTES

Each dimension table contains attributes. Attributes are often used to search, filter, or classify facts. *Dimensions provide descriptive characteristics about the facts through their attributes.* Therefore, the data warehouse designer must define common business attributes that will be used by the data analyst to narrow a search, group information, or describe dimensions. Using a sales example, some possible attributes for each dimension are illustrated in Table 13.11.

TABLE 13.11   Possible Attributes for Sales Dimensions

DIMENSION NAME	DESCRIPTION	POSSIBLE ATTRIBUTES
Location	Anything that provides a description of the location. For example, Nashville, Store 101, South Region, and TN	Region, state, city, store, and so on
Product	Anything that provides a description of the product sold. For example, hair care product, shampoo, Natural Essence brand, 5.5-oz. bottle, and blue liquid	Product type, product ID, brand, package, presentation, color, size, and so on
Time	Anything that provides a time frame for the sales fact. For example, the year 2008, the month of July, the date 07/29/2008, and the time 4:46 p.m.	Year, quarter, month, week, day, time of day, and so on

These product, location, and time dimensions add a business perspective to the sales facts. The data analyst can now group the sales figures for a given product, in a given region, and at a given time. The star schema, through its facts and dimensions, can provide the data in the required format when the data are needed. And it can do so without imposing the burden of the additional and unnecessary data (such as order number, purchase order number, and status) that commonly exist in operational databases.

Conceptually, the sales example's multidimensional data model is best represented by a three-dimensional cube. Of course, this does not imply that there is a limit on the number of dimensions that can be associated to a fact table. There is no mathematical limit to the number of dimensions used. However, using a three-dimensional model makes it easy to visualize the problem. In this three-dimensional example, the multidimensional data analysis terminology, the cube illustrated in Figure 13.14 represents a view of sales dimensioned by product, location, and time.

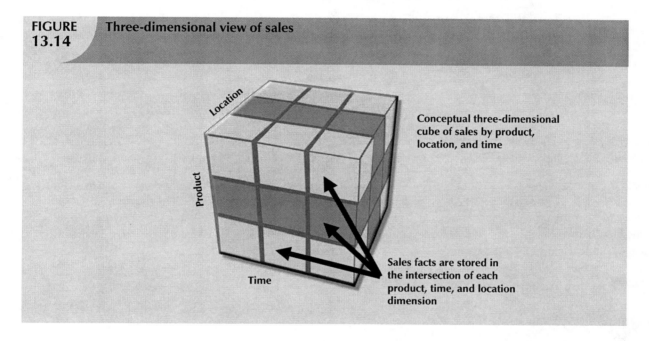

FIGURE 13.14   Three-dimensional view of sales

Conceptual three-dimensional cube of sales by product, location, and time

Sales facts are stored in the intersection of each product, time, and location dimension

Location

Product

Time

Note that each sales value stored in the cube in Figure 13.14 is associated with the location, product, and time dimensions. However, keep in mind that this cube is only a *conceptual* representation of multidimensional data, and it does not show how the data are physically stored in a data warehouse. A ROLAP engine stores data in an RDBMS and uses its own data analysis logic and the end-user GUI to perform multidimensional analysis. A MOLAP system stores data in an MDBMS, using proprietary matrix and array technology to simulate this multidimensional cube.

Whatever the underlying database technology, one of the main features of multidimensional analysis is its ability to focus on specific "slices" of the cube. For example, the product manager may be interested in examining the sales of a product while the store manager is interested in examining the sales made by a particular store. In multidimensional terms, the ability to focus on slices of the cube to perform a more detailed analysis is known as **slice and dice**. Figure 13.15 illustrates the slice-and-dice concept. As you look at Figure 13.15, note that each cut across the cube yields a slice. Intersecting slices produce small cubes that constitute the "dice" part of the "slice-and-dice" operation.

To slice and dice, it must be possible to identify each slice of the cube. That is done by using the values of each attribute in a given dimension. For example, to use the location dimension, you might need to define a STORE_ID attribute in order to focus on a particular store.

Given the requirement for attribute values in a slice-and-dice environment, let's reexamine Table 13.11. Note that each attribute adds an additional perspective to the sales facts, thus setting the stage for finding new ways to search, classify, and possibly aggregate information. For example, the location dimension adds a geographic perspective of where the

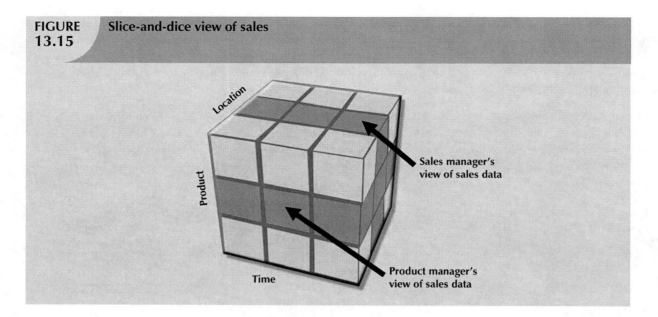

FIGURE
13.15   Slice-and-dice view of sales

Sales manager's
view of sales data

Product manager's
view of sales data

Location

Product

Time

sales took place: in which region, state, city, store, and so on. All of the attributes are selected with the objective of providing decision support data to the end users so that they can study sales by each of the dimension's attributes.

Time is an especially important dimension. The time dimension provides a framework from which sales patterns can be analyzed and possibly predicted. Also, the time dimension plays an important role when the data analyst is interested in looking at sales aggregates by quarter, month, week, and so on. Given the importance and universality of the time dimension from a data analysis perspective, many vendors have added automatic time dimension management features to their data warehousing products.

13.7.4 ATTRIBUTE HIERARCHIES

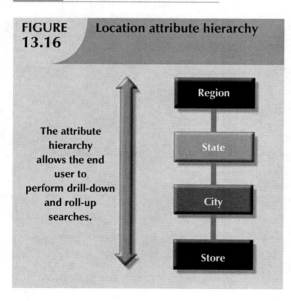

FIGURE
13.16   Location attribute hierarchy

The attribute hierarchy allows the end user to perform drill-down and roll-up searches.

Region

State

City

Store

Attributes within dimensions can be ordered in a well-defined attribute hierarchy. The **attribute hierarchy** provides a top-down data organization that is used for two main purposes: aggregation and drill-down/roll-up data analysis. For example, Figure 13.16 shows how the location dimension attributes can be organized in a hierarchy by region, state, city, and store.

The attribute hierarchy provides the capability to perform drill-down and roll-up searches in a data warehouse. For example, suppose a data analyst looks at the answers to the query, How does the 2007 month-to-date sales performance compare to the 2008 month-to-date sales performance? The data analyst spots a sharp sales decline for March 2008. The data analyst might decide to drill down inside the month of March to see how sales by regions compared to the previous year. By doing that, the analyst can determine whether the low March sales were reflected in all regions or in only a particular region. This type of drill-down operation can even be extended until the data analyst identifies the store that is performing below the norm.

The March sales scenario is possible because the attribute hierarchy allows the data warehouse and OLAP systems to have a defined path that will identify how data are to be decomposed and aggregated for drill-down and roll-up operations. It is not necessary for all attributes to be part of an attribute hierarchy; some attributes exist merely to provide narrative descriptions of the dimensions. But keep in mind that the attributes from different dimensions can be grouped to form a hierarchy. For example, after you drill down from city to store, you might want to drill down using the product dimension so the manager can identify slow products in the store. The product dimension can be based on the product group (dairy, meat, and so on) or on the product brand (Brand A, Brand B, and so on).

Figure 13.17 illustrates a scenario in which the data analyst studies sales facts, using the product, time, and location dimensions. In this example, the product dimension is set to "All products," meaning that the data analyst will see all products on the y-axis. The time dimension (x-axis) is set to "Quarter," meaning that the data are aggregated by quarters (for example, total sales of products A, B, and C in Q1, Q2, Q3, and Q4). Finally, the location dimension is initially set to "Region," thus ensuring that each cell contains the total regional sales for a given product in a given quarter.

FIGURE 13.17   Attribute hierarchies in multidimensional analysis

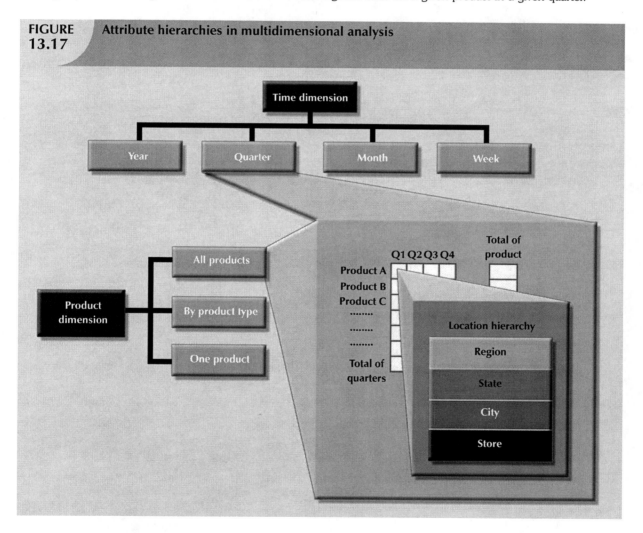

The simple data analysis scenario illustrated in Figure 13.17 provides the data analyst with three different information paths. On the product dimension (the y-axis), the data analyst can request to see all products, products grouped by type, or just one product. On the time dimension (the x-axis), the data analyst can request time-variant data at different levels of aggregation: year, quarter, month, or week. Each sales value initially shows the total sales, by region, of each product. When a GUI is used, clicking on the region cell enables the data analyst to drill down to see sales by states within the region. Clicking again on one of the state values yields the sales for each city in the state, and so forth.

As the preceding examples illustrate, attribute hierarchies determine how the data in the data warehouse are extracted and presented. The attribute hierarchy information is stored in the DBMS's data dictionary and is used by the OLAP tool to access the data warehouse properly. Once such access is ensured, query tools must be closely integrated with the data warehouse's metadata and they must support powerful analytical capabilities.

13.7.5 STAR SCHEMA REPRESENTATION

Facts and dimensions are normally represented by physical tables in the data warehouse database. The fact table is related to each dimension table in a many-to-one (M:1) relationship. In other words, many fact rows are related to each dimension row. Using the sales example, you can conclude that each product appears many times in the SALES fact table.

Fact and dimension tables are related by foreign keys and are subject to the familiar primary key/foreign key constraints. The primary key on the "1" side, the dimension table, is stored as part of the primary key on the "many" side, the fact table. *Because the fact table is related to many dimension tables, the primary key of the fact table is a composite primary key.* Figure 13.18 illustrates the relationships among the sales fact table and the product, location, and time dimension tables. To show you how easily the star schema can be expanded, a customer dimension has been added to the mix. Adding the customer dimension merely required including the CUST_ID in the SALES fact table and adding the CUSTOMER table to the database.

FIGURE 13.18   Star schema for SALES

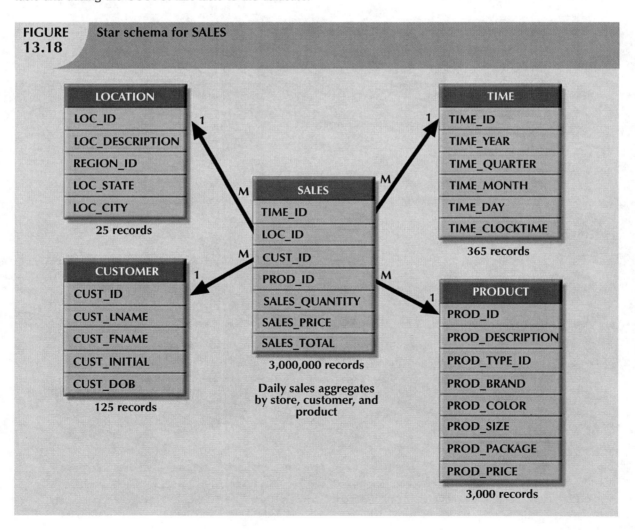

The composite primary key for the SALES fact table is composed of TIME_ID, LOC_ID, CUST_ID, and PROD_ID. Each record in the SALES fact table is uniquely identified by the combination of values for each of the fact table's foreign keys. *By default, the fact table's primary key is always formed by combining the foreign keys pointing to the dimension tables to which they are related.* In this case, each sales record represents each product sold to a specific customer, at a specific time, and in a specific location. In this schema, the TIME dimension table represents daily periods, so the SALES fact table represents daily sales aggregates by product and by customer. Because fact tables contain the actual values used in the decision support process, those values are repeated many times in the fact tables. Therefore, the fact tables are always the largest tables in the star schema. Because the dimension tables contain only nonrepetitive information (all unique salespersons, all unique products, and so on), the dimension tables are always smaller than the fact tables.

In a typical star schema, each dimension record is related to thousands of fact records. For example, "widget" appears only once in the product dimension, but it has thousands of corresponding records in the SALES fact table. That characteristic of the star schema facilitates data retrieval functions because most of the time the data analyst will look at the facts through the dimension's attributes. Therefore, a data warehouse DBMS that is optimized for decision support first searches the smaller dimension tables before accessing the larger fact tables.

Data warehouses usually have many fact tables. Each fact table is designed to answer specific decision support questions. For example, suppose you develop a new interest in orders while maintaining your original interest in sales. In that scenario, you should maintain an ORDERS fact table and a SALES fact table in the same data warehouse. If orders are considered to be an organization's key interest, the ORDERS fact table should be the center of a star schema that might have vendor, product, and time dimensions. In that case, an interest in vendors yields a new vendor dimension, represented by a new VENDOR table in the database. The product dimension is represented by the same product table used in the initial sales star schema. However, given the interest in orders as well as sales, the time dimension now requires special attention. If the orders department uses the same time periods as the sales department, time can be represented by the same time table. If different time periods are used, you must create another table, perhaps named ORDER_TIME, to represent the time periods used by the orders department. In Figure 13.19, the orders star schema shares the product, vendor, and time dimensions.

Multiple fact tables also can be created for performance and semantic reasons. The following section explains several performance-enhancing techniques that can be used within the star schema.

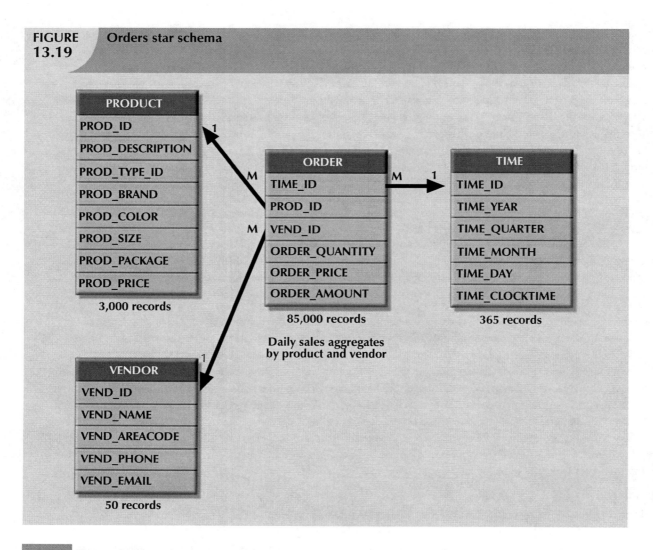

FIGURE 13.19   Orders star schema

PRODUCT

PROD_ID
PROD_DESCRIPTION
PROD_TYPE_ID
PROD_BRAND
PROD_COLOR
PROD_SIZE
PROD_PACKAGE
PROD_PRICE

3,000 records

ORDER

TIME_ID
PROD_ID
VEND_ID
ORDER_QUANTITY
ORDER_PRICE
ORDER_AMOUNT

85,000 records

Daily sales aggregates
by product and vendor

TIME

TIME_ID
TIME_YEAR
TIME_QUARTER
TIME_MONTH
TIME_DAY
TIME_CLOCKTIME

365 records

VENDOR

VEND_ID
VEND_NAME
VEND_AREACODE
VEND_PHONE
VEND_EMAIL

50 records

13.7.6 PERFORMANCE-IMPROVING TECHNIQUES FOR THE STAR SCHEMA

The creation of a database that provides fast and accurate answers to data analysis queries is the data warehouse design's prime objective. Therefore, performance-enhancement actions might target query speed through the facilitation of SQL code as well as through better semantic representation of business dimensions. Four techniques are often used to optimize data warehouse design:

- Normalizing dimensional tables.
- Maintaining multiple fact tables to represent different aggregation levels.
- Denormalizing fact tables.
- Partitioning and replicating tables.

Normalizing Dimensional Tables

Dimensional tables are normalized to achieve semantic simplicity and facilitate end-user navigation through the dimensions. For example, if the location dimension table contains transitive dependencies among region, state, and city, you can revise those relationships to the 3NF (third normal form), as shown in Figure 13.20. (If necessary, review normalization techniques in Chapter 5, Normalization of Database Tables.) The star schema shown in Figure 13.20 is known as a **snowflake schema**, which is a type of star schema in which the dimension tables can have their own dimension tables. The snowflake schema is usually the result of normalizing dimension tables.

FIGURE 13.20 Normalized dimension tables

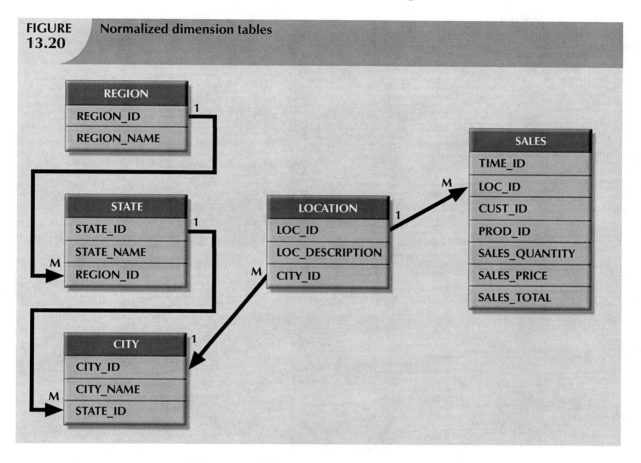

By normalizing the dimension tables, you simplify the data-filtering operations related to the dimensions. In this example, the region, state, city, and location contain very few records compared to the SALES fact table. Only the location table is directly related to the sales fact table.

> **NOTE**
>
> Although using the dimension tables shown in Figure 13.20 gains structural simplicity, there is a price to pay for that simplicity. For example, if you want to aggregate the data by region, you must use a four-table join, thus increasing the complexity of the SQL statements. The star schema in Figure 13.18 uses a LOCATION dimension table that greatly facilitates data retrieval by eliminating multiple join operations. This is yet another example of the trade-offs that designers must consider.

Maintaining Multiple Fact Tables that Represent Different Aggregation Levels

You can also speed up query operations by creating and maintaining multiple fact tables related to each level of aggregation (region, state, and city) in the location dimension. These aggregate tables are precomputed at the data-loading phase rather than at run time. The purpose of this technique is to save processor cycles at run time, thereby speeding up data analysis. An end-user query tool optimized for decision analysis then properly accesses the summarized fact tables instead of computing the values by accessing a lower level of detail fact table. This technique is illustrated in Figure 13.21, which adds aggregate fact tables for region, state, and city to the initial sales example.

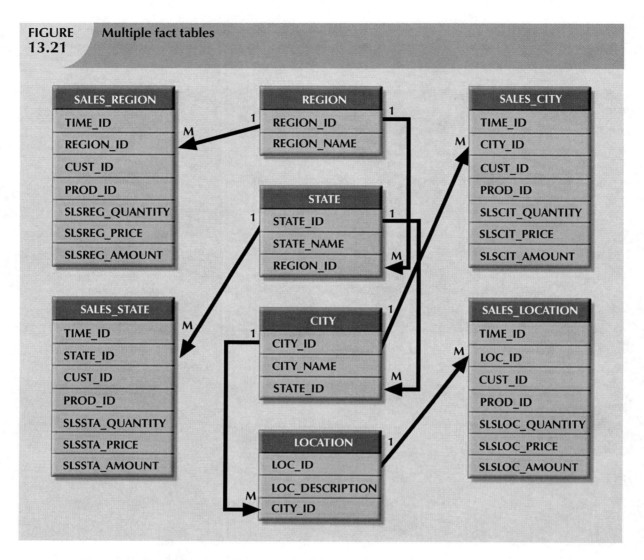

FIGURE 13.21 Multiple fact tables

The data warehouse designer must identify which levels of aggregation to precompute and store in the database. These multiple aggregate fact tables are updated during each load cycle in batch mode. And because the objective is to minimize access and processing time, according to the expected frequency of use and the processing time required to calculate a given aggregation level at run time, the data warehouse designer must select which aggregation fact tables to create.

Denormalizing Fact Tables

Denormalizing fact tables improves data access performance and saves data storage space. The latter objective, however, is becoming less of an issue. Data storage costs decrease almost daily, and DBMS limitations that restrict database and table size limits, record size limits, and the maximum number of records in a single table have far more negative effects than raw storage space costs.

Denormalization improves performance by using a single record to store data that normally take many records. For example, to compute the total sales for all products in all regions, you might have to access the region sales aggregates and summarize all of the records in this table. If you have 300,000 product sales, you could be summarizing at least 300,000 rows. Although this might not be a very taxing operation for a DBMS, a comparison of, say, 10 years' worth of previous sales begins to bog down the system. In such cases, it is useful to have special aggregate tables that are denormalized. For example, a YEAR_TOTALS table might contain the following fields: YEAR_ID, MONTH_1, MONTH_2 ... MONTH_12, and each year's total. Such tables can easily be used to serve as a basis for year-to-year comparisons at the top month level, the quarter level, or the year level. Here again, design criteria, such as frequency of use and performance requirements, are evaluated against the possible overload placed on the DBMS to manage the denormalized relations.

Partitioning and Replicating Tables

Because table partitioning and replication were covered in detail in Chapter 12, Distributed Database Management Systems, those techniques are discussed here only as they specifically relate to the data warehouse. Table partitioning and replication are particularly important when a BI system is implemented in dispersed geographic areas. **Partitioning** splits a table into subsets of rows or columns and places the subsets close to the client computer to improve data access time. **Replication** makes a copy of a table and places it in a different location, also to improve access time.

No matter which performance-enhancement scheme is used, time is the most common dimension used in business data analysis. Therefore, it is very common to have one fact table for each level of aggregation defined within the time dimension. For example, in the sales example, you might have five aggregate sales fact tables: daily, weekly, monthly, quarterly, and yearly. Those fact tables must have an implicit or explicit periodicity defined. **Periodicity**, usually expressed as current year only, previous years, or all years, provides information about the time span of the data stored in the table.

At the end of each year, daily sales for the current year are moved to another table that contains previous years' daily sales only. This table actually contains all sales records from the beginning of operations, with the exception of the current year. The data in the current year and previous years' tables thus represent the complete sales history of the company. The previous years' sales table can be replicated at several locations to avoid remote access to the historic sales data, which can cause slow response time. The possible size of this table is enough to intimidate all but the bravest of query optimizers. Here is one case in which denormalization would be of value!

13.8 IMPLEMENTING A DATA WAREHOUSE

Organization-wide information system development is subject to many constraints. Some of the constraints are based on available funding. Others are a function of management's view of the role played by an IS department and of the extent and depth of the information requirements. Add the constraints imposed by corporate culture, and you understand why no single formula can describe perfect data warehouse development. Therefore, rather than proposing a single data warehouse design and implementation methodology, this section identifies a few factors that appear to be common to data warehousing.

13.8.1 THE DATA WAREHOUSE AS AN ACTIVE DECISION SUPPORT FRAMEWORK

Perhaps the first thing to remember is that a data warehouse is not a static database. Instead, it is a dynamic framework for decision support that is, almost by definition, always a work in progress. Because it is the foundation of a modern BI environment, the design and implementation of the data warehouse means that you are involved in the design and implementation of a complete database-system-development infrastructure for company-wide decision support. Although it is easy to focus on the data warehouse database as the BI central data repository, you must remember that the decision support infrastructure includes hardware, software, people, and procedures, as well as data. The argument that the data warehouse is the only *critical* BI success component is as misleading as the argument that a human being needs only a heart or a brain to function. The data warehouse is a critical component of a modern BI environment, but it is certainly not the only critical component. Therefore, its design and implementation must be examined in light of the entire infrastructure.

13.8.2 A Company-Wide Effort That Requires User Involvement

Designing a data warehouse means being given an opportunity to help develop an integrated data model that captures the data that are considered to be essential to the organization, from both end-user and business perspectives. Data warehouse data cross departmental lines and geographical boundaries. Because the data warehouse represents an attempt to model all of the organization's data, you are likely to discover that organizational components (divisions, departments, support groups, and so on) often have conflicting goals, and it certainly will be easy to find data inconsistencies and damaging redundancies. Information is power, and the control of its sources and uses is likely to trigger turf battles, end-user resistance, and power struggles at all levels. Building the perfect data warehouse is not just a matter of knowing how to create a star schema; it requires managerial skills to deal with conflict resolution, mediation, and arbitration. In short, the designer must:

- Involve end users in the process.
- Secure end users' commitment from the beginning.
- Solicit continuous end-user feedback.
- Manage end-user expectations.
- Establish procedures for conflict resolution.

13.8.3 Satisfy the Trilogy: Data, Analysis, and Users

Great managerial skills are not, of course, solely sufficient. The technical aspects of the data warehouse must be addressed as well. The old adage of input-process-output repeats itself here. The data warehouse designer must satisfy:

- Data integration and loading criteria.
- Data analysis capabilities with acceptable query performance.
- End-user data analysis needs.

The foremost technical concern in implementing a data warehouse is to provide end-user decision support with advanced data analysis capabilities—at the right moment, in the right format, with the right data, and at the right cost.

13.8.4 Apply Database Design Procedures

You learned about the database life cycle and the database design process in Chapter 9, Database Design, so perhaps it is wise to review the traditional database design procedures. These design procedures must then be adapted to fit the data warehouse requirements. If you remember that the data warehouse derives its data from operational databases, you will understand why a solid foundation in operational database design is important. (It's difficult to produce good data warehouse data when the operational database data are corrupted.) Figure 13.22 depicts a simplified process for implementing the data warehouse.

As noted, developing a data warehouse is a company-wide effort that requires many resources: human, financial, and technical. Providing company-wide decision support requires a sound architecture based on a mix of people skills, technology, and managerial procedures that is often difficult to find and implement. For example:

- The sheer and often mind-boggling quantity of decision support data is likely to require the latest hardware and software—that is, advanced computers with multiple processors, advanced database systems, and large-capacity storage units. In the not-too-distant past, those requirements usually prompted the use of a mainframe-based system. Today's client/server technology offers many other choices to implement a data warehouse.
- Very detailed procedures are necessary to orchestrate the flow of data from the operational databases to the data warehouse. Data flow control includes data extraction, validation, and integration.
- To implement and support the data warehouse architecture, you also need people with advanced database design, software integration, and management skills.

FIGURE 13.22   Data warehouse design and implementation road map

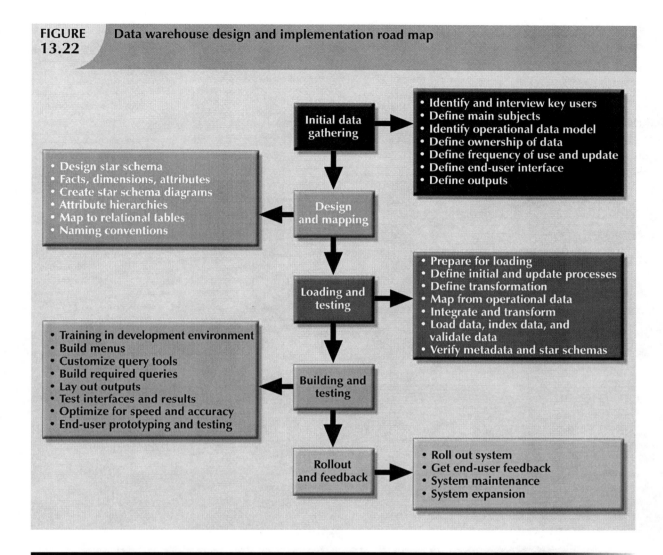

13.9 DATA MINING

The purpose of data analysis is to discover previously unknown data characteristics, relationships, dependencies, or trends. Such discoveries then become part of the information framework on which decisions are built. *A typical data analysis tool relies on the end users to define the problem, select the data, and initiate the appropriate data analyses to generate the information that helps model and solve problems that the end users uncover.* In other words, the end user reacts to an external stimulus—the discovery of the problem itself. If the end user fails to detect a problem, no action is taken. Given that limitation, some current BI environments now support various types of automated alerts. The alerts are software agents that constantly monitor certain parameters, such as sales indicators and inventory levels, and then perform specified actions (send e-mail or alert messages, run programs, and so on) when such parameters reach predefined levels.

In contrast to the traditional (reactive) BI tools, data mining is *proactive*. Instead of having the end user define the problem, select the data, and select the tools to analyze the data, *data-mining tools automatically search the data for anomalies and possible relationships, thereby identifying problems that have not yet been identified by the end user.* In other words, **data mining** refers to the activities that analyze the data, uncover problems or opportunities hidden in the data relationships, form computer models based on their findings, and then use the models to predict business behavior—requiring minimal end-user intervention. Therefore, the end user is able to use the system's findings to gain knowledge that might yield competitive advantages. Data mining describes a new breed of specialized decision support tools that automate data analysis. In short, data-mining tools *initiate* analyses to create knowledge. Such knowledge can be used to address any number of business problems. For example, banks and credit card companies use knowledge-based analysis to detect fraud, thereby decreasing fraudulent transactions.

To put data mining in perspective, look at the pyramid in Figure 13.23, which represents how knowledge is extracted from data. *Data* form the pyramid base and represent what most organizations collect in their operational databases. The second level contains *information* that represents the purified and processed data. Information forms the basis for decision making and business understanding. *Knowledge* is found at the pyramid's apex and represents highly specialized information.

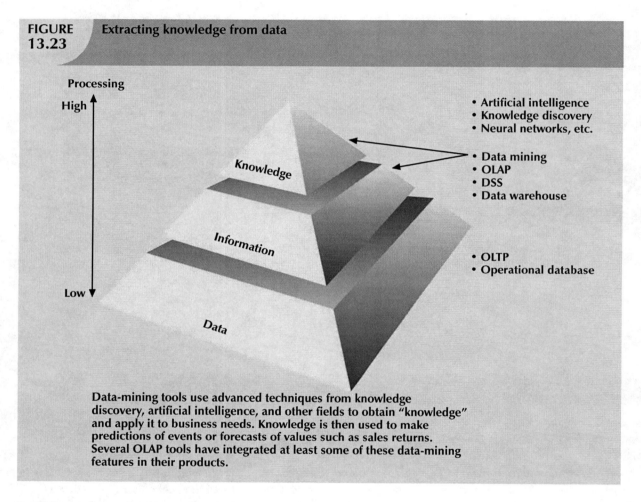

FIGURE 13.23   Extracting knowledge from data

Data-mining tools use advanced techniques from knowledge discovery, artificial intelligence, and other fields to obtain "knowledge" and apply it to business needs. Knowledge is then used to make predictions of events or forecasts of values such as sales returns. Several OLAP tools have integrated at least some of these data-mining features in their products.

It is difficult to provide a precise list of characteristics of data-mining tools. For one thing, the current generation of data-mining tools contains many design and application variations to fit data-mining requirements. Additionally, the many variations exist because there are no established standards that govern the creation of data-mining tools. Each data-mining tool seems to be governed by a different approach and focus, thus generating families of data-mining tools that focus on market niches such as marketing, retailing, finance, healthcare, investments, insurance, and banking. Within a given niche, data-mining tools can use certain algorithms, and those algorithms can be implemented in different ways and/or applied over different data.

In spite of the lack of precise standards, data mining is subject to four general phases:

1. Data preparation.
2. Data analysis and classification.
3. Knowledge acquisition.
4. Prognosis.

In the *data preparation phase*, the main data sets to be used by the data mining operation are identified and cleansed of any data impurities. Because the data in the data warehouse are already integrated and filtered, the data warehouse usually is the target set for data mining operations.

The *data analysis and classification phase* studies the data to identify common data characteristics or patterns. During this phase, the data-mining tool applies specific algorithms to find:

- Data groupings, classifications, clusters, or sequences.
- Data dependencies, links, or relationships.
- Data patterns, trends, and deviations.

The *knowledge acquisition phase* uses the results of the data analysis and classification phase. During the knowledge acquisition phase, the data-mining tool (with possible intervention by the end user) selects the appropriate modeling or knowledge acquisition algorithms. The most common algorithms used in data mining are based on neural networks, decision trees, rules induction, genetic algorithms, classification and regression trees, memory-based reasoning, and nearest neighbor and data visualization. A data-mining tool may use many of these algorithms in any combination to generate a computer model that reflects the behavior of the target data set.

Although many data-mining tools stop at the knowledge-acquisition phase, others continue to the *prognosis phase*. In that phase, the data mining findings are used to predict future behavior and forecast business outcomes. Examples of data mining findings can be:

- Sixty-five percent of customers who did not use a particular credit card in the last six months are 88 percent likely to cancel that account.
- Eighty-two percent of customers who bought a 27-inch or larger TV are 90 percent likely to buy an entertainment center within the next four weeks.
- If age < 30 and income <= 25,000 and credit rating < 3 and credit amount > 25,000, then the minimum loan term is 10 years.

The complete set of findings can be represented in a decision tree, a neural net, a forecasting model, or a visual presentation interface that is used to project future events or results. For example, the prognosis phase might project the likely outcome of a new product rollout or a new marketing promotion. Figure 13.24 illustrates the different phases of the data mining techniques.

Because data mining technology is still in its infancy, some of the data mining findings might fall outside the boundaries of what business managers expect. For example, a data-mining tool might find a close relationship between a customer's favorite brand of soda and the brand of tires on the customer's car. Clearly, that relationship might not be held in high regard among sales managers. (In regression analysis, those relationships are commonly described by the label "idiot correlation.") Fortunately, data mining usually yields more meaningful results. In fact, data mining has proved to be very helpful in finding practical relationships among data that help define customer buying patterns, improve product development and acceptance, reduce healthcare fraud, analyze stock markets, and so on.

Ideally, you can expect the development of databases that not only store data and various statistics about data usage, but also have the ability to learn about and extract knowledge from the stored data. Such database management systems, also known as inductive or intelligent databases, are the focus of intense research in many laboratories. Although those databases have yet to lay claim to substantial commercial market penetration, both "add-on" and DBMS-integrated data mining tools have proliferated in the data warehousing database market.

FIGURE 13.24   Data–mining phases

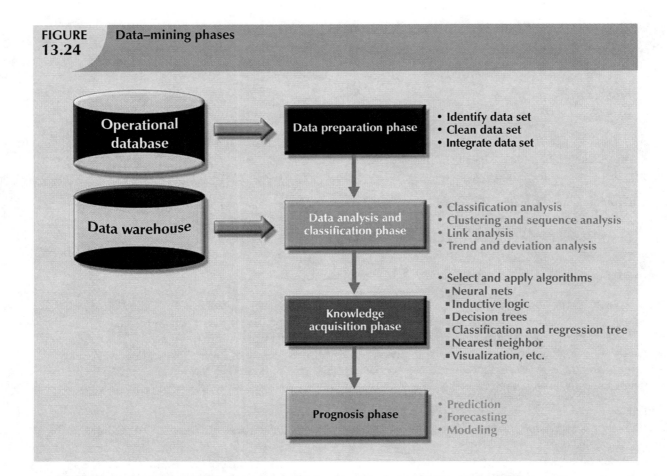

13.10 SQL EXTENSIONS FOR OLAP

The proliferation of OLAP tools has fostered the development of SQL extensions to support multidimensional data analysis. Most SQL innovations are the result of vendor-centric product enhancements. However, many of the innovations have made their way into standard SQL. This section introduces some of the new SQL extensions that have been created to support OLAP-type data manipulations.

The SaleCo snowflake schema shown in Figure 13.25 will be used to demonstrate the use of the SQL extensions. Note that this snowflake schema has a central DWSALESFACT fact table and three dimension tables: DWCUSTOMER, DWPRODUCT, and DWTIME. The central fact table represents daily sales by product and customer. However, as you examine the star schema shown in Figure 13.25 more carefully, you will see that the DWCUSTOMER and DWPRODUCT dimension tables have their own dimension tables: DWREGION and DWVENDOR.

Keep in mind that a database is at the core of all data warehouses. Therefore, all SQL commands (such as CREATE, INSERT, UPDATE, DELETE, and SELECT) will work in the data warehouse as expected. However, most queries you run in a data warehouse tend to include a lot of data groupings and aggregations over multiple columns. That's why this section introduces two extensions to the GROUP BY clause that are particularly useful: ROLLUP and CUBE. In addition, you will learn about using materialized views to store preaggregated rows in the database.

FIGURE
13.25

SaleCo snowflake schema

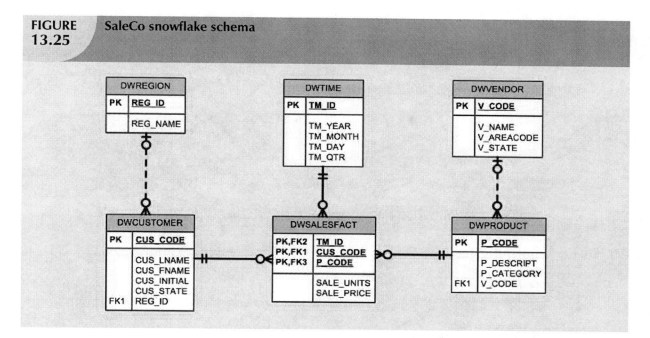

ONLINE CONTENT

The script files used to populate the database and run the SQL commands are available in the Student Online Companion.

NOTE

This section uses the Oracle RDBMS to demonstrate the use of SQL extensions to support OLAP functionality. If you use a different DBMS, consult the documentation to verify whether the vendor supports similar functionality and what the proper syntax is for your DBMS.

13.10.1 THE ROLLUP EXTENSION

The ROLLUP extension is used with the GROUP BY clause to generate aggregates by different dimensions. As you know, the GROUP BY clause will generate only one aggregate for each new value combination of attributes listed in the GROUP BY clause. The ROLLUP extension goes one step further; it enables you to get a subtotal for each column listed except for the last one, which gets a grand total instead. The syntax of the GROUP BY ROLLUP is as follows:

```
SELECT      column1, column2 [, ...], aggregate_function(expression)
FROM        table1 [,table2, ...]
[WHERE      condition]
GROUP BY    ROLLUP (column1, column2 [, ...])
[HAVING     condition]
[ORDER BY   column1 [, column2, ...]]
```

The order of the column list within the GROUP BY ROLLUP is very important. The last column in the list will generate a grand total. All other columns will generate subtotals. For example, Figure 13.26 shows the use of the ROLLUP extension to generate subtotals by vendor and product.

Note that Figure 13.26 shows the subtotals by vendor code and a grand total for all product codes. Contrast that with the normal GROUP BY clause that will generate only the subtotals for each vendor and product combination rather than the subtotals *by vendor* and the grand total for *all products*. The ROLLUP extension is particularly useful when you want to obtain multiple nested subtotals for a dimension hierarchy. For example, within a location hierarchy, you can use ROLLUP to generate subtotals by region, state, city, and store.

FIGURE 13.26   **ROLLUP extension**

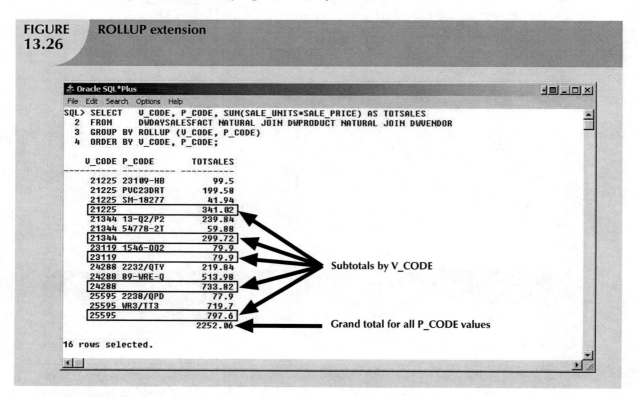

13.10.2 THE CUBE EXTENSION

The CUBE extension is also used with the GROUP BY clause to generate aggregates by the listed columns, including the last one. The CUBE extension will enable you to get a subtotal for each column listed in the expression, in addition to a grand total for the last column listed. The syntax of the GROUP BY CUBE is as follows:

```
SELECT      column1 [, column2, ...], aggregate_function(expression)
FROM        table1 [,table2, ...]
[WHERE      condition]
GROUP BY    CUBE (column1, column2 [, ...])
[HAVING     condition]
[ORDER BY   column1 [, column2, ...]]
```

For example, Figure 13.27 shows the use of the CUBE extension to compute the sales subtotals by month and by product, as well as a grand total.

In Figure 13.27, note that the CUBE extension generates the subtotals for each combination of month and product, in addition to subtotals by month and by product, as well as a grand total. The CUBE extension is particularly useful when you want to compute all possible subtotals within groupings based on multiple dimensions. Cross-tabulations are especially good candidates for application of the CUBE extension.

FIGURE 13.27   CUBE extension

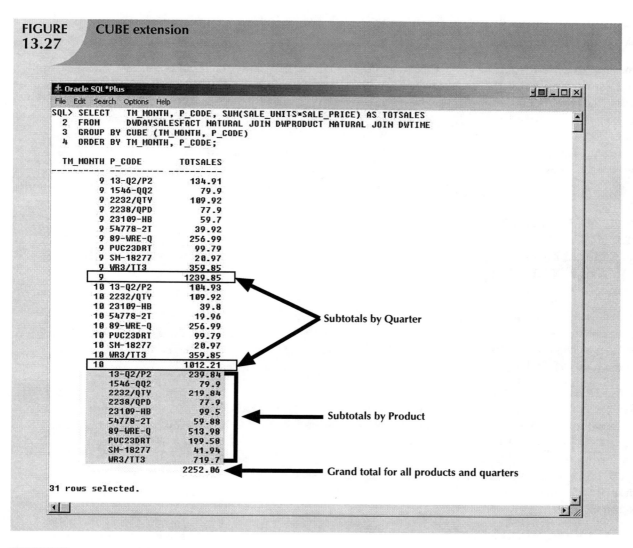

```
Oracle SQL*Plus
File  Edit  Search  Options  Help
SQL> SELECT    TM_MONTH, P_CODE, SUM(SALE_UNITS*SALE_PRICE) AS TOTSALES
  2  FROM      DWDAYSALESFACT NATURAL JOIN DWPRODUCT NATURAL JOIN DWTIME
  3  GROUP BY CUBE (TM_MONTH, P_CODE)
  4  ORDER BY TM_MONTH, P_CODE;

TM_MONTH P_CODE       TOTSALES
-------- ----------   ----------
       9 13-Q2/P2       134.91
       9 1546-QQ2        79.9
       9 2232/QTY       109.92
       9 2238/QPD        77.9
       9 23109-HB        59.7
       9 54778-2T        39.92
       9 89-WRE-Q       256.99
       9 PVC23DRT        99.79
       9 SM-18277        20.97
       9 WR3/TT3        359.85
       9                1239.85
      10 13-Q2/P2       104.93
      10 2232/QTY       109.92
      10 23109-HB        39.8
      10 54778-2T        19.96
      10 89-WRE-Q       256.99
      10 PVC23DRT        99.79
      10 SM-18277        20.97
      10 WR3/TT3        359.85
      10                1012.21
         13-Q2/P2       239.84
         1546-QQ2        79.9
         2232/QTY       219.84
         2238/QPD        77.9
         23109-HB        99.5
         54778-2T        59.88
         89-WRE-Q       513.98
         PVC23DRT       199.58
         SM-18277        41.94
         WR3/TT3        719.7
                        2252.06

31 rows selected.
```

Subtotals by Quarter

Subtotals by Product

Grand total for all products and quarters

13.10.3 MATERIALIZED VIEWS

The data warehouse normally contains fact tables that store specific measurements of interest to an organization. Such measurements are organized by different dimensions. The vast majority of OLAP business analysis of "everyday activities" is based on comparisons of data that are aggregated at different levels, such as totals by vendor, by product, and by store.

Because businesses normally use a predefined set of summaries for benchmarking, it is reasonable to predefine such summaries for future use by creating summary fact tables. (See Section 13.5.6 for a discussion of additional performance-improving techniques.) However, creating multiple summary fact tables that use GROUP BY queries with multiple table joins could become a resource-intensive operation. In addition, data warehouses must also be able to maintain up-to-date summarized data at all times. So what happens with the summary fact tables after new sales data have been added to the base fact tables? Under normal circumstances, the summary fact tables are re-created. This operation requires that the SQL code be run again to re-create all summary rows, even when only a few rows needed updating. Clearly, this is a time-consuming process.

To save query processing time, most database vendors have implemented additional "functionality" to manage aggregate summaries more efficiently. This new functionality resembles the standard SQL views for which the SQL code is predefined in the database. However, the added functionality difference is that the views also store the preaggregated rows, something like a summary table. For example, Microsoft SQL Server provides indexed views, while Oracle provides materialized views. This section explains the use of materialized views.

A **materialized view** is a dynamic table that not only contains the SQL query command to generate the rows, but also stores the actual rows. The materialized view is created the first time the query is run and the summary rows are stored in the table. The materialized view rows are automatically updated when the base tables are updated. That way, the data warehouse administrator will create the view but will not have to worry about updating the view. The use of materialized views is totally transparent to the end user. The OLAP end user can create OLAP queries, using the standard fact tables, and the DBMS query optimization feature will automatically use the materialized views if those views provide better performance.

The basic syntax for the materialized view is:

CREATE MATERIALIZED VIEW view_name
BUILD {IMMEDIATE | DEFERRED}
REFRESH {[FAST | COMPLETE | FORCE]} ON COMMIT
[ENABLE QUERY REWRITE]
AS select_query;

The BUILD clause indicates when the materialized view rows are actually populated. IMMEDIATE indicates that the materialized view rows are populated right after the command is entered. DEFERRED indicates that the materialized view rows will be populated at a later time. Until then, the materialized view is in an "unusable" state. The DBMS provides a special routine that an administrator runs to populate materialized views.

The REFRESH clause lets you indicate when and how to update the materialized view when new rows are added to the base tables. FAST indicates that whenever a change is made in the base tables, the materialized view updates only the affected rows. COMPLETE indicates that a complete update will be made for all rows in the materialized view when the select query on which the view is based is rerun. FORCE indicates that the DBMS will first try to do a FAST update; otherwise, it will do a COMPLETE update. The ON COMMIT clause indicates that the updates to the materialized view will take place as part of the commit process of the underlying DML statement, that is, as part of the commit of the DML transaction that updated the base tables. The ENABLE QUERY REWRITE option allows the DBMS to use the materialized views in query optimization.

To create materialized views, you must have specified privileges and you must complete specified prerequisite steps. As always, you must defer to the DBMS documentation for the latest updates. In the case of Oracle, you must create materialized view logs on the base tables of the materialized view. Figure 13.28 shows the steps required to create the MONTH_SALES_MV materialized view in the Oracle RDBMS.

FIGURE 13.28 Creating a materialized view

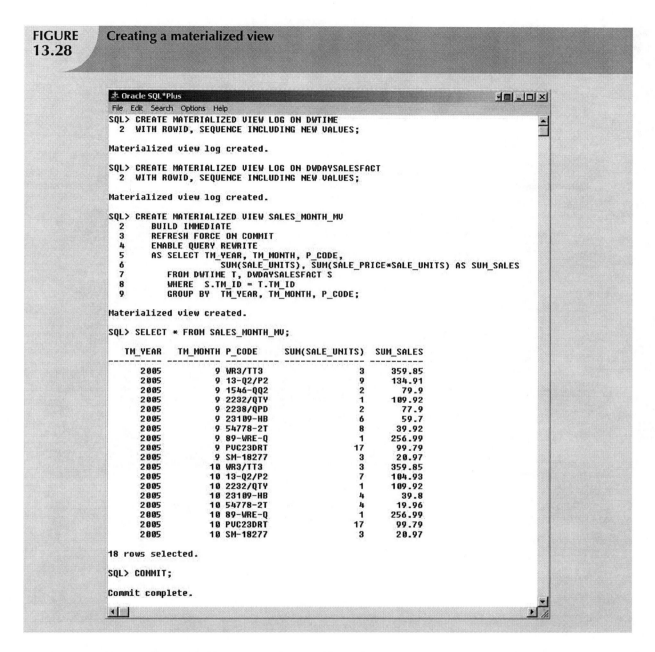

The materialized view in Figure 13.28 computes the monthly total units sold and the total sales aggregates by product. The SALES_MONTH_MV materialized view is configured to automatically update after each change in the base tables. Note that the last row of SALES_MONTH_MV indicates that during October, the sales of product 'SM-18277' are three units, for a total of $20.97. Figure 13.29 shows the effects of an update to the DWDAYSALESFACT base table.

FIGURE
13.29

**FIGURE
13.29**   **Refreshing a materialized view**

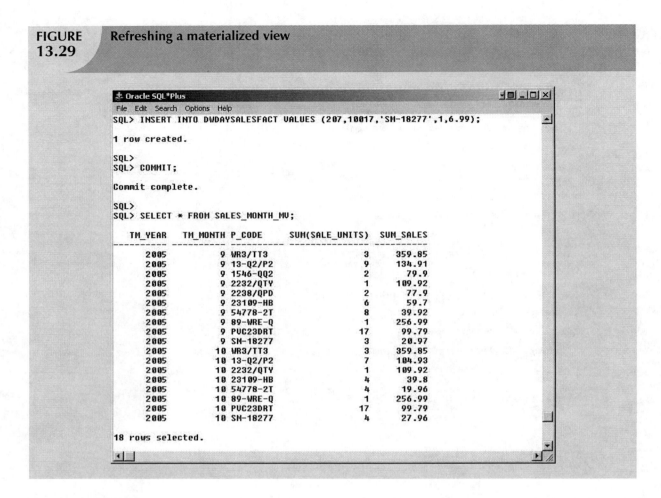

Figure 13.29 shows how the materialized view was automatically updated after the insertion of a new row in the DWDAYSALESFACT table. Note that the last row of the SALES_MONTH_MV now shows that in October, the sales of product 'SM-18277' are four units, for a total of $27.96.

Although all of the examples in this section focus on SQL extensions to support OLAP reporting in an Oracle DBMS, you have seen just a small fraction of the many business intelligence features currently provided by most DBMS vendors. For example, most vendors provide rich graphical user interfaces to manipulate, analyze, and present the data in multiple formats. Figure 13.30 shows two sample screens, one for Oracle and one for Microsoft OLAP products.

FIGURE 13.30   **Sample OLAP applications**

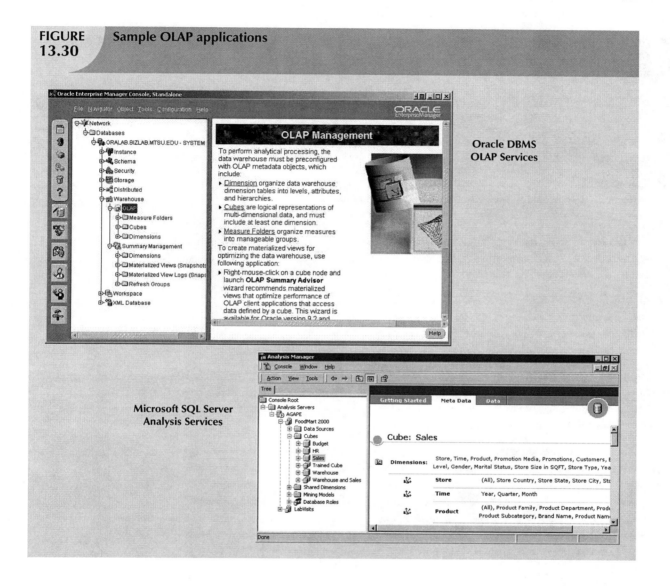

SUMMARY

- Business intelligence (BI) is a term used to describe a comprehensive, cohesive, and integrated set of applications used to capture, collect, integrate, store, and analyze data with the purpose of generating and presenting information used to support business decision making.

- BI covers a range of technologies and applications to manage the entire data life cycle from acquisition to storage, transformation, integration, analysis, monitoring, presentation, and archiving. BI functionality ranges from simple data gathering and extraction to very complex data analysis and presentation.

- Decision support systems (DSS) refers to an arrangement of computerized tools used to assist managerial decision making within a business. DSS were the original precursor of current generation BI systems.

- Operational data are not well-suited for decision support. From the end-user point of view, decision support data differ from operational data in three main areas: time span, granularity, and dimensionality.

- The requirements for a decision support DBMS are divided into four main categories: database schema, data extraction and loading, end-user analytical interface, and database size requirements.

- The data warehouse is an integrated, subject-oriented, time-variant, nonvolatile collection of data that provides support for decision making. The data warehouse is usually a read-only database optimized for data analysis and query processing. A data mart is a small, single-subject data warehouse subset that provides decision support to a small group of people.

- Online analytical processing (OLAP) refers to an advanced data analysis environment that supports decision making, business modeling, and operations research. OLAP systems have four main characteristics: use of multidimensional data analysis techniques, advanced database support, easy-to-use end-user interfaces, and client/server architecture.

- Relational online analytical processing (ROLAP) provides OLAP functionality by using relational databases and familiar relational query tools to store and analyze multidimensional data. Multidimensional online analytical processing (MOLAP) provides OLAP functionality by using multidimensional database management systems (MDBMSs) to store and analyze multidimensional data.

- The star schema is a data-modeling technique used to map multidimensional decision support data into a relational database with the purpose of performing advanced data analysis. The basic star schema has four components: facts, dimensions, attributes, and attribute hierarchies. Facts are numeric measurements or values representing a specific business aspect or activity. Dimensions are general qualifying categories that provide additional perspectives to a given fact. Conceptually, the multidimensional data model is best represented by a three-dimensional cube. Attributes can be ordered in well-defined attribute hierarchies. The attribute hierarchy provides a top-down organization that is used for two main purposes: to permit aggregation and to provide drill-down/roll-up data analysis.

- Four techniques are generally used to optimize data warehouse design: normalizing dimensional tables, maintaining multiple fact tables representing different aggregation levels, denormalizing fact tables, and partitioning and replicating tables.

- Data mining automates the analysis of operational data with the intention of finding previously unknown data characteristics, relationships, dependencies, and/or trends. The data mining process has four phases: data preparation, data analysis and classification, knowledge acquisition, and prognosis.

- SQL has been enhanced with extensions that support OLAP-type processing and data generation.